THE ANATOMY OF
NEOPLATONISM

THE
ANATOMY
OF
NEOPLATONISM

A. C. LLOYD

CLARENDON PRESS · OXFORD

1990

Oxford University Press, Walton Street, Oxford OX2 6DP
Oxford New York Toronto
Delhi Bombay Calcutta Madras Karachi
Petaling Jaya Singapore Hong Kong Tokyo
Nairobi Dar es Salaam Cape Town
Melbourne Auckland
and associated companies in
Berlin Ibadan

Oxford is a trade mark of Oxford University Press

Published in the United States
by Oxford University Press, New York

British Library Cataloguing in Publication Data

Lloyd, A. C. (Anthony Charles) 1916–
The anatomy of neoplatonism.
1. Neoplatonism
I. Title
186'.4
ISBN 0-19-824229-8

Library of Congress Cataloging in Publication Data

Lloyd, A. C. (Antony C.)
The anatomy of neoplatonism/A. C. Lloyd.
Includes bibliographical references.
1. Neoplatonism.
I. Title.
B517.A52   1990   186'.4—dc20   89-35812
ISBN 0-19-824229-8

Typeset at the Alden Press
Oxford London and Northampton

Printed in Great Britain by
Biddles Ltd., Guildford and King's Lynn

PREFACE

To name friends and scholars to whom I have been indebted
for criticism and encouragement in writing this book would be
either invidious or impracticable. It is built on work which extends
over many years. Some of that work found its way into articles; and
sometimes, I should mention, these now seem to me to contain
significant errors. But sometimes they contain in greater detail the
arguments for claims I make in the present book—hence the inor-
dinate number of my own articles in the bibliography. By and large
neither the text nor consequently the bibliography (which includes
only publications that are mentioned in the text) follows the
practice of providing information for information's sake about
further treatment of topics in question. The general index too is
restricted because it complements the sub-headings of the table of
contents.

References to texts follow, I hope, accepted custom. In the
absence of one for Proclus I refer to his *Platonic Theology* by Book
and chapter followed, where needed, by page and line numbers of
the Saffrey–Westerink edition. The numbers for the *Elements of
Theology* are those of the propositions, but the lines are those of
corresponding pages in Dodds' text since that is how he numbered
them. The initial Roman numbers of the *Timaeus* commentary
indicate Diehl's volumes, not Proclus' Books.

Last and least, ' ∼ ' means 'corresponds to'.

A.C.L.

Hove, E. Sussex
December 1988

CONTENTS

I
ATTITUDES TO LOGIC

Opening at random a few pages in any of the major Neoplatonic works, someone unfamiliar with them would perhaps expect to find hypostases and analogies, processions and reversions, the ascent of the soul and a vision of the One. Some of these he would be likely to find without reading far. But anyone with experience of the subject will know that he would find mingled with them wholes and parts, for instance, genera and species, and, less often but significantly, references to dialectic. These have an uninteresting place in the formal deductive logic of the ancients, although their place in semantics is an essential one, and we shall see how semantics provides the substructure for much of what is familiar Neoplatonism. Neoplatonists' attitudes to logical form and validity are therefore described in this first chapter more because, having been rather neglected by other writers, they may be of interest to the reader, who can make his own assessment of them.

The topic which occupies more space, the nature of the Greek logical commentaries, does so because it is in them that Neoplatonists described and, what is more important, argued for the substructure which I have mentioned. Secondly, that very fact raises the question whether the philosophy itself was affected by it. On this the chapter must speak for itself.

Commentaries and scholia

It need hardly be said that the Neoplatonists' attitude to logic is chiefly to be found in the *Commentaria in Artistotelem graeca*, which include extracts from additional scholia and anonymous commentaries. Certain other logical commentaries, roughly speaking Neoplatonic, have been edited. The most important of these are still the Latin texts which depend on Greek originals. For the present purpose Boethius' are foremost because they reproduce the most influential semantic theory of Imperial philosophy, that of

Porphyry. I will make an exception of describing them briefly, for the modern work on them which will justify our use of them to reconstruct Porphyry's semantics is complicated. We have modern editions of Boethius' commentaries on the *Isagoge, Categories,* and *De interpretatione.* If he ever completed one on the *Prior Analytics* it has not survived. A first stage of it, however, has been identified as scholia or marginalia found in a Latin version of Aristotle's text and edited in *Aristoteles latinus.*[1] The version is by Boethius; and the scholia are a very literal translation of Greek scholia which we do not possess as a collection but which are very close to Philoponus' *In Analytica priora,* without depending directly on that or any other commentary we know. (I cannot find anything intrinsically interesting in them: but they are at least evidence of material which Philoponus had at his disposal, over and above Ammonius.)

Comparisons at a linguistic level point to Boethius' other commentaries being based entirely on Greek scholia, which he translated and wove into a more literary and continuous form but with no additions of his own. The evidence is against his having used at first hand any of the commentaries known to us.[2] But unquestionably the notes he used come largely from Porphyry.[3] Boethius' second editions are only fuller versions of the first editions, and there is no reason to suppose that they drew on any different material. He sometimes makes this clear himself (see Shiel, 1958, 233 = Fuhrmann-Gruber, 1984, 171).

---

[1] *Ps.-Philoponi aliorumque scholia,* in L. Minio Paluello (ed.), *Aristoteles latinus,* III/4 (1962). The identification had been suggested in Minio Paluello (1970) col. 15 A and has been convincingly confirmed by J. Shiel (1982; 1984). But see further S. Ebbesen (1981).

[2] In particular Porph., *In Cat.* (*pace* Bidez, 1923) or Amm., *In Cat.,* and *In De int.* (*pace* Courcelle, 1944). But the same holds for the lost Iambl., *In Cat.* (*pace* Pfligersdorffer, 1953) and Porphyry's longer commentary on the *Categories,* the *In Gedalium.* Evidence first in Shiel (1958), discussed at length and mostly accepted by Obertello (1974), and not refuted by Chadwick (1981), 627 ff. For the vexed question of the conventional introductory 'heads' or 'didascalica' see I. Hadot (1982), 101–6. Boethius provides a good warning, often unheeded by scholars, against inferences which assume that a commentator is speaking *in propria persona.* A famous case is his 'promise' to show elsewhere the agreement of Aristotle and Plato, when all he has probably done in making it is to translate what he found in his scholia (*In De int.*[2], 80. 1–7). Thus the use of cross-references in commentaries, whether for inferences about chronology or for other purposes, must often be hazardous. Cf. Shiel (1958), 243 = Fuhrmann-Gruber (1984), 180.

[3] But *In De int.,* Bk. VI is not Porphyrian, for Porphyry, like Ammonius— though apparently no one else—thought the last two chapters of *De int.* spurious.

Of Greek logical commentaries published outside the Berlin Academy corpus (*CAG*) I will say only that the reader may be disappointed to find how elementary as well as derivative they are but should not be surprised. There was always a demand for easy expositions of works belonging to a difficult curriculum: they were easy because they ignored difficulties, and they are consequently uninteresting to us. It would, of course, be impracticable, even if it were sufficiently relevant to the present purpose, to produce a list of published texts, as this could not be counted on to remain up to date. For the same reason I omit the fund of unedited manuscripts which may or not be rewarding.

What is to my purpose is to indicate some features which are common to all the logical commentaries and which sometimes affect their content, and more often affect, or rather ought to affect, our understanding of their content. They are a genre, many of whose conventions depend not just on tradition but on external and institutionalized circumstances. As far back as their natural starting-point in the publication of the *Organon* the genre spanned a wide range. A fourteenth-century Byzantine makes a partial division which is probably Alexandrian (cf. Simplicius, *In Categoris, ad init*). There is, he says, *exegesis*, which usually follows the text (i.e. with lemmata) and tries to clarify it from the standpoint of the commentator; examples given are Alexander and the Alexandrians, including Ammonius, Simplicius, and Philoponus. Secondly, there is *paraphrasis*, which presents the text in a continuous form but simplifies it when it is too difficult, regardless of whether the simplification is the commentator's own; examples given are Themistius and Psellus.[4] But in fact there is something like a spectrum running from scattered notes on a text to paraphrase (often in effect a text which has taken account of clarification from such notes), and then through increasing proportions of explicit exegesis (i.e. formally distinct from the text) to quite lengthy discussions of alternative interpretations, as well as excursuses on whatever were considered crucial topics.

Scholia and commentary differed all the less for the scholia's being on the whole in sentences, not the grammatical shorthand

---

[4] Sophonias, *In De an.* (*CAG*, XXIII/1), 1.1; 2.12 ff; cf. 2.28 ff. Simpl., *In Phys.*, 918. 11–15 distinguishes *synopsis* from *paraphrase*: the first certainly implies abridgement but, *pace* F. Romano (1985), 54–6, it is questionable whether the second implies expansion.

which a modern annotator is accustomed to use.[5] Collections of scholia were common. As an illustration of the practice, Proclus annotated Syrianus' commentary on the Orphic writings, and this work was kept in the school (Marinus, *Vita Procli*, § 27). But these collections can only be distinguished from 'commentaries' by the comparative independence from one another of the units which compose them and the comparative comprehensiveness with which they cover a text. This applies to commentaries which have the additional marks of being lectures. Moreover, the researcher of manuscripts will soon learn not to rely on titles which apparently distinguish these degrees under the names 'scholia', 'paraphrase', and the like. Still less, of course, are the attributions to authors reliable.[6]

To the extent, which is a very large one, that all 'commentaries' are expansions of 'scholia', Sophonias' phrase, 'from the stand-point of the commentator', would be wrong if it were taken to imply that we could *expect* originality or even, as we shall see, unqualified commitment on the part of commentators.

The Neoplatonic curriculum

Although not all Neoplatonic commentaries were lectures, they presuppose the existence of a philosophical curriculum which affects not only their form but the Neoplatonic treatment of logic. In Alexandria (we can infer from Elias) the course in Aristotle would start from logic, without, however, neglecting moral advice (of the kind, I suppose, that we might find in Isocrates); the end or goal of Aristotelian philosophy is to know that there is one ἀρχή (see *Metaphysics* Λ) which is the Good (see *Nicomachean Ethics* proem). But between this metaphysics ('theology') and logic come ethics,

---

[5] The comparison is not exact, because (as Ebbesen informs me) until the Middle Ages scholars did not annotate texts in the margins but on separate wax tablets, which might be copied as a result of the fame, wealth, or vanity of the scholar. Points of reference would be indicated by lemmata. Logical diagrams go back at least to the sixth century.

[6] His successors had a habit of attributing comments, often wrongly, to Ammonius. Cf. Busse, in *CAG* IV/5, p. xlii. Though the reason why Philop., *In Cat.*, passed, pretty well until Busse, under Ammonius' name lies in marginal titles added to the otherwise anonymous text of the Aldine eds. (Venice, 1503 etc.).

physics, and mathematics.[7] The same order had probably held in fifth-century Athens. E. Westerink has extrapolated the following organization of the quadrivium in sixth-century Alexandria (Westerink, 1971). Three years, say, would first be spent on Aristotelian philosophy, in the order: logic (including Porphyry's *Isagoge*), ethics (but not theoretical, at most the *Carmen aureum* or a little Epictetus), physics (i.e. *De caelo, De generatione et corruptione, Meteorologica, De anima*), mathematics (selected from Nicomachus, Euclid, Aristoxenus, and Ptolemy or Paulus Alexandrinus), theology (*Metaphysica*). This would be followed by another say three years' study of Platonic philosophy, consisting of the twelve dialogues in Iamblichus' canon.

The same curriculum, I believe, continued in Constantinople, as it did in other disciplines (cf. Praechter, 1910*a*, 314–29: Mango, 1975, 9). M. Treu (1898) published an early medieval Byzantine text containing a list of philosophers to be studied, as he plausibly surmised, in an 'encyclopaedic education'. It is sometimes quoted as a curriculum: but since, starting with the *Organon* and *Physics*, it includes the commentators Alexander, Ammonius, Porphyry, Philoponus, 'and many others' and goes on to Plato's works with *his* commentators, Proclus and Iamblichus, common sense shows that 'curriculum' is an exaggeration, except in the sense that it includes books which will be referred to.[8] Nevertheless, it shows how completely the Alexandrian tradition had survived.

Ebbesen produces evidence for believing that the *Posterior Analytics* as well as the *Topics* had been omitted from the normal curriculum from the tenth to the thirteenth centuries 'and probably much longer' (1981, 264). But the evidence suggests to me rather a state of affairs which existed even in Alexandria, namely that indolence or incapacity prevented most, if not all, students from reaching the last stages of the logic syllabus. It is perhaps surprising that the *Posterior Analytics* was considered especially difficult, but it was (Ammonius, *In Isagogen*, 38. 16–17). Possibly they stopped even sooner: is it an accident that there was no surviving, non-Byzantine commentary on *Prior Analytics II*?

---

[7] Elias, *In Cat.*, 113. For the conventional discussion where we should start in Aristotle's works see also Philop., *In Cat.*, 5, 15 ff.

[8] It must be borne in mind that the form of Treu's text is more or less literary: a professor is supposed to be questioning a pupil, who does not, however, open his mouth.

Let us look at the order of study at Alexandria. In logic this had a rationale which went back several centuries. Logic is concerned with demonstration (sometimes called 'method'), which is the subject of the *Posterior Analytics*. The student therefore starts with the three concepts which are involved in demonstration and which have three other treatises devoted to them. These are: propositions, because a syllogism is composed of them; terms, because propositions are composed of terms; and names, because that is what terms were before they were elements of propositions. These three—names, terms, and propositions—are respectively the subject-matter of *Categories*, *De interpretatione*, and the *Prior Analytics*. Elias calls these three treatises 'the works preliminary to demonstration' (*In Categorias*, 116. 20). But it was also traditional that the *Posterior Analytics* were heuristic, rules for the discovery of middle terms (Eustratius, *In Analytica posteriora 11*, 6. 32; 7. 7). The *Topics* dealt with only probable inference ('dialectical syllogism'), was not considered central to logic, and was read at the end of the *Organon*, with *Sophistici elenchi* as a kind of appendix on fallacies ('sophistical syllogism').[9] Neoplatonists followed Porphyry in objecting to an alternative title for the *Categories*, 'preliminary to the Topics'.[10] What they were objecting to was the notion that to understand a demonstrative proof the student needed first to understand a probable proof, instead of proof (i.e. syllogism) as such, which they thought Aristotle dealt with in the *Prior Analytics*. But more than that their objection was really based, as we can see in Simplicius, on Porphyry's semantics of names, terms, and propositions. It was considered not only to be consistent with this but to follow from it that the *Categories* was also the proper introduction to the whole of philosophy (e.g. Simplicius, op. cit., 15. 34–5).

Conventional features of lectures

The teaching was based on lectures; and those commentaries which were lectures (as most of the Alexandrian were) follow formal

---

[9] Cf. Amm., *In An. pr.*, 2; 'Apodeictic' and 'Dialectic' became jargon terms for *Posterior Analytics* and *Topics* respectively.
[10] Porph., *In Cat.*, 56. 23–31; Elias, *In Cat.*, 132. 26–8; Simpl., *In Cat.*, 15. 30–16. 16.

conventions which have been described more than once.[11] But the practice of improvisation needs some remarks, for it may account for not infrequent deficiencies and anacolutha in the content which are puzzling to the reader. It is a logistical fact that many lectures —and not merely reported ones, which might be expected to be abridged—are simply not long enough to fill the time without unwritten material. It must be wrong, even in the case of lectures divided into θεωρία and λέξις, to say that the comments which followed the reading of the lemma were always extempore. But there is one circumstance which does entail some extemporizing. Of all teachers, the Platonist was the most likely to leave room for students' questions; and he did. Here is an example, which comes, incidentally, from 'undivided' lectures and can correct any impression that the formal division of lectures implies a change of method. At the end of an excursus covering a logical aporia about the differentia Ammonius says, 'We have now laid all the foundation. Otherwise, the text is clear. So let us read it, and if anything does come up, let us make *that* clear' (*In Isagogen*, 105). Certainly it does not follow that it was the students who would put the questions. But we possess an example of that too in Ammonius' class. Asclepius (the later medical writer) raised a problem with Ammonius, and his fellow student reports, 'Our philosopher replied to him as follows . . .' (Asclepius, *In Metaphysica*, 143. 31–5). Syrianus had allowed it, as we can see from the interventions of his two outstanding auditors, Hermias and Proclus (see Hermias, *In Phaedrum*). To add an instance from Byzantium, Psellus is asked during a lecture to explain the physics of the rainbow, but in this case says—as many an experienced lecturer has had to say—that the explanation must be deferred to another day (*ap*. Bidez, 1928, 55).[12]

As well as formal conventions attaching to a commentary there are fairly flexible conventions of content. The most prominent of these are the 'heads' (κεφάλαια) of the introduction. These cover two lists of topics: those which belong to logical commentaries

---

[11] For the division, said to have started with Olympiodorus, into θεωρία and λέξις see bibliographical notes in Devreesse (1954), 67–72; Westerink (1976), 25 n. 42; Hunger (1978), 26. Here, I confine myself to the warning against a common error that the comments included in λέξις deal with problems of text, not content.

[12] This fact was kindly supplied to me by I. Pontikos. Questions were sometimes confined to a session after the day's lectures, as in Calvisius Taurus' school (2nd cent.), (Aul. Gell., I. 26, cited by Donini, 1982, 68 n. 28).

because these commentaries introduce the student to the study of Aristotle in general, and those which are better known because they belong to the study of any Aristotelian book. If it is a logical work, there will be a place in the second list, under 'position of the work in Aristotle's philosophy', for the function of logic—the question whether it is a part or an instrument of philosophy. The standard lists have been amply described elsewhere. But there is an addition to it which we sometimes find and which bears on one of the less well-explored byways in the Neoplatonists' conception of logic.[13]

The dialectic methods and the meaning of 'analysis'

This is 'the method of teaching' adopted by the work in question. For behind this topic lies the fact that the Neoplatonists were faced by two conceptions of logic—that is, of proof: the method of syllogism and the method of classification, which, following Plato, they called dialectic. It may seem confusing that the same term was also used, following Aristotle, for the *Topics*. But once it is conceded that the genus is the disjunction (in class logic the sum) of its species, the deductive logic in those parts of the *Topics* concerned with genera and species is part of elementary Boolean class logic, with its ordinary rules of transitivity for class inclusion and so on. It is what collection and division represent, and, if we allow for the anachronistic description, the best of the Imperial philosophers took it this way, since for the purpose of logic they tended to ignore extra-logical restrictions on what counted as genera and species. 'The teaching methods' were sometimes called the 'dialectical methods' because they corresponded to branches of dialectic, namely division, definition, demonstration, analysis. This division of 'dialectic' was itself a commonplace in commentaries on Plato and Aristotle alike; and it was usually described in terms which would fit either philosopher.[14] Division divides genera into species, definition corresponds to collection by gathering the

---

[13] Amm., *In Isag.*, 26. 5; Amm., *In De int.*, in *CAG* iv/5, p. xix n. 1 and ib. xxi; *ad init.*

[14] Porphyry, like Albinus, omitted analysis. But Albinus (*Isag.*, § 3 *ad init.*) had included induction. This is not as divergent as it may look: some later Neoplatonists required analysis to start from sense perception, so that it was equivalent to induction and called τεκμηριωδήc by Damascius (*In Phileb.*, § 68).

properties of something so as to distinguish it from other things.[15] Demonstration shows that one thing belongs to another, but it does so by a process from causes to effects. (Notice that this description is not just that of Neoplatonic metaphysics but that of syllogistic in the *Posterior Analytics*.) Analysis is a process from effects to causes. Ammonius informed his students of this division of dialectic in his introduction to the *Prior Analytics* (7. 26–8. 14), Elias, under the head of 'utility' in his introduction to Porphyry's *Isagoge* (37. 13–38. 15). Both these Alexandrians connect their description to the question whether analysis (or analytic) is merely the contrary of synthesis or is also the contrary of each of the first three methods of dialectic. I propose to devote one paragraph to explaining their question, which has no merit other than unwittingly to illustrate a congenital blemish of Imperial commentaries.

Ammonius is the most puzzling, because, after talking quite predictably about analysis under the head of 'title of the book' (viz. *Prior Analytics*), he abruptly says, 'So much for the title. But is analysis the opposite of synthesis or of other things too? We say, of other things too. For there are four methods of dialectic . . .'— which he then proceeds to describe in such a way as to show that analysis is the opposite of each of the other methods. But why on earth should one want to know that it is? (It can have nothing to do with a contrast between Aristotle's 'Analytics' and Plato's dialectic, for analysis belongs to the latter and demonstration is among its opposites.) How can it be relevant? It isn't. It does nothing but illustrate how the well-oiled cogs of the genre 'commentary' turn out material from a stockpile while the author, if such he can be called, has no means of stopping the machinery. What has happened here is that a sub-topic or commonplace has become detached from the context which gave it its point, and turns up because of its association in Ammonius with the topic of analysis and in Elias with that of dialectical methods. This context, which it may already have lost in Ammonius' and Elias' source, was in Proclus' *Parmenides* commentary and depended entirely on the Platonic lemma.[16] That lemma was Parmenides' famous claim that

---

[15] For 'definition' corresponding to collection, not division, Procl., *In Parm.*, 650–1; 656. 3–4; cf. Syrian., *In Met.*, 56. 3.
[16] Something of the sort would have been repeated in his *Philebus* commentary (cf. Dam., *In Phileb.*, § 53), but for reasons which I pass over this is a less likely origin of Ammonius' scholium.

without the Ideas there would be no faculty or capability of dialogue (135 B). Proclus supported this by arguing as follows (982. 11–36): Dialogue uses the four methods of dialectic (ll. 21–2); the first three of these depend on the 'forms in us', which depend on the Ideas; the fourth, analysis, is the opposite of each of the others, and opposites are destroyed simultaneously. (This last dictum is not explicit in the argument but is clearly implicit at ll. 23–4.)

But we must return to matters of content. First, what does 'analysis' mean in our context? The standard explanation of going *up*, i.e. back, from an end to a beginning, is Peripatetic as well as Platonist. Alexander instances its meaning in geometry of working through steps from the conclusion of a proof to the original problem but says that in syllogistic the term has several applications. These are (1) analysis of (a) compound syllogisms (i.e. polysyllogisms) to simple ones or (b) simple syllogisms into propositions and premisses, (2) reduction (ἀνάγειν/ἀναγωγή) of an imperfect syllogism to a perfect one, (3) reduction of a given syllogism to its appropriate figure.[17] The technical usages are accepted by all later logicians. (2) and (3) belong to proof theory, as they are (Peripatetic) methods of validation. For (1)(b) Imperial logicians were ready to assume that when '*p* and *q*, therefore *r*' was asserted '*r*, if *p* and *q*' could be asserted; and this is why analysis was called 'the converse of demonstration' (Elias, *In Isagogen*, 37. 22). But, more important, it was seen epistemologically: someone who knew what premisses yielded a given conclusion was in possession of a proof form, which was simply the synthesis that was the *converse* of the analysis.[18] So a definition of it in geometry (attributed to the first-century BC mathematician Geminus) as 'the discovery of a demonstration' was equally apt (Ammonius, *In Analytica priora*, 5. 22–31). This was to be expected in geometry, for there theorems were put alongside problems which were apparently practical— how is a square to be constructed on a given straight line, as one might ask how is a house to be constructed? But comparatively speaking this was just how Peripatetics and Platonists did see logic. The comparison lies between how they saw it and their picture of how Stoics saw it. All this implies a greater attachment than we find in Aristotle's own *Prior Analytics* to the dialectic of the *Topics*,

---

[17] *In An. pr.*, 7. 11–82. (2) and (3) are also called ἀναγωγή.
[18] Ib. Cf. ἀναστρέφοντα, ἀνεστροφάν, Procl., *In 1 Eucl.*, 57. 26; 69. 17–24.

where the *problem* was prior to the *proposition/premiss* of a proof.[19] The way to that had been opened for the Platonists by the authoritative Alexander (*In Analytica priora*, 44; cf. Tae-Soo Lee, 1984). These commentators display their Platonism by recognizing and approving a species of 'analysis' outside deductive logic. It was the 'ascent' from the sensible to the intelligible forms: its pre-eminent example was to be found in the *Symposium* and even counted as a subordinate species called 'erotic analysis' (Ammonius, op. cit., 5. 24). But it was not subjected to the the programme of harmonizing Aristotle with Plato. It was simply put alongside the application in syllogistic and other sciences as 'in philosophy': there was the generic concept of analysis as finding the simple components of a compound, and there were its species in the sciences (ib., p. 5) For of course the ascent from sensible universals was nothing in Neoplatonic metaphysics if it was not an ascent from the compound to the simple.

Proclus' comparison of Aristotelian and Parmenidean logic

On the other hand, Aristotelian commentaries did not normally indulge in derogatory comparison of Aristotelian syllogistic with Platonic dialectic. Others did. Plotinus' version, although he was well aware of what he was doing, was too eccentric to be relevant to a conception of logic.[20] Dexippus repeats Platonist debating-points: for example a very bad one to the effect that, unlike division, syllogistic proofs are impossible in the case of categories or summa genera (*In Categorias*, 53). In a conventionally rhetorical introduction to the *Cratylus*, Proclus contrasts the dialectic of the *Republic*, which we shall find in our Dialogue, with the empty dialectical methods of the Lyceum, which deal in names, not in what they stand for: syllogistic is easy to learn and perfectly clear for anyone, he says, who has steady nerves and a good memory (*In*

---

[19] Problem distingushed from proposition *Top.*, I. 4; see further P. Moraux (1968). *Dialectical* problem defined *Top.*, I. 10–11. Ammonius discusses the dialectical proposition in this context in an excursus of his *De int.* commentary, 199. 19–203. 20.

[20] This will be touched on in ch. 7. G. Leroux (1974) bases his account on a 'descending' and an 'ascending' dialectic, which he attributes to Plotinus but which I can find no word of in the *Enneads*.

Cratylum, 1. 10–2. 4). He mentions also the *Parmenides* as exempli-
fying non-empty dialectic as well as representing, although
inexactly, the collection and division of the *Phaedrus* and *Sophist*
(ib., 2. 28–3. 12; *In Parmenidem*, 650). This does not make it any
easier to make much sense of his claim that categorical syllogistic
is heuristically the inferior, less 'neat' for dispensing with hypotheses in the discovery of the 'connections and differences of things'.
For he is obviously trying to do something more interesting than
to repeat the claim that syllogistic was a posteriori because its premisses came from sense-perception (as in Damascius, *In Philebum*,
§ 68). He tells us in his commentary what he takes Parmenides'
logic to be. It shows the relations to itself, i.e. *per se* properties, and
to 'the other things', i.e. relational properties, of anything that is.

In a model of it, soul is taken as what is and bodies as the other
things (1004 ff). Its framework is twenty-four hypotheses of the
following form:

1. *a*. If soul exists, *P Q R* are consequent *per se* properties of
soul
   b. If soul exists, *S T U* are incompatible *per se* properties of
soul
   c. If soul exists, *V W X* are consequent and incompatible
properties of soul
2. If soul exists, (... are properties of soul in relation to bodies,
repeated as in 1. *a*, *b*, and *c*)
3. If soul exists (... are *per se* properties of bodies, again
divided into *a*, *b*, and *c*)
4. If soul exists (... are properties of bodies in relation to soul,
again divided into *a*, *b*, and *c*)
5–8. If soul does not exist (..., repeated as in 1–4.)

Unfortunately, Proclus does not express himself rigorously. But
the consequents of 5–8 are apparently the negations of those
mentioned in the affirmative hypotheses. We must also understand
that possessing a property (say life) in relation to other things is
equivalent to causing them to possess a similar property. So among
relational properties we can infer as follows (cf 1006. 19–26):

soul is the cause of *P Q R* for bodies,

for

if soul exists, *P Q R* follow for bodies
and if soul does not exist, not -*P*, not-Q not-*R* follow for
bodies
therefore soul is the only cause of *P Q R* for bodies

He points out that in order to start from the more familiar we
should expect to discover the relational, that is causal, properties
first, and from them to demonstrate the intrinsic properties. But
equally, of course, one property may have to be deduced from
another of the same kind.

I am aware [he admits (1007)] that copying this method Aristotle requires
the logician to propound the predicates and the subjects and what is
inappropriate to a given subject and what is inappropriate to a given
predicate, i.e. stating both their consequent and their incompatible properties . . .

But our method, he claims, is a more finished one because all its
moods (Proclus means the twenty-four types of hypothesis) are
propounded as a result of division; proceeding through all the
hypotheses is a neater way of reaching what we are looking for,
namely the truth about things.

And for the most part we use hypothetical deductions, which direct our
attention especially well to the connection of things—their interrelations
and their mutual divisions. But we shall use categoricals too when we need
to argue for the conditional or for the minor premiss in each hypothesis.[21]

The trouble is that all this still leaves the reader uncertain—and
Proclus himself seems uncertain—whether the Parmenidean
method is superior on account of its deductive virtues or on some
other grounds which are at best heuristic and perhaps only psychological. As for deduction, it is in fact logically indifferent (since
existential import is not particularly relevant) whether we demonstrate a property of a subject by a categorical syllogism of the form
'*bAa, cAb*, therefore *cAa*', by a hypothetical syllogism of the form,
'if *bAa* and *cAb* then *cAa*, but *bAa* and *cAb*, therefore *cAa*', or by
a proof in class algebra of the form '$\beta \subset \alpha$, $\gamma \subset \beta$, therefore $\gamma \subset \alpha$'.

---

[21] For example, 'if soul exists, sympathy is a property of bodies' (3*a*) will be
proved by their participation in life-giving, which is a property of soul in relation
to bodies (2*a*). Cf. 1004. 39–1005. 1. The reference to the minor premiss follows the
accepted Peripatetic doctrine which stems from Ar., *An. pr.*, *1*. 44. See, for example,
Ps.-Amm., *In An. pr.*, 65. 37–66. 2.

The hypothetical form would be represented by the Parmenidean method, the class algebra by Plato's collection and division. The equivalence of the last form to a categorical syllogism in Barbara was implicit in the passage of the *Prior Analytics* (43^b1 ff.) some of whose actual words Proclus repeated when he admitted that Aristotle copied 'our' method. Then what can he mean at the end of his explanation by preferring hypothetical deductions for directing our attention to the interrelations of the forms? Certainly he put weight on the Parmenidean matching of the affirmative by negative conditionals, for this made for the exhaustiveness of division and so for its validity as a deductive method. (He named it as a formal reason why Parmenides was superior to Zeno.) But suppose we take a simplified version of his own example,

> if soul exists, life belongs to bodies
> if soul does not exist, life does not belong to bodies
> therefore soul is the sole cause (sufficient and necessary condition) of life in bodies:

we can start by substituting for the first premiss

> all bodies with soul are living bodies,

and no student with steady nerves and a good memory will be unable to complete a categorical polysyllogism yielding the equivalent conclusion. (Again, dropping the reference to existence is irrelevant to the present comparison.)

On the other hand, the substitution of what belongs apparently to a propositional logic of the form '$p \rightarrow q$' by what apparently belongs to a logic of terms of the form 'aAb' is feasible only when 'p' and 'q' happen to be restricted to a form which already belongs to the logic of terms, i.e. when '$p \rightarrow q$' is restricted to

> if anything is f it is g.

It is not feasible for 'if the sun is above the earth it is day' or, more relevantly, for 'if equals are added to equals the result is equals'.[22]

---

[22] Explicit identification of aAb (or its 'indefinite'/unqualified form) with a conditional is not normal among the ancients, presumably because of the question of existential import. But as Barnes points out (1983, 312), it is allowed by Galen, XI. 499K.

But Proclus claims another merit for his method; and this does depend on the non-formal restriction of the conditionals. The types of hypothesis are propounded, he claims, as a result of division. This can and should be taken generally. It can be stated as an abstract framework of the twenty-four hypotheses in which there are no constants, so that 'soul' is replaced by a class-variable, 'K', and the other bodies by 'K''' (the complement class). For a class and its complement are an obvious division; and the property variables can be defined or introduced as being ordered by a stemma (as in a division). And these structural relations, of course, can be stated as applying to the particular example which contains the values 'soul', 'bodies', 'motion', 'life', and so on. This merit is associated with Proclus' insistence on the correct order in the use of the dialectical methods, first division, then definition, then demonstration (e.g. *Parmenides Commentary*, 982. 11–15; *Platonic Theology*, I. 9. 40. 10–12). But again the trouble is that Aristotle's use of syllogistic in *Posterior Analytics* recommended just such an ordering on hierarchy of predicates in any science—first a genus or species from the definition, then a proprium, which is first the major term of a first syllogism which demonstrates it, and then middle term of a second syllogism which demonstrates a second proprium (and major term), to become middle term of a third syllogism, and so on. No doubt this does not occur in any actual Aristotelian science. But if it does not, that is not due to the logic. It is a matter of something prior to the logic, namely the choice of primitive premisses, including definitions. Here Proclus has emphasized one method of teaching definitions, namely Division. The method was rejected by Aristotle because Platonic division meant more than arranging a class or genus in a stemma: it required there to be one *fundamentum divisionis* (in other words no cross-division) throughout the classes *and subclasses* (*subordinate species*). He thought this was not to be found universally in nature. His logical objection to earlier Platonists' belief that division could be demonstrative is not to the point, for the Neoplatonists distinguished it from demonstration.

Still less can any superior 'power to direct our attention to the connections of things' be validly claimed for hypothetical deductions. These connections are only what the logical constants of the propositions stand for; and, as we have seen, it makes no logical difference whether we express a universal proposition by using

mutatis mutandis 'all . . . are . . .' or by using 'if something is . . .
it is . . .'. In any case, if there is something defective about categorical deductions, how do they lose that defect when they are used 'to argue for the conditions or for the minor premiss'?

To sum up the value of Proclus' comparison of the two logics, we have to conclude that his criticism of Aristotelian formal logic is mostly too confused to amount to anything. He has in effect three complaints about the Peripatetics. First, the complaint in his introduction to the *Cratylus* that their logic is about empty names. 'Empty' does not mean devoid of significance or of reference but in abstraction from them. This is the complaint usually made about Stoic logic by the Aristotelians and by Platonists expounding Aristotle: but by what might be called an extrapolation of convention it could be applied to Peripatetic logic in a commentary on Plato for no other motive than that that logic was not Platonic dialectic. The burden of it is an objection to formalism, and we shall consider it more generally quite soon.

Secondly, in the context of the *Parmenides* he says that to follow a chain of Parmenidean hypotheses is a neater way of arriving at the truth. Since such hypotheses can be transposed into equivalent categorical syllogisms, Proclus' claim must be invalid; for his example is restricted to cases of 'if anything is *f* it is *g*'. But a glance at his context will suggest that, if we wish to be charitable, we can suppose that his ground is a third argument for the superiority of Parmenidean dialectic; this would be that its premisses are reached by division. As for this, we have to notice that it does not concern the deductive logic and that there is equal room for it in the preliminaries to categorical syllogistic. It is, of course, true that the Peripatetics did not avail themselves of this possibility precisely because they did not think that Platonic divisions represented the facts about natural kinds.

This summary is, I believe, confirmed by another description which Proclus gives, in the *Platonic Theology*, of the Parmenidean dialectic (I. 10. 45. 19–46. 22). On the face of it, it is rather different, but that is mainly because it is much less rhetorical. I will summarize this too.

The series of hypotheses in the *Parmenides* (he asserts) represent a chain of demonstrations in which

1. the first are deduced from premisses which contain (*a*) the fewest, (*b*) the simplest, and (*c*) the most familiar or self-evident

ideas which might be called 'common notions';
2. the next are (*a*) greater in number, and (*b*) less simple;
3. prior conclusions (i.e. ones demonstrated in prior hypotheses) are used to make the next in order, as in geometry;
4. the order represents the order of procession among the divine realities.[23]

The logical order of the properties, which are forms or Ideas, is of paramount significance to Neoplatonists. For participation is the converse relation of procession or generation. That is why they say division corresponds to procession and analysis to reversion (e.g. Damascius on the *Philebus*, 54 Westerink, followed by Olympiodorus, 246 Stallbaum). And the significance of this to anyone wanting to understand them is that it reveals their metaphysics not so much as idealist but as rationalist: the metaphysical order is the rational order.

The Alexandrian conception of logic

Conventions of the genre which I have stressed in the Aristotelian commentaries were influential also in the Platonic commentaries. There is no reason to suppose that Proclus' commentaries on the *Organon*, which were extensive but have not survived, were not sympathetic as well as scholarly. The question of *sincerity* on the part of an author who expressed such different points of view is not, as we shall see later, as simple as it might seem. The Alexandrian commentaries on the *Organon* present a certain conception of logic which ought now to be given a brief description.

One of the required topics for an introductory course, and one not confined to the Platonists, was the question whether logic is a part or an instrument of philosophy.[24] Several of the arguments given for each answer are reasonable, but they can be found repeated so often in the commentaries that they need not be repeated here. What must not continue to escape notice is a misunderstanding of the thesis that logic is a part of philosophy. This thesis is generally recognized, as it was by the Alexandrian

---

[23] The properties of the One and the others in the *Parmenides* were also gods according to Proclus.

[24] It was covered by Alexander (*In An. pr.*, *1*. 1. 3–4. 29). A list of its occurrences in the commentators can be found in Westerink (1961), 131–2.

commentators, to be something that the Stoics had said; and modern students of ancient philosophy infer that the commentators were objecting to the Stoic conception of dialectic and its relation to other branches of philosophy. No doubt this is how the debate had started centuries before: but study of the arguments will show that they contribute nothing to it, and one wonders whether the later commentators had any idea what the Stoics meant by 'part' of philosophy. They hadn't because they didn't know what Stoic 'dialectic' was but took it to mean formal logic.[25] Even Alexander had taken 'part' for no more than the vague negation of 'instrument' (cf. *In Analytica priora*, 3. 4–6), and the Alexandrians did the same. But they accepted also his account of proof, or syllogism; and the significance of this fact has been explained by Tae-Soo Lee in a valuable contribution to the history of logic (1979, particularly 46–54, 72–3).

The theory, as Lee argues, depended on presuming a picture of syllogism not merely as argument, 'so and so, therefore so and so', rather than a conditional, 'if so and so, then so and so', but as argument for a purpose. 'What has no use is not a proof ('syllogism') either' (Alexander, *In Analytica priora*, 18. 21). Consequently the basic notion was not so much conclusion as 'problem' (cf. Lee, 72–3). We saw earlier that logic is analysis because analysis is the discovery of proof, but that technically it was the problem which was supposed to be analysed in order to discover premisses. In fact Alexander was much closer than Aristotle to considering logic as a method of discovery rather than proof. And the theory inherited from him produced large gaps in the Alexandrian commentaries. For example, the broad neglect of Book II of the *Prior Analytics* and, when it was not neglected, its treatment as an introduction to the dialectical syllogism meant that syllogisms with false premisses and syllogisms with contradictory premisses received very little attention from them or their Byzantine successors (ib., 48). These gaps probably had other causes as well: but Lee is correct in complaining that modern historians who treat the controversy over 'instrument or part' as a tedious one of words have lost sight of the connection between the definition as instru-

---

[25] Only a little later the exceptionally well-informed Simplicius complained that he had no access to 'Stoic doctrine and the majority of their works' (*In Cat.*, 334. 2–3).

ment and a conscious restriction of the field of formal logic (ib., 49). How did Alexander understand logic as part of philosophy? In view of his negative definition of 'part' it could only be as a logic without use; which he quite reasonably—and here at least as a good Aristotelian—took as one studied for its own sake. And to be accurate, what was debated was rather alternative ways of studying logic than alternative logics. The ancient commentators did not even distinguish a Peripatetic calculus of terms from a calculus of propositions. Alexander illustrated the subject studied without an ulterior use by the presence of trivial theorems, such as ones of the form 'p or p, p, therefore p' and 'p or q, q, therefore q'. These had, of course, been long associated with the Stoics; and we owe a good deal of our evidence about Stoic formal logic to the fact that Alexander was at pains to illustrate the concept of vain labour.

Whether or not the Neoplatonists inherited this general prejudice in favour of logic as serving a purpose, Ammonius' treatment of the conventional dispute is quite different from Alexander's, and it is left virtually unaltered by his successors. The formalist version of logic turns out to be the 'instrument' version, which, in direct contradiction of Alexander, is that of Aristotle's syllogistic. Concrete philosophical arguments belong to the 'part' version, are attributed to Plato, and have nothing to do with Stoicism. There is nothing strange in this, once a number of facts are appreciated. First, by this time, Stoicism was only of antiquarian interest, and the need to restrict the field of formal logic was no longer a live issue. In the second place, Ammonius professed to be dealing with a different claim, attributed to Platonists; and he defined 'part' less artificially than Alexander. Fourthly, the Athenian school had paved the way for an interpretation of the *Parmenides* of the kind which we described in the case of Proclus.

What does Ammonius actually say? As well as attributing the 'part of philosophy' claim to the Stoics and the 'instrument' claim to the Peripatetics, he states that some Platonists believed that according to Plato logic was the most valuable part of philosophy (*In Analytica priora*, 8. 15 ff.). They were in fact quoting *Philebus*, 57E–58E. He defines 'part' as 'what helps to complete something and whose removal entails the removal of that whole'. Some of the traditional arguments from the second-century debate are rehearsed; they concern such questions as whether that debate should be about 'part' or 'subpart'. But Ammonius returns to the

suggestion of 'some Platonists', and asserts that in spite of what the
Phaedrus and the *Philebus* said about dialectic it is not the most
valuable part of philosophy. Nor should it in fact be called part, but
part *and* instrument.

As part, he explains, the logic has content or reference—it is
'with the things'. As instrument it is 'without the things'—empty
rules, or canons. An example of the latter is '*A* is predicated of all
B, *B* is predicated of all *C*, therefore *A* is predicated of all *C*.' Plato,
however, sometimes uses the kind of logic which is a part of
philosophy, that is, when he applies such canons to things and
makes syllogisms about things, e.g. 'soul is self-moving, what is
self-moving is always moving, what is always moving is immortal,
therefore soul is immortal'. But sometimes he asserts mere rules, or
canons which are empty because without content or reference, 'the
things'. Ammonius gives no example from Plato of this.

According to Lee, Ammonius' thesis was due to a misunderstanding of Alexander which, it appears, can have been inspired
only by Plotinus' essay on dialectic. As the reader will have
inferred, it is not my view that Ammonius has misunderstood
Alexander but that he has found another hare to chase. Plotinus
certainly referred to 'empty theorems and canons', but that was a
cliché. His essay (as we shall see when we consider the stages of
knowledge) has in any case a subject which is far removed from that
of Ammonius. In fact the Alexandrians had little acquaintance with
the *Enneads*. And if another 'source' has to be found, it could better
be found in Proclus, with the proviso that he is unlikely to have
gone so far as Ammonius in amalgamating Plato's and Aristotle's
logic. But this is not the place to pursue that.

The official Neoplatonic account is now that Plato's dialectic is
both part *and* instrument of philosophy inasmuch as he *sometimes*
used it about things, *sometimes* about rules.[26] For a conception of
what logic is, this is disappointing. No attempt has been made
—nor will it be made for centuries—to suggest a theoretical relation
between the two beyond the fact, which is taken for granted, that
the use about things is making true inferences about them and the

---

[26] The anonymous *De arte logica*, which tends to copy Ammonius, names the
Parmenides for 'instrument' (ed. Busse, *CAG*, xii/1, p. x.), Olympiodorus the
Phaedo.

rules are rules for making these true inferences. The form or expression of the rules seems to have been thought unimportant.

The criterion of validity

Neither Platonist nor Aristotelian distinguished rules of inference from major premisses. This is borne out by the hopeless, if often ingenious, efforts to turn hypothetical, relational, and other arguments into categorical syllogisms.[27] Familiar as this is to historians of logic, they have perhaps neglected the influence of Euclid. What he called axioms and used as premisses seemed to be just the kind of highly general proposition which provided schemata of inferences: and I think that they were often not distinguished from what Aristotle called axioms. Among many Stoic concepts which had become common currency was that of 'common notions', and it was under this head that axioms were included by the later Neoplatonists.[28] But to demand a general distinction between a principle of inference and a premiss may be to have too limited a historical sense. Aristotle recognized it in the case of some 'common principles', namely the laws of contradiction and of excluded middle, but not, it seems, in the case of 'equals taken from equals leave equals', which can and do occur within a geometrical proof (cf. Lear, 1980, 102 n. 9).

We might, however, ask, What was their criterion of validity? Their remarks about Platonic division and dilemmas are superficial, so we should confine ourselves to syllogism. They assumed that, so far as he had one, Aristotle's criterion was *contained in* the theory of perfect syllogism and the transposition of syllogisms in the second and third figures (the fourth not being admitted) to the perfect moods of the first. Obviously, however, the very possibility of this transposition makes the perfect moods logically equivalent to the imperfect (save for two in the third figure). This objection had been met by Peripatetic commentators who claimed that whether or not the first figure was logically prior it was prior in

---

[27] e.g. Al., *In An. pr.*, 262 ff; 344. 7 ff.
[28] e.g. Procl., *In Eucl.*, I. 56. 28; 240. 11–241. 5. These refer to geometry. But Olympiodorus, *In Gorg.*, 20. 17–18 Norvin, describing the place of demonstration among the 'dialectical methods', says quite generally that 'starting from the definition it proceeds from the common notions and demonstrates'.

nature. What can this mean? Themistius in the fourth century explained that, quite apart from the question of formal logic, it was the cause inasmuch as it was the 'generator' of the other figures.[29] What was in their opponents' minds, I think, is that we might just as well have said that the other figures 'generated' the first inasmuch as the first-figure moods can be inferred from them.[30] Themistius gives two grounds for his position. The first, that the more perfect 'engenders' the less perfect, begs the original question. But secondly, the first figure alone contains the middle term in its natural position. This presumably refers to the *Prior Analytics*' explanation of the self-evidence of its moods (25^b32-5). But it is far from clear—at least from this Arabic version, which is all we have—that when Themistius says that the other figures 'participate in', i.e. share a property of, the first, he means the property of being evidently necessary, and not the property of being necessary, i.e. syllogistic. If he means the latter, he is open to the charge of having confused the concept of *perfect* with the concept of *valid*. His insistence that the 'engendering' does not hold between the moods but between the figures could be interpreted either way.[31] For he could be trying to distinguish the relation between the figures in respect of their self-evidence from their formal relation. More conclusive is his reply to a question of his chief opponent.[32] The Neoplatonist Maximus asked, 'Is the value of the proof given by an argument derived by conversion from the first figure the same as, or less than, or greater than that of an argument in the first figure?' Themistius replied, 'The same, for there are more ways of killing a cat than drowning' (loc. cit.,

---

[29] *Traité de Thémistius en réponse à Maxime au sujet de la réduction de la deuxième et la troisième figures à la première* (tr. from Arabic), in A. Badawi (1968). Badawi's text and translation were criticized as unreliable by P. Moraux in an apparently unpublished paper. But, with this warning Themistius' arguments seem to me sufficiently repetitive and sufficiently, if indirectly, corroborated to justify my use of them.

[30] Only Darapti and Felapton in the third figure are not logically equivalent to a first-figure mood; for the reduction of these (to Darii and Ferio respectively) depends on the conversion of A to I which is, of course, not reciprocal. But the exceptions only enhance the opponents' case, since their first-figure opposite numbers *cannot*, as logically prior, or implicates, generate them, while there are no cases of this in the reverse direction.

[31] This claim, he adds, is not stated by Aristotle or by Theophrastus but by the modern Peripatetics.

[32] For the controversy behind Themistius' treatise see Amm., *In An. pr.*, 31. 18–22.

169). The point is of some significance, for it implies that Patzig's strictures on writers who call the figure rather than moods perfect are either exaggerated or do not apply to all such writers.[33] Thus Themistius may have seen that the relation between the figures in respect of their self-evidence is the one relevant to Aristotle's notion of a perfect syllogism. But to describe it as 'generating' or 'engendering' less self-evident but not less valid figures does not encourage one to suppose that he was very clear about his own claim. Whatever the meaning of the Neoplatonizing rule to which he appeals and which makes the more 'perfect' engender the less perfect, it must be out of place here.

But Alexander had already gone half-way down this path (*In Analytica priora*, 42. 27 ff.). On the one hand he distinguished 'generating', which (as J. Barnes suggested to me) is not an inference, since it consists only in converting the subject and predicate *expressions*, from 'reduction', in which the conversion is a logical operation on the subjects and predicates (cf. op. cit., 327). And he supposes that perfection is concerned with reduction. This distinction may have been neglected by some of his successors. But at the same time Alexander had claimed that the first figure was 'first' *because* it generated the others (48. 11–12). And he gilds the lily with a misplaced ingenuity by continuing a hierarchy of figures that looks more Neoplatonic than Aristotelian. The second is 'superior' to the third by containing universal (though negative) conclusions, while the third is superior to the second by containing affirmative (though particular) conclusions. But *universal* is more of a proprium of an apodeictic syllogism than *affirmative*; in fact, he says, the second figure is appropriate to dialectical syllogisms on account of its negative (corresponding to destructive) conclusions, and the third to sophistical syllogisms on account of its particular (corresponding to indefinite) conclusions (ib., 48. 21–49. 17).

It is perhaps an unexpected pleasure to be able to report that this inept tale initiated by the two leading Peripatetics since Theophrastus was not repeated by any Neoplatonist known to us on this subject.

As for perfection, Alexander seems to have understood quite well that, according to *Prior Analytics* 24[b]16–26 and 25[b]32 ff., Barbara and Celarent were perfect because the inferences in them were self-evident without additional support (54. 2–21 and 25).

[33] G. Patzig (1968), 43, 44, 74. Cf. Them., loc. cit., 170.

Philoponus adds nothing save the phrase, rightly admired by Patzig, that in the perfect syllogism the conclusion is for anyone to grasp, while in the imperfect form it needs the expert.[34] And all commentators knew quite well that the second- and third-figure forms of perfect syllogisms were still syllogisms: they could read it in Aristotle at 27^a1-2 and 28^a1-7. But they find it difficult to avoid saying things which imply or are close to implying the opposite. Some of the inconsistencies are due, I suspect, to the piecemeal treatment of their sources which I have earlier attributed to commentators; and this must include the mixture, which we cannot always dissolve, of their own views and their exposition of Aristotle's.

There is, however, a more significant factor within logic which made them liable to confuse perfection and validity. The self-evidence of an inference in Barbara or Celarent, in which the perfection of these moods as proof forms consists, is not in fact independent of its validity. What those proof forms 'make evident' is the 'necessity' of the other forms or moods, and in this context 'necessity' is Aristotle's term for validity. The self-evidence of the perfect forms is thus a criterion—or better, perhaps, a guarantee —of validity. (The *dictum de omni et nullo* can be seen as resting on identifying the relation of subject to predicate with the relation of part to whole, or the application of Euler diagrams.) But it is a non-formal guarantee. Had Aristotle used it as, or in, a definition, it could have counted as a non-syntactic but semantic criterion (on a par with truth tables). But he was unwilling to do that. It would have seemed to him an epistemological not a logical property. Consequently it is not a necessary condition of validity. But to expect such a necessary condition is an involuntary impulse on the part of a logician. Hence Maximus' question to Themistius about the comparative 'value' or 'worth' of the imperfect moods. He wants to ask about validity but knows he cannot call it 'necessity' because it is common ground that the Aristotelian theory attributed that to the imperfect mood *per se*, not by way of reduction.

The logical commentators' expectation, conscious or unconscious, of more system in the logic than Aristotle was willing to espouse betrays itself by an inappropriate epithet. Starting at least from Alexander (op. cit., 54) they called the first figure or its moods

---

[34] *In An. pr.*, 54. 2–21; Patzig, op. cit., 72–3. But Patzig's opinion that Philoponus is a better logician than Ammonius is hardly tenable.

not just perfect and convincing but ἀναπόδεικτος. This mistakenly suggests that the imperfect moods required demonstration, that they were theorems whose necessity derived from axioms (the perfect moods), in other words that the perfect moods corresponded to the Stoics' famous 'indemonstrables' or 'undemonstrated' and reduction to the Stoic 'analysis'.

We do not possess Ammonius' comments on *Prior Analytics* 25ᵇ32 ff., which is the normal lemma for a discussion of perfect syllogisms; but we know that he followed an alternative Peripatetic tradition which argued, against Aristotle, that perfect moods belonged to all the figures (*In Analytica priora*, 14. 31–3). The arguments have to be inferred from the counter-arguments of Themistius: but it should now be easy to see from Maximus' question how simple the case is. A perfect syllogism, Ammonius would have said, must by the force of the term be one which is more of a proof (συλλογισμός) than an imperfect one; on Aristotle's own showing a second- or third-figure mood is no less of a proof than a first-figure mood; so he should not have said that perfect syllogisms are confined to the first figure.[35] Philoponus may have believed this too. There is no reason why he should not have done; and had he not, he would have departed from the mainstream of Neoplatonist logicians (ib. ll. 15–25).

Logical form

Problems of validity are problems of logical form. Let us try asking what conception the commentators had of that. To recognize logical form, it is necessary to recognize logical constants, that is, to distinguish them from variables and constants. But it should go without saying that having or not having these concepts is not an all-or-none affair. Take the question of variables first. It may well be thought that the limitations of ancient Greek mathematics—no differential calculus, no algebra, no conic sections—were due to the lack of this concept. Were the letters which Aristotle used for a syllogistic schema variables? Well, he did not have quantifiers as such—this is specially evident in the case of the particular quanti-

---

[35] The argument is not affected by the fact that, perversely construing 24ᵇ16–26, he took the *An. pr.*, ch. 1 description of perfect syllogisms to be intended only to exclude enthymemes (op. cit., 31).

fier. Secondly, we have a more formal criterion in the fact that there is no sign of his having been willing to substitute one such letter for another where there are two in one open sentence, and there are signs that he was not willing to.[36] For these reasons alone his letters are closer to abbreviations or pronouns than to variables. On the other hand, the *De interpretatione* touched real profundity in logic by claiming that the terms 'no' and 'every' are not names which, in the scholastic Latin, 'significant' but like 'is' and 'is not' 'adsignificant' (προσσημαίνει); they do not indirectly indicate the universal subject but indirectly indicate that it is universal, i.e. distributed (16^{b}19–25; 20^{a}9–14). This does not make the 'A' and 'I' modern quantifiers, but it gives them an essential character of these, which is to be logical constants or operators.

The commentators made major advances towards the idea of logical form. First, as for variables, Łukasiewicz pointed out that Alexander did substitute one letter for another in a syllogistic schema, which implies identifying two variables, when he was proving the convertibility of universal negative premisses.[37]

As for logical form itself, no one is going to say that it was not recognized implicitly by Aristotle and by many of his ancient readers. To know that a given proof is a syllogism in the first figure is enough for that. But we are looking for an explicit idea of it which connects it with the ideas of variables, constants, and operators. Something of this kind can be attributed to Alexander, although doubtless the question of his originality cannot be settled. He

[36] At least that is what Łukasiewicz (1951), 9, inferred from his constructing a syllogism with opposite premisses (*An pr.*, II. 64^{a}23–32) 'by the heavy roundabout way ... of concrete terms'.

[37] Al., *In An. pr.*, 34; Łukasiewicz, op. cit., 10. Alexander's argument, which is compressed, is a *reductio:* Suppose *b*E*a* is not convertible, it is compatible with *a*I*b*; but these two would yield the following first-figure syllogism, whose conclusion is absurd. (I have used a notation in which the first term is the subject term, as more familiar to non-Aristotelious.)

$$bEa$$
$$aIb$$
therefore *a*O**a**

Alexander must have begun with a syllogism in Ferio, viz.

$$bEa$$
$$cIb$$
therefore *b*O*a*

from which he obtains the required syllogism by substituting *a* for *c*.

explained, as Aristotle did not, that letters were used for the terms of syllogism to represent its figure as contrasted with its matter (*sic*), so that whatever the matter that is substituted for them it does not affect their validity (53. 28–54. 2). Ammonius rightly thought the distinction important enough and intelligible enough to introduce in the proëm to his *Prior analytics* commentary (p. 4). But he introduces the pair as 'what is analogous to matter' and 'what is analogous to form' and uses these expressions for the rest of the paragraph. Analogous to form are the figures (and presumably moods), analogous to matter are the 'underlying things' (ὑποκείμενα πράγματα), which means what is signified or referred to by the three terms. They are underlying in the technical sense of being the subject of the propositions, but also in the modern sense of being what these are about.[38] He therefore uses the distinction to explain how dialectical and demonstrative syllogisms differ in their matter, not their form: demonstrative syllogisms are about 'necessary' objects (19. 15–17; 20. 33 ff.). Evidently it applies also to that *use* of syllogism which Ammonius called logic as instrument of philosophy. For the 'rules or canons', which are better described as schemata and whose terms (letters) had no signification or reference, represented only the forms of arguments.[39] So we have a recognition of logical form which, with the possible, but no more than possible, exception of Stoicism, is the most explicit in the ancient world.[40]

---

[38] Cf. Ps.-Amm. Scholia ad *An. pr.*, I; ib., 71. 15–16; conversely, arguments are the matter of logic according to the Stoics (Amm., op. cit., 9. 26–7). For πράγματα as what the propositions are about (περί), 19. 16–17. There is only one point here at which Ammonius is careless about use and mention and speaks as though the matter were the concrete *terms* (4. 14–15).

[39] So Philoponus, *In An. pr.*, *I*. 46. 24–47. 11. But he departs from his master at 9. 9–11 by giving an example in a metalinguistic form. This departure is judiciously assessed by Lee (1979), 42–43.

[40] *Logical form in Arabic philosophy*: this is an extension of the Alexandrian Neoplatonists' commentaries. However: (i) Arabic resembles, much more than Greek does, the artificial languages of logicians, since the words indicate their form independently of their meaning. Hence the distinction of form and matter had long been familiar from the well-developed subject of Arabic grammar. (ii) On the other hand, the Aristotelian–Porphyrian tradition taught that logic was about thought, not expressions. (iii) The *De int.* (*ad init.*) also said that thought or meaning was distinct from its expression by being universal, not restricted to a linguistic group. (iv) Thus it was concluded, and endorsed by al-Farabi, that logic is universal grammar.
  I have summarized this from Zimmermann's invaluable introduction to his translation of al-Farabi on *De int.* (1981, xxxviii ff.; cf. cxxvii–cxxxix). But (a minor point) Alexander of Aphrodisias' and Ammonius' general application of 'matter', which I have referred to, make it unnecessary for Zimmermann to suppose (xxxix–xl) that al-Farabi, extrapolated this application from the separate and restricted one which Ammonius also made in connection with modality (*In De int.*, 215).

How much did Neoplatonism influence the logical commentaries?

How much does their Neoplatonism influence the Aristotelian logic of the commentators? Very little. Without pronouncing on the correct shape of Aristotle's own logic, it is not, of course, possible to be sure about distortions: but distortions or developments, these were mostly inherited from Peripatetics, chiefly Theophrastus and Alexander. The well-known goal of harmonizing Aristotle and Plato had been increasingly accepted since Porphyry had firmly established the *Categories* in the curriculum. Their agreement had in any case been a commonplace in the Middle Academy, except for rigorists like Atticus. It was also a convention in Alexandria that lectures on either author should not be from a *parti pris*. Here is part of Elias' rather complacent version:

He must not range himself with the authors he may be commenting on, like an actor on the stage who puts on different masks for representing different characters, becoming an Aristotelian when he is expounding Aristotle's works and declaring that there never was a philosopher like him, and when he is expounding Plato becoming a Platonist and declaring that there never was a philosopher to compare with Plato ... He must not share the feelings of any one school, as happened to Iamblichus; for, sympathizing with Plato, Iamblichus concedes to Aristotle that he, Aristotle, does not contradict Plato over the Ideas. He must not have an antipathy to a school, like Alexander; for Alexander being antipathetic to the immortality of the rational soul tries every turn in the game [Elias is quoting the *Republic*] to throw the claims made in the third argument of *On the immortality of the soul*. He must know all the work of Aristotle so that, after showing that Aristotle is consistent with himself, he can expound Aristotle's work by means of Aristotle's work. He must know all the work of Plato so that he can demonstrate Plato's consistency with himself by making the work of Aristotle an introduction to that of Plato. (*In Categorias*, 122. 27–123. 11)

Simplicius repeats Elias' points, showing thereby that they were commonplaces of the genre, but he is more committed to the programme of harmonization:

With respect to the things which Aristotle says against Plato, I think that the commentator should not simply look at the text and declare the disagreement of the two philosophers but, by having regard to the thought, should track down the agreement which does in most cases hold between them. (*In Categorias*, 7. 29–32)

A notable case of such reconciliation was provided by Ammonius when he settled the question of the status of logic. Olympiodorus comments that the ancients, meaning Plato, knew how to demonstrate but not how to construct a demonstration, like people who know how to wear shoes but not how to make them. But he finds it necessary to add that this does not make Plato inferior to Aristotle. On the contrary, Aristotle needed Plato's actual demonstrations from which to abstract for his science, but Plato did not need Aristotle's science in order to demonstrate: their relation was the same as the relation between Homer or Demosthenes and the author of *On poetry* or Hermogenes (*Categorias* [*Prolegomena*], 17).

The Neoplatonists rejected the priority of the first figure of syllogism, but they accepted the dependence on categoricals for the proof of hypothetical arguments. And in general they had no quarrel with Aristotle's formal logic. In the wider field of the *Organon*, however, the field of semantics, they drew on some of the major logico-metaphysical themes of Neoplatonism. They could be said to have been obsessed by universals—not unnaturally, since it is in problems raised by predication that everyone, including Aristotle, had placed the gulf between Platonists and Aristotelians. Perhaps the two principal themes with which they attempted to bridge the gulf were the Neoplatonic multiplication of the universal and the recognition of genus which was *ad unum* or *ab uno*. Assuming the accepted picture of a universal as a whole, the first theme distinguished three kinds of whole reflected by a general idea: the whole before, i.e. prior to, the parts; the whole in, i.e. composed of, the parts; and the whole of (meaning 'said of') or after the parts. If a universal in a given Aristotelian passage had unacceptable properties, it could be claimed that they were unacceptable only because the kind of universal had been misidentified. The second theme was believed to rebut the constant dilemma between inseparability and unequivocal predicability: Aristotle's genus was unequivocally predicable of its species but thereby reducible to them by being simply the class which included them extensionally. Neoplatonists built on Aristotle's own *tertium quid* between equivocal and unequivocal to have, in addition, a Platonic-style genus which was not so reducible. Both these themes, because of their importance to the structure of their metaphysics, will figure among those which are dealt with in detail in later chapters.

Finally, there was a methodological principle which applied to all philosophical enquiry and which could not fail to serve the aim of reconciling apparently inconsistent theses. This was Iamblichus' attempt to put some order into the practice of allegorical interpretation. Porphyry, he believed, offered alternative interpretations—whether of features in the cave of the nymphs or features in Egyptian theosophy—which were arbitrary and, more important, unrelated. Philosophical questions should be treated philosophically, theurgical questions theurgically, ethical questions ethically (*De mysteriis*, I. 2 *ad fin.*; and I. 4 for physical questions). When questions could fall under more than one of these categories there was immediate opportunity for harmonization. Aristotle had, of course, already used the notion, distinguishing, for instance, 'logical' from 'physical' analysis; and Porphyry's application of specifically Neoplatonic levels of interpretation to a literary text was more systematic than Iamblichus implies (cf. Lamberton, 1986, 127).

Iamblichus' disciple the Emperor Julian provided an application to philosophy and religion which became a comonplace. In Julian's *Hymn to King Helios* 'the sun' is the name (1) of the first (Plotinian) hypostasis, or Idea of the Good, the (2) 'intelligibly' in the second hypostasis, of the good which causes existence, beauty, and the like for thought, then (3) 'intellectually' in the second division of the hypostasis, of good considered as an act instead of object of thought, and finally (4) as the sun in the sky (Oratio IV.).). (2) and (3) are each it seems, identified with a Mithras, and (4) is a visible god.

Moreover, this methodological principle, which had been implicit in Plotinus and was enthusiastically embraced by the Athenian school, can almost be counted as a structural element in Neoplatonic metaphysics. For, as the example shows, the categories or modes of interpretation correspond to hypostases and other intermediate levels of reality which have an hierarchical order. It follows that the different interpretations are no longer, as Iamblichus found them in Porphyry, independent. So, from the point of view of knowledge, there is an analogical chain of inference from the lower to the higher. For the same attribute will appear in its 'appropriate' form on all the different levels. K. Praechter, who was the first to have noticed both the importance and the details of Iamblichus' method, argued plausibly that in recommending the commentator to look not merely for the particular 'scope' or aim of a passage in his author but for a single scope of the whole work, Iamblichus had in mind the kind of analogical chain that I have just mentioned (Praechter, 1910*b*, especially 138). He quotes a clear example from Hermeias' account of the subject-matter of the *Phaedrus*, that is, 'beauty in all its forms', and claims also Iamblichus' own account of the *Categories* as being about all three of the conventionally proposed subjects: words, concepts, and things.[41] It is the meaning of Proclus' complaint that Porphyry gave a 'more particular' (i.e. less universal) exposition than Iamblichus of the *Timaeus*.[42] What Iamblichus described as the 'intellectual theory', and therefore the highest discursive interpretation of a given notion, means what we should call the metaphysical interpretation and is commonly approved by Simplicius. It embraces just this demonstration that the same notion appears in different and appropriate forms at the different levels. The excursus on place recorded in his *Categories* commentary is only one if many express examples.

Before the question of Neoplatonic influence is left, one prominent feature should be mentioned. All over the commentaries on Plato and Aristotle alike one finds concepts or objects being classified by division. The process is often both artificial and unfruitful. Here are some examples taken at random from the logical commentaries. To begin with, Aristotle's own writings are divided into 'particular', 'universal', and 'intermediate'; the universal are subdivided into 'memoranda' and 'collections', and memoranda into those which are 'monographs' and those which 'have various subjects' . . . and so on with some alternative classifications.[43] Division itself is divided into four (Ammonius, *In Isagogen*, 81. 16 ff.) or seven kinds (Elias, *In Isagogen*, 67. 22 ff.). Aristotle's categories are fitted into a complicated tree of genus and species (Simplicius., op. cit., 67. 26–68. 16).

Is this not a typical manifestation of Neoplatonic dialectic? Certainly: but that is only an incidental cause and not the origin of the use and abuse of division. It was the practice almost without

---

[41] Herm., *In Phaedr.*, 13. 6 ff.; Philop., *In Cat.*, 129. 9 ff.; 136. 29 ff.; Simpl., *In Cat.*, 13. 16 ff.; Olympiod., *Proleg.*, 18. 23 ff.

[42] *In Tim.*, 204. 24–7. Iamblichus' was ἐποπτικώτερος, which is the Platonic equivalent, in the context, of the Neoplatonic νοερός.

[43] Simpl., *In Cat.*, 4. 10–5. 2. Ilsetraut Hadot (1984, 339–40) has some remarks, with which I do not wholly agree, about the 'ontological significance' of the first stage in the division. See also P. Moraux (1973), 67 ff.

exception in what today would be classed an educational books. This had been so at least since the early Peripatos, and it applied to all subjects, as M. Fuhrmann (1960) showed in his work on 'handbooks'. 'Introductions to', 'Arts of' rhetoric, philosophy, ethics, grammar, medicine, and so on, divide their topics or familiar concepts into 'parts', 'genera', 'species' without an agreed logical vocabulary but with the ideal of defining everything by genus and differentia. Ever since the *Topics* there had been an interchange between philosophers and rhetoricians. The author of an introduction to Hermogenes' Στάσεις writes,

... the philosophers propound definitions or at least descriptions of every object: so let us define each of the pair which we have mentioned . . . Now since definitions have to consist of a genus and differentiae . . . (Rabe, *Prolegomena*, 184. 1 ff.).

All this was only reinforced, in no way started, by the addition or assimilation of Platonic dialectic.

The mechanical recourse to it, however, could have unfortunate results. To confine examples to logic, Galen did less than assist the subject of fallacies with a division which 'proved' that there are exactly six fallacies of diction (*De captionibus*, cc. 2–3, 14. 585 ff. K., on Aristotle, *Sophistici elenchi* 165^b24–30). Ammonius supposed that *Categories*, 6^a20 ff. was providing an 'analogy to definition' of *in a subject* and found himself having to make *in something* 'analogous to a genus' (*In Categorias*, 26. 31–2). But a much worse instance is provided by his pupil Philoponus (cf. Lee, 1984, 59–61).

This concerns the definition of πρότασις, which sometimes means any proposition but usually means a proposition in a syllogism. Ammonius had again found only a concept which was 'analogous to a differentia', and there were two of them at that, but at least what he proposed was a further step towards making explicit a formal structure which we now represent by variables and a logical constant. For he decided on quantity and quality, in the technical sense of the terms. But Philoponus first chooses *affirming or denying* them, then more Aristotelian than Aristotle, comes to grief at the obstacle that (being co-extensive with the definiendum) it should be a proprium not a differentia. By means of a blunder in logic he argues that it should be understood as the conjunction *affirming and denying* but in the end defines πρότασις as λόγος τινὸς κατά τινος—

which fails to distinguish it from assertion/statement (*In Analytica priora* I, 16–18).[44]

A comment on consistency and originality

A good deal of this chapter has been devoted to showing that the ancient commentaries are pervaded by various conventions of the genre. Before finishing it, it might be as well to mention some features which resulted from this fact and some inferences which are not always drawn from it by modern readers. It will not be necessary to repeat the relevant conventions.

First, we should expect to find and do find numerous inconsistencies in different commentaries under the same author's name, and even in a single work. This follows from the manner in which lectures were constructed to one degree or another out of scholia which were to hand, and sometimes from the extemporizing which went on in them and would be included in reports of lectures. But inconsistencies will also arise from differences between points of view. These points of view were determined particularly by the curriculum, and secondly by the *Problematik* suggested, for example, by applying Iamblichus' method. But they were determined accidentally, as it were, by a third factor, the 'authenticity' of the commentary: many lectures of Philoponus consist for the most part of Ammonius' views, but every so often he gives his own without marking the distinction. The effect is the same as that of constructing commentaries from scholia. In both cases the conventions were familiar to readers and audiences, so that, while no philosopher would totally ignore inconsistency, it would not worry him as it would a modern philosopher, since the reasons for it were understood.

Moreover, there are two kinds of inconsistency: there is the

---

[44] This scholastic use of classification by division has survived into the twentieth century. Writing of Rome in the 1950s, A. Kenny says in *A Path from Rome* (London, 1985, 97) that in the current Catholic breviary: 'saints who were not important enough to have their own office written were celebrated by an office common to the class to which they belonged. For this purpose men were divided first into martyrs and non-martyrs and then into bishops and non-bishops. Women were divided first into virgins and non-virgins and after that into martyrs and non-martyrs.'

inconsistency of the text and there is the inconsistency of the writer. For the latter depends on the writer's commitment to the text. Most of the conventions of the genre, both external and internal, make it reasonable quite often to doubt this commitment and to look for corroborating evidence of it, even if only indirect evidence, whereas with few exceptions we can take it for granted in the case of modern texts.

It should also be clear that originality is another goal which authors of these commentaries can be expected to have sought less urgently than modern authors. This, however, is not to say that we do not find it there. It is a commonplace that the Empire was an age in which philosophy was propounded by the means of commentary, although most philosophers wrote monographs as well. If one of them had original thoughts, none of the conventions of the genre prevented him from expressing those thoughts in a commentary. Porphyry, Syrianus, Proclus, and probably Ammonius did so. It is simply that, if one of them did not have such thoughts, all the conventions of the genre made it easy for him to write a commentary. Not, of course, to write a good commentary. Bringing its comparatively mechanical aspects into the foreground may have given an exaggerated impression that its author lost his individuality. To redress the balance let us look for a moment at two lecture courses which are on the same subject and in which the content of the second is almost entirely copied from the first.

The *Isagoge* is the first book in the logic course, which is the first philosophy course. Ammonius' first question in his lectures on the *Isagoge* is therefore 'What is philosophy?' ... Or not quite. For we answer a 'What is *x*?' question by a definition. We ask first therefore, 'What is a definition?' Similarly, the next question, whether philosophy has divisions, implies the question, what are division, supplementary division, and subdivision. (Anyone who knows the *Isagoge* will recognize a skilful 'lead in' to it, as well as the communication of some elementary philosophical notions and jargon which the lecturer will need later.) The first definition of philosophy—'knowledge of the things that there are'—will bring him to a simple account of categories as highest universals, mentioning them as predicates but carefully avoiding anything more about that, which would be too difficult or too lengthy. Then— 'Aristotle wrote a book about them', and our book, the *Isagoge*, is an introduction to that with the purpose of clarifying five important terms in it which are not familiar from ordinary usage. Then the standard headings of utility, authenticity, and so on are covered.

Contrast Elias. Unlike Ammonius, he follows the conventional practice of beginning with the standard headings of a proëm before giving his students any idea of the *content*, that is, what the course is going to be about—the order in fact of philology, not philosophy. Elias does not even interpret the 'scope' correctly; and he is generally inferior to Ammonius, whom he follows, though not slavishly, and he is less elementary. The excursus on the status of universals is made before genera and species have been introduced, because he is following mechanically the order of the lemmata. Ammonius' students had been told in a previous lecture what 'universals and particulars', 'genera and species' mean; the examination of their formal properties would come later, with the lemmata. Like Porphyry, he declined 'on the present occasion' to decide between Aristotle and Plato. Elias has no such hesitation. His excursus on the supposed genus of being (67–9) contains four points which are additional to those in Ammonius (81–3): it can hardly be a coincidence that they are the only ones which are dubious from an Aristotelian point of view. He does, however, add the clearest and most explicit excursus (70–1), save for Simplicius', on (1) the *ab uno* notion of a genus and (2) its attribution to Plato. This derives perhaps directly from Proclus.

2

PORPHYRIAN SEMANTICS

Imposition of names

Introducing the curriculum of Aristotelian logic, I said that Neo-platonists saw its order as justified by Porphyry's semantics. But that appeal to this semantic theory was not simply to decide a question of educational practice but to decide questions of far-reaching theoretical importance. Let us start from the theory known as 'imposition of names'. All schools had continued to debate the question, which was traditional in Plato's day, whether the words of a language were assigned to their objects by nature or by convention. But in his commentary on the *Categories* this is ignored by Porphyry: instead we find him making a distinction we do not hear of before him but which became widely disseminated. The first imposition (also called more simply 'first use') of names is the assignment, for example, of the word 'bench' or 'man' to the thing in the lecture room, and of the words 'black' and 'a foot long' to other kinds of thing, and so on.[1] Then at a second approach the words themselves were given names according to their form classes, for example 'noun' and 'verb'. Whereas in their first im-position names belong to non-linguistic objects and are therefore used semantically (συμβολικῶc), those of the second imposition name words—the objects which, as Boethius' version describes them, are inflected.[2]

In the *Isagoge* Porphyry also ignores any intermediary between

---

[1] Verbs could be included, but with tenses removed (Boeth., *In Cat.*, 159 C–D, as well as Elias, *In Cat.*, 131. 19 and Simpl., *In Cat.*, 15), i.e. as names of actions and the like. The commentators had in mind Ar., *De int.*, 16ᵃ20.

[2] *First and second imposition*: see Porph., *In Cat.*, 57. 29–58. 3; Boeth., *In Cat.*, PL 64, 159 B–C. The *Principia dialecticae* attributed to Augustine does combine 'imposition' with a 'natural origin of language' theory which is probably Stoic (cf. Lloyd, 1971b; Pépin, 1976). As for antecedents, Epicurus mentions two stages in the imposition of names, but whatever his second stage is it is not Porphyry's. Por-phyry's theory is the remote cause of the scholastic distinction between terms of first and second intention.

a name and what it is the name of. Neither Aristotle nor Chrysippus had described words as directly representing things: what they directly represented was either mental effects or impressions, or else elements of abstractions called 'what was said'. Porphyry offers here no such analysis or dissolution of the semantic relation, which is simply that of standing for things (παραστατικὴ τῶν πραγμάτων, 58. 1). This is usually put down to his professed avoidance of topics too deep for beginners. This topic does not seem to me to be in the technical sense deep, that is metaphysical, for it can be treated independently of the 'status of universals'; and silence about it can as well be explained by the *Isagoge*'s relative independence of Aristotle, which we shall see in other matters. And this omission is probably more interesting than his omission of the nature–convention controversy. For, put alongside similar moves which he makes elsewhere towards a logician's approach, it can be seen as part of the recognition of logic as an autonomous subject, divorced from psychology, epistemology, and metaphysics. This development had already taken place in the Stoa, but to nothing like the same extent among Peripatetics or Platonists; and so influential was Porphyry that in cases where it was not followed by his successors this was generally because they did not understand him.

But he writes as a lecturer introducing texts, and his contribution is shaped by the conventions of the genre. Formally speaking, the theory of names is introduced to solve the conventional questions of the scope of Aristotle's logical texts and the order in which they should be read. The subject of the *Categories* is single words (i.e. unrelated to other words), while that of the *De interpretatione* is words as constituents of sentences and assertions, whether as subjects and predicates or as nouns and verbs; and the first treatise corresponds to the first imposition, the second to the second imposition. We can see in Table 1 how the scheme was developed and how it systematically divided the *Organon*. Porphyry's contribution, whether or not original, is column D.[3] Logicians found it difficult, however, to define the basic terms of columns A and B. Either they were at a loss to find differentiae— e.g. Philoponus' struggle to define πρότασις—or else had to say just

---

[3] For A and B see e.g. Amm., *In De int.*, 10; for C, ib., 1. 21–4. 24; Porph., *In Cat.*, 58. 30–59. 2; Dexipp., 11; for D, Porph., *In Cat.*, 57 and Boeth., *In Cat.*, 159 B–C; for E, Amm., *In De int.*, 4. 5–10.

TABLE 1. Systematic division of the *Organon*

	A	B	C	D	E
1	ἁπλαι φῶναι		~ *Cat.*	~ 1st imposition of names	
2	ὀνόματα/ ῥήματα	i.e. constituents of λόγος (sentence)	*De int.*	~ 2nd imposition of names	~ 1st σύνθεσις φωνῶν
3	φάσεις	i.e. constituents of ἀπόφανσις (assertion)	*De int.*		
4	ὅροι	i.e. constituents of συλλογισμός (inference)	~ *An pr.*		~ 2nd σύνθεσις φωνῶν

that a ὅρος is an ὄνομα when it is in a λόγος, which is a πρότασις when it is in a syllogism. Ammonius thinks to avoid the triviality of this (I believe) not by saying anything different from it but by saying it systematically, i.e. having some sort of theory to offer. The theory amounts to fitting it in three recognizable models: (1) the method of synthesis (column E above), (2) the imposition of names, and (3) the order of Aristotle's logical works.

The long-standing dispute whether the *Categories* was about concepts or names (expressions) or the objects named will be virtually settled in Porphyry's commentary by his formula that it was about 'expressions *qua* signifying objects' (*In Categorias*, 58. 3–6).

'Genus' and 'species'

Among the terms of second imposition are 'genus' and 'species'. These figure in the solution of a paralogism which can be repeated for a range of similar terms. Aristotle had written, 'whenever one thing is predicated of another as of a subject, everything said of what is predicated can be said of the subject also' (*Categories*, 3.1ᵇ10–12). Neoplatonic commentators were agreed that he meant by 'said of a subject' 'said in the category of substance'. But this left the objection that Socrates is a man and man is a species while the inference 'Socrates is a species' is false. (Similarly, of course, substituting 'animal' and 'genus'.) Porphyry replied that the transitivity rule did not apply because 'species' and 'genus' were not predicated in the category of substance. For they did not indicate part of man's or animal's essence, but the fact that *man* and *animal* 'belong to the class of things named in respect of a common property' (or perhaps just '. . . named in common, κατὰ κοινόητα καταγορευομένων, not 'individually' like *Socrates*); and this fact, namely that *man* and *animal* can be said of more than one individual, is in a certain sense an accident of them (*In Categorias*, 80. 32–81. 22). This is a little below Porphyry's usual standard of clarity. He is in fact relying on Alexander's interpretation of Aristotle's definition of a genus: 'what is predicated essentially of many which differ in species' (*Topics*, 102ᵃ31–2; cf. *Isagoge*, 2. 15–17). Alexander had argued that *animal* is *per se* universal, for it would exist if there were only one animal, but it would not be a genus; its being a genus consists in the contingent fact that there are several species for it to be predicated of (see e.g. *Quaestiones*, I. xi).

But later writers claimed that *species* and *genera* were not only accidents but terms of second imposition: when they were predicated of *man* or *animal* these were the words 'man' and 'animal'. And it is probable that this was not merely Porphyrian semantics but Porphyry's own view, expressed in his larger, lost commentary. There are strong grounds for inferring this in the fact that both Dexippus' and Boethius' commentaries call genera and species 'names of names' (26. 33 and 176 D *ad fin.*, Boethius: 'quodammodo'). Dexippus' account of the matter amounts otherwise only to an expansion without blunders of the Porphyry text we have, and Boethius' to an abbreviation of it. And the independent evidence that Boethius depended only on material derived from Porphyry is cogent. Secondly, Dexippus introduces some terminology which is additional to that of our shorter commentary. 'Genus' and 'species' 'indicate the imposition of the name κατὰ κοινὴν σχέσιν', that is to say they indicate 'according to what relation Socrates has been named "man" or "animal"' (26. 29–33). Porphyry's predilection for the concept and the term σχέσις is well known.[4] Ammonius and Philoponus say without explaining it that the genus (*animal*) is predicated accidentally καὶ κατὰ σχέσιν/ σχετικῶς (*In Categorias*, 31. 12 and 39. 3 respectively). Similarly, supposing

Agamemnon is an animal,

Philoponus distinguishes (1) 'animal' as predicated of the object Agamemnon (2) 'disyllable' as predicable of the word ζῷον, and (3) 'genus' of the relation (*In Categorias*, 39). Relation of *what*? we may ask in the case of (3). Philoponus does not say. It is reasonable to suppose that he meant what Dexippus meant. This is almost certainly the word ζῷον, for it is the relation of being common, equivalent to being predicable of many. Porphyry had introduced the *first* imposition of names as concerned with their 'relation to the objects' (*In Categorias*, 57. 24).

We must not lose sight of the distinction between (*a*) predicating

---

[4] Busse's statement (ad loc., *CAG*, IV/2, 26. 30) that what Dexippus says here is incompatible with Porph. 81. 18 seems to me just a mistake.

genus/species of some subject and (*b*) predicating the genus/species of some subject. (I use italics where it is inappropriate to decide between use and mention, as in the case of Aristotelian terms, or where I simply wish to be non-committal.) In (*a*) the predicate expression is 'genus', in (*b*) it is (say) 'animal' or 'man'. We are concerned with (*a*), which is, as it were, a comment on cases of (*b*). The Porphyrian theory which is found in Dexippus and apparently assumed by the Alexandrians can be put as follows. Predicating *species* of man indicates what type of word 'man' is. This is tantamount to indicating in respect of what relation the name 'man' has been assigned to (imposed on) men; and that relation is the relation of its being common to all men (26. 27–30). It is a relation inasmuch as it is not an intrinsic property of the name *qua* letters, such as being a disyllable. Or rather, it is not even an intrinsic relation of names. For some parts of speech are straightforward terms of second imposition and might be said to stand for the relation of one name to another. But being a species is not in this context a syntactic but a semantic property. Nor, except in the rather abbreviated or jargon version of Philoponus, is *genus* or *species* described as a relational property of a predicate expression. It is described as 'indicating a predicate expression in respect of' a certain semantic relation; and one understands why its meaning is seen as a property of the imposition of a name (26. 30).

Use and mention?

It is clear that the importance of distinguishing the logician's use and mention is diminished when we try to make one class out of the range of predicates falling under the second imposition. Even 'whole' and 'part' are attributed to the second imposition by Dexippus (15. 16–31); and Porphyry himself seems wrong to count metaphor under it (*In Categorias*, 58. 22–59. 2). In fact it is almost certainly a mistake to suppose that our use and mention is what Porphyry intended by his distinction. Both impositions are restricted to syncategorematic words—in effect words which can be subjects and predicates. I suggest that (1) the second imposition refers to those which are definable morphologically. Putting this more strictly, names belonging to the second imposition are names of word classes which are definable morphologically. For instance,

'verb' is the name of words which conjugate. This is clearly a
feature of the word as composed of letters and therefore overlaps
our *mention*. (2) But of such words some also satisfy a second
criterion: they can be defined or at least partly described syntactically—a verb for instance as a predicate. This can still be called a
property of the word, but not simply of the word as composed of
letters since it is a function which is observable only when it is
being used, not mentioned. The class satisfying this criterion
consists largely of those syncategorematic words that interest
logicians, at least logicians of the Empire, which in turn means
primarily those considered in the *De interpretatione*; and it overlaps
the class covered by (1). Consequently (1) and (2) are treated as
though they were extensionally equivalent. This assumed equivalence is expressed by the ambiguity of the terms χαρακτήρ and
τύπος, which are used both by grammarians and by philosophers
sometimes to mean the word *qua* letters, sometimes its word class,
such as noun. More important, it has the consequence that (1) and
(2) come to be treated as implying *equal* or *alternative* criteria for
the second imposition. This allows on the one hand 'monosyllable'
or 'disyllable', which concern a physical characteristic of what they
describe and which are prime examples of our 'mention', to count
as second imposition, and on the other hand also 'genus' or
'species'. For although 'genus' and 'species' are based on an existential fact which accounts for their semantic idiosyncrasy betrayed by
the paralogism, they have also a syntactic function which stops
them from being an example of our 'mention'. 'Predicable of many'
can name a semantic relation of sign to things or a syntactic relation
of sign to signs. We shall see more of this ambiguity shortly.
Dexippus, or his source, presumably saw 'whole' and 'part' as (in
this sense) syntactical words.

Most writers tried to follow Porphyry's nominalist approach to
predication by supposing that in the second imposition expressions
would somehow *signify* types of linguistic expression. But this will
not cover Dexippus' extensive and confusing list of expressions
which do not fall into the class of categories/predicates (pp. 11–12),
although he seems to assume that they belong to the second imposition (cf. 11. 14–17). He classifies them as those which are 'studied
as' types of linguistic expression (12. 10–15), for they fall under the
study of grammar, poetry, and the like. This may well be Porphyrian in origin, for it accounts for the inclusion of metaphor in

the second imposition (cf. 12. 20–1). The theory clearly cannot do as much as Dexippus expects of it. But it seems to reappear in al-Farabi (see Zimmermann, 1981, xxxi–xxxiv).

Genus and species, it was argued, were not properties of animals or men (and not, therefore, said πραγματικῶς like terms of the first imposition), for no actual animal is a genus, nor Ajax nor Agamemnon a species. If one asks whether it would not have been more plausible and more fruitful to have inferred simply that they were properties/classes of properties/classes, the short answer must be, yes. Unlike the nominata of both 'verb' and 'disyllable', the nominatum of 'genus' or 'species' is not distinguishable morphologically. But this fact was probably indicated by Porphyry's qualifying the second imposition in their case as κατὰ σχέσιν. Defining them syntactically is his intention rather than achievement; for although he has identified the class, that of common or general names, in which they are included, he has not offered a syntactic but non-circular description of the subclass which they constitute. But it is the formal approach, the implied programme, which is significant.

Singular terms, individuals and bundles of properties

There could be no clearer indication of Porphyry's programme of a semantics which excludes extra-logical considerations than his admission of singular terms as predicates. He does this without apology. Plato's belief that the dialectician should ignore individuals because they are indefinite in number, and hence not embraced by a science, is mentioned in the *Isagoge* but not discussed (6. 12–16). As for definite descriptions, Aristotle claimed that where, as in 'the son of Sophroniscus' or 'the white thing', they conceal an accidental predication (such as 'the thing which *is* son of Sophroniscus' or '. . . *is white*') they are not proper subject terms. From this it follows that they cannot be proper predicate terms either; for the only subjects they could have would be either proper names, which are not terms at all for Aristotle, or other such definite descriptions, which *ex hypothesi* are improper subjects. Porphyry, who knows this very well, passes it by in silence.

Indeed, he finds room for the predication of these singular terms (as we may call them provisionally) by repeating the familiar rule that what is predicated is a term which is either wider than the subject-term or equal to it in extension. The predicates equal in extension will be by definition the propria of the subjects (or their definitions, if these are counted, as they were not normally, as predicates): for instance, *risible* said of *man*. The effect of Porphyry's theory is to class singular terms, whether represented by proper names or by definite descriptions, with propria. The lowest species, he states, is said of all its individuals but the individual is said of one, and only one, particular (*Isagoge*, 7. 18–19). In the *Categories* commentary singular terms are neither admitted nor excluded as predicates: they are merely excluded as predicates said of a subject, because the restricted interpretation of the phrase restricted it to universals (76. 30–77. 12). Names are allowed to be convertible with definitions or descriptions. But the decision not to carry this explicitly to its logical conclusion is best explained by the fact that where there is an Aristotelian text to be expounded the writer is more faithful to Aristotle's thought.

To return to the *Isagoge*, Porphyry continues:

Socrates and this pale thing and this son of Sophroniscus who is approaching (if Socrates is his only son) are called individuals. Now such things are called individuals because each of them consists of properties forming a collection that would not be the same if it belonged to someone else. (7. 19–23)

This concludes a passage the point of which has been to define an individual solely by the way in which it can be predicated. Following (as we have seen) Aristotle's *Topics*, Porphyry has already done this for genus and species; and individuals are added to them as the immediate subjects for species. This follows smoothly and persuasively from the Tree of Porphyry, which is itself disingenuously introduced as though it were the most natural way in the world for beginners to understand predication; for it makes substance a highest genus, and, at the bottom, Socrates a division of Man. And it is reinforced, equally disingenuously, by its description as a series of wholes and parts in which class membership is not distinguished from class inclusion (7. 27–8. 3).

Porphyry is pursuing the plan which he stated in his short proëm. The so-called predicables are to be explained in so far as the explanation is needed to understand the *Categories* and is useful for division and demonstration. (Those who believe that he is following the treatment of the predicables in the *Topics* have regularly complained that he added species to Aristotle's four. Why do they not complain of a sixth predicable, individual?) Anyway, the plan will ignore problems of their metaphysical status and describe the treatment of them chiefly on the part of the Aristotelians and in the context of logic.

It follows that it is *terms* and their syntactic and semantic relations which we should expect to find him treating. He himself thought that the *Categories* was about expressions (φῶναι), or rather expressions *qua* signifying things, and the *Isagoge* came to be called the Πέντε φῶναι quite early. I hope it will emerge that this is what he understood terms to be. In the passage which I have just quoted about individuals, M. Mignucci has recently argued that what is meant is the expressions, or what we should call the definite descriptions, not the things or persons referred to.[5] But in fact Porphyry's language is ambiguous. It is not enough to infer that individuals cannot be physical objects because, or when, they are predicated. For Aristotle had expressly distinguished 'things that are' from 'things that are said' but had gone on to describe how they are predicated (*Categories*, 2 *ad init.*). Porphyry uses the word 'individuals' (ἄτομα) quite often as a synonym for 'individual sub stances' (ἄτομοι οὐσίαι), as well as interchangeably with 'particulars' (τὰ κατὰ μέρος and τὰ καθ᾽ ἕκαστα). The result is that we find 'individuals' replaced by 'the many men', which can hardly refer to terms or expressions, only to be contrasted with 'the man in common (universal)', which can hardly refer to anything else.[6] In my opinion it is not necessary to decide whether the Porphyry passage refers to singular terms or individual objects. For if it is thought objectionable to have the latter reduced to a bundle of

---

[5] He construes it so that 'such things' refers only to 'this pale thing' and 'this son of Sophroniscus who is approaching', not to Socrates, whom Porphyry takes for granted as an individual. This meets the objection that Porphyry's audience would have supposed that the expression/name 'Socrates' was composed of syllables and letters. It still leaves him calling names of properties, such as 'son of Sophroniscus', properties. But that licence is taken by most Greek logicians. Or better, we should suppose him to be referring to terms rather than expressions. As I understand him, Mignucci objects only to supposing a reference to the physical objects.

[6] Similar indifference in Porphyry's (admittedly *ad hominem*) argument against the inference from 'Socrates is white' that Socrates is many (*ap.* Simpl., *In Phys.*, 93–4; e.g. 93. 16 and 94. 33). Such oscillation or ambiguity is an obstacle to translation into grammatical English, but it is familiar in Aristotle, to whom many (if few English) scholars have attributed a novel but deliberate language that will have one foot in an ontological (extra-linguistic) 'order' and one foot in a logical ('judgemental') 'order', or perhaps unite them. Cf. Mansion (1946), 354; Coulou-baritsis (1980), 110–11.

properties, this is because such a description has been misunderstood by most modern critics (myself, 1956, included) and taken to be asserting more than it does. This matter had best be disposed of immediately.

When we look later at Plotinus' radical criticism of Aristotle's account of genus, differentia, and substance, we shall find the theory that a sensible individual is a bundle of qualities without genuine substance. It excludes a core self of form and matter for Socrates or Dion which would have been a substrate for their accidents. But, although it is *ad hominem* against Aristotle, it seems to me that the spirit of Plotinus' argument is so alien to Aristotelian logic as to make it unlikely that it would have been acceptable in any commentary on Aristotle, including the *Isagoge*. In fact the standard meaning of the widely accepted description of individuals as bundles of properties was that they were bundles of properties *qua individuals*; and this meant no more than that uniquely instantiated sets of accidents were the principle of individuation. The factor which has been overlooked, and which left the individuals still Aristotelian substances, is that the collection of properties '*composing*' as opposed to individuating the individuals included the specific and substantial ones, two-footedness, animality, and so on. Indeed, one can surmise that Neoplatonists were simply following a Peripatetic version of Aristotle's principle of individuation. Aristotle had said several times that it was matter, but he had said even more frequently that matter was the 'principle' of accidents. Alexander (or the author of *Quaestiones*, 7. 21–3 and 8. 1–3) suggested that it was the collection of accidents 'which go with the material circumstances' that individuated. But there is also an obvious overlap with the Stoic category of ἰδίως ποιός[7]

Again, either interpretation of *Isagoge*, 7. 19–23 will leave the

---

[7] *Bundle of properties as individuating principle*: See Porph., *In Cat.*, 129. 8–10; Boeth., *In Is.*², 235. 5–236. 6; Simpl., *In Cat.*, 229. 17–18. At *Isag.*, 7. 22 the 'because', which explains why *this pale thing* etc. are called individuals, does not refer to their consisting of properties but to their consisting of properties forming a unique collection.

For inclusion of specific and substantial properties in the bundle which *composed* the individual see particularly Philop., *In An. post.*, 437. 17–24 and 32.

Alexander (*De an.*, 85. 15–16) takes up a half-way position about the principle of individuation: it is just 'the material circumstances'. Ammonius (*In Isag.*, 60. 19 and 21) told at least his beginners that it was matter. Some Neoplatonists rejected both parties; Dexippus (*In Cat.*, 30. 20–4) argued that countability was what individuated. Standard amalgamation in Jo. Dam., *Dial.*, c. 30: individuals necessarily differ in number and in accidents. For Stoic overlap cf. Dexipp., 30. 23–26.

non-Aristotelian consequence that proper names as well as definite descriptions are reducible to properties or classes. For this follows not from the statement about the composition of *individuals* but from the fact that they can be predicate terms. Otherwise, such apparent predications would really be statements of identity. It is interesting that Porphyry counts even the demonstrative, or perhaps the demonstrative adjective, 'this' among predicates (2. 17–18); I think that he takes 'pointed at' and the like to be its connotation. The reducibility of proper names is the natural conclusion of a logic that concerns itself with classes—or in Porphyry's terms wholes and parts. As I have previously suggested (Lloyd, 1956, 159), it puts one in mind of W. V. Quine's treatment of singular terms. Boethius in fact describes 'Platonitas' as a made-up name (just like 'Pegasizing') standing for the unique property, itself compound, of Plato.[8]

Predication

While there was nothing to prevent Porphyry from including in his account of singular predicates a statement about the individuals on which they depend, it remains true that in his semantic theory what is predicated is 'an expression *qua* signifying'. This is implied throughout the *Isagoge* because 'the things said without combination' which are the subject of Aristotle's *Categories* are interpreted as significant names, and he has been at pains to distinguish these from non-significant names or nonsense-words. The significant names are the ones which have been imposed, i.e. assigned.[9] Moreover, the *Categories* is about names 'in respect of' their signifying things—that is, only to the extent that they signify things.[10]

How did he think names did signify? According to the imposition theory, by being used to call things by those names. But in the

---

[8] *In De int.*[2], 137. 7 ff. (463 A Migne). 'Incommunicabilis proprietas' means of course that it is 'non communis', not that it is ineffable!

[9] There would seem to be some confusion in equating 'unassigned' with 'nonsensical'; if so, it is due to the fact that the standard example, βλίτυρι, does not purport to be a 'name'. It is (at least in origin) an imitation of the twang of a stringed instrument, so that it would have a usage (exclamatory?) like that of 'Woof! Woof!' Cf. Ax (1986), 194–9.

[10] καθό, implying the exclusion of other aspects, just as the *De int.* deals with names only as (καθό) word classes (Porph., *In Cat.*, 58.36).

predication theory, which is explicit only in the *Categories* commentary, a further element was introduced. Predicating was 'calling something in accordance with something (τι) signified' (58. 16–17). In this definition what is signified cannot be the thing, the physical object. (Apart from other objections, it would follow that true predicative statements were tautologies, and false ones not predications.) Certainly, when he returns to the definition, the physical object is called the thing (πρᾶγμα) signified. But Porphyrian semantics always referred to two objects of signifying, the direct and the indirect. This feature can be seen in the illustration which introduced the definition:

Any simple significant expression [λέξις] when it is spoken [applied to?] and said of the thing signified is said to be a predicate. Suppose for instance a thing which is this stone that is being indicated (that we are touching or looking at): when we say of it, 'This is a stone', the expression 'stone' is a predicate. For it signifies a thing of that kind and is spoken of the thing being indicated.[11]

Here the predicate expression is spoken of, or applied to (αγορευεται), the thing which is indicated, but 'signifies *such* a thing' or 'a thing of that kind'.[12] I say 'but' because it does not make sense, and Porphyry would not have thought it did, to *identify* 'such a thing as *A*' with '*A*'. Nor can it *denote*, or refer to, *A*, since it is not a referring expression in the way that a definite description is. I shall use the term 'significatum' for the abstract object represented by 'such a thing'. Where the Neoplatonists' apparently ambiguous use of 'signify' causes ambiguity for the reader, I shall call the external objects 'nominata'. Only the Stoics confined what was 'signified' to the abstract *lekton*.

So predicates are expressions used in accordance with a significatum, or *qua* signifying not merely a nominatum but also a significatum. The important point is that the significatum is indispensable; in a natural language it is required logically by a predicate. Someone might after all suggest that Porphyry regarded it as a psychological accompaniment to the use of general names and verbs, like images. This would leave him to define predicates

---

[11] 56.8–13. 'Simple' expression means one which is not a statement.

[12] τὸ τοιόνδε πρᾶγμα can, of course, mean 'the thing of such a kind'. But when in English we say 'a thing of such a kind' the Greek idiom uses the definite article. Logicians unfamiliar with the idiom must not be misled by it.

as expressions applicable to many objects. But even if we put aside
the problem of proper names, which were predicates according to
Porphyry, such a definition would be inadequate, for there would
be no criterion for the applicability of a given predicate to some
individual object to which it had not already been assigned according to the similarly inadequate imposition theory. The significatum
can be called an intension or a connotation: but, while it is indispensable for explicating 'predicate', it is immaterial what
non-formal explication, if someone chooses to give one, is given of
'intension'.

In a proposition, that is to say what is meant or stated by some
class of sentences composed of expressions, the predicate is a term
(ὅρος) which does not refer to any nominatum. (Even a singular
predicate *contains* a general term.) *Qua* predicate all that it determines is a 'such' not a 'this'. Consequently, while in a sentence the
predicate expression signifies some significatum, the predicate
term of a proposition *is* that significatum. But the syntactic behaviour of these terms is for the most part isomorphic with that of the
expressions which signify them; and they normally have the same
names. Nor is this an accident. A 'that . . .' clause, which expresses
a proposition, is a 'that' + a sentence. This has two consequences.
First, it is systematically hard to tell which some ancient logician
is speaking of, and secondly, it does not usually matter. Logic can
be expounded equally as the logic of propositions and their component terms or as that of significant sentences *qua* significant and
their component expressions. Either, for instance, can be called the
truth-bearers. By and large we know how to translate from one
mode to the other. The same does not hold if we are explaining
metre: but that is because metre belongs to expressions but not to
expressions *qua* signifying.

Predicates as concepts

Porphyry does expound a non-formal explication of intension that
is best understood, in logicians' terminology, as an interpretation
of the class of significata.

Following the famous opening of *De interpretatione*, Neoplatonists of the third century onwards accepted a formula according to
which subject and predicate expressions signified things by the

mediation of thoughts (concepts).[13] It is, in fact, Porphyry's own view; and his description of it confirms what we could have supposed—that the 'such' signified by the predicate word 'stone' coincided with Aristotle's distinction between the universal and the individual which is a 'this'. Porphyry writes in his commentary:

It is impossible to conceive of an ox or a man or a horse apart from the particular ones. But by starting from the perception of the particulars we can arrive in thought at the common/universal ox (or man and so on), which we no longer conceive as a 'this' but a 'such' . . . (91. 1–4)

Dexippus has a similar account, which in any case could just as likely have come from Alexander as from Porphyry. But he deals more directly with our question what exactly a predicate is, and his vocabulary is interesting (*In Categorias*, 7–10).

To say that animal is predicated of man is to say that the significant expression for an animal, viz. the noun 'animal' is predicated [in the first place, according to Dexippus] of the thought signified by the expression 'man' and also [in the second place] of the thing which is the object of this thought. For to be predicated is a proprium of significant sounds—they signify the concepts and the things. (*In Categorias*, 10. 27–32)

He distinguishes, however, the things said, which is what Aristotle, of course, called his predicates, from the words used to say them; or, as one might put it, he distinguished predicate expressions from what they predicated. But, departing, it would seem, from Aristotle, Dexippus calls the expressions 'predicates' (κατηγορίαι) and what they predicate (i.e. say *of* something) 'the things said' (τὰ λεγόμενα). One of his arguments for distinguishing his predicates and the things said is the existence of ambiguous expressions. One and the same expression can 'say' two non-identical things, which produces a contradiction if the expression is identified with the thing said. Instead, Dexippus identifies the things said with the things signified, which as he has already claimed are 'in the first

---

[13] *Verba significant res mediantibus conceptis*: at least in the context of the *Categories* the formula is attributed to Iamblichus by Olympiodorus (*In Cat.*, 41. 12) and Elias (*In Cat.*, 130. 14). Ammonius, who is briefer and mentions few authorities, only uses it, but at *In An. pr.*, 1. 7–11 associates it with Iamblichus' pupil Theodorus. Dexippus had propounded the theory on the same lines as Porphyry without mentioning him (*In Cat.*, 7–10). After a successful career in the Middle Ages, it continues in Bacon (e.g. *De augm. sci.*, V, ch. 2), Hobbes (*Leviathan*, I, ch. 4) and Locke ('Words are the sensible signs of his ideas who uses them', *Essay*, III, ii, § 2) and is popular today in elementary textbooks of linguistics.

place' concepts or thoughts. These concepts, as in Porphyry's, or for that matter Aristotle's, account, are distinct from, but not separated from, the things, the physical objects; for they are *of* the things and *from* the things.

When they are the significata of expressions combined so as to form statements, these things said are also the bearers of truth or falsity, 'for the true or false is not to be found in things but in thought and the excursions of mind' (9. 24–10. 5).

How does Dexippus differ from Porphyry? Only in a way which may be accidental and insignificant, but which, I suspect, is not. Dexippus expounded the significatum early in his commentary because it falls under the introductory topic of his author's scope. Porphyry omitted it altogether from the *Isagoge*, gave it a bare mention (58) in his predication theory—where a reader knowing only the imposition theory might even have interpreted it as the physical nominatum—and himself interpreted it (91) as the conceptual universal. But he produced this interpretation only under the 'Plato versus Aristotle' question why it is the particulars instead of the universals that are called first substances.

This does not mean, however, that Dexippus was not copying from Porphyry, whether or not by way of Iamblichus' reports. There are several indications of this. A substantial one is that Porphyry's defence of the priority of individuals in the *Categories* also depends expressly on the scope or subject-matter of the book. But it is important to notice that what he undertakes to rebut is not Platonism but a logical and *ad hominem* objection to Aristotle. According to this objection, the removal of the universal *man* which is essential to Socrates entails the removal of Socrates, and the removal of *animal* entails the removal of *man* and therefore of Socrates, while the converse entailments do not hold. Porphyry's reply may be surprising, although it was gratefully followed by later lecturers anxious to defend Aristotle. It is not the individual which is the primary substance but all the men/animals from which we got the thought of the *man/animal* that is predicated in common (90. 12–34). And he concludes from the genetic account of universals which we have already quoted that 'if the particular animals were removed, there would equally be no universal to predicate of them' (91. 4–5).

Nevertheless, he does not distinguish this argument from the argument from the order of imposition of names—these being first imposed on individuals. And it is the imposition of names which brings him to the scope or subject-matter of the *Categories*.

Now since the subject of the *Categories* is significant expressions and these were first imposed on the objects of perception—these being the first we encountered—it was these which Aristotle called first substances too, in accordance with his subject; that is, corresponding to the fact that the objects of perception were the first to be named he has the thesis that by reference to ($\pi\rho\delta s$) significant expressions the individual substances are first . . . (91. 7–12)

Since it is not clear exactly what this passage implies, it is best to quote also his summary:

The upshot is that, while by reference to significant expressions the first substances are the individual and perceptible substances, by reference to natural priority ($\pi\rho\delta s$ $\tau\dot{\eta}\nu$ $\phi\dot{\upsilon}\sigma\iota\nu$) they are the intelligible ones. But the programme is to distinguish the kinds of things by reference to the significant expressions for them, and the expressions are first of all those that are significant of the individual perceptible substances. (91. 23–7)

Let us first dismiss from our minds the notion that Porphyry is appealing to a unique series of historical events called the imposition of names. He has clearly been saying something along the lines of Aristotle's account of the abstraction of universals. That described what psychologists call concept formation, and which is supposed to be repeated more or less by every child born. Porphyry can be presumed to be doing the same thing for the formation, that is learning, of meanings of words. The absence of any description of the process itself (such as a behaviourist account) is irrelevant because it was not needed for his purpose: all that was needed was for his audience to accept the empiricist order of learning. And this appears to be all that Porphyry meant by his defence of Aristotle. Someone might object that it is weak, because it amounts only to the empirical fact, if it is one, that we are first acquainted with perceptible objects. But Porphyry the Platonist might accept the objection and point out that he had said himself that the perceptible objects were not prior in nature (which usually meant in essence or existence).

It is tempting to notice that he and Dexippus do not refer directly, as their successors would have done, to the predicates as concepts or thoughts but use phrases such as 'the man thought of as universal', which is ambiguous between the psychological phrase, 'the thought of the universal man' and the logical 'the man *qua* universal'. One can object that there is a simple reason for this: if he is to argue from the subject-matter or programme of the *Categories*, he will have to avoid talk about concepts, for he has already rejected the theory that the *Categories* was about concepts. But, while quite correct, this makes the strongest point on the other side. For, equally, Porphyry's expository parameters are the significant expressions. He continues to say that what they signify is the nominata or external things—they signified them 'according to' what I called the significatum or connotation—and it would at least be consistent for him to have envisaged all his explicanda as terms of propositions, if not expressions of sentences. The '*man*' predicated in common' will turn up later in this chapter as the 'unallocated *man*', and both should be understood either as expressions or, better, as terms.

Porphyry's two programmes

All in all, we may wonder whether Porphyry has not in mind two programmes for a theory of meaning, or at least the possibility of two programmes. One would be the conventional programme, where predicates were explicated by reference to psychological, metaphysical, or at any rate extra-logical elements such as abstraction, concepts, universals, none of which would figure among the 'things' or nominata of the terms of first imposition. This would be the approach which we find half-way through the *Categories* commentary, and indirectly at that, since it is not made primarily for the purpose of explicating predicates. A second programme would be a pure logician's programme, suggested by the *Isagoge*. This would not dispense with a significatum, and the significatum would still not be identical with any of the nominata but would be explicated in terms only of the names and nominata. Ideally, it would be what some modern logicians call a semantic representation.[14]

For the speculation to be justified, it has to be shown against the background of Porphyry's own order of exposition. To show this will also sum up the chapter so far. Porphyry expounds predicates in three stages, of which I remind the reader only in rough terms.

[14] U. Egli (1970; 1978) has essayed a translation of Stoic syntactic and semantic theory into a modern model which incorporates this notion.

The first stage is the imposition of names. Here

1. Certain expressions have a property, 'being the name of'.
2. 'Name of' is unanalysed, defined just as 'assigned to'.
3. Individuals are names which are distinguished from general names by being names of only one object.
4. Species and genera are names which are distinguished as correlates: e.g. all nominata of a species are nominata of a genus, but only some nominata of a genus are nominata of a species . . .

This stage is thus nominalist inasmuch as it deals with sentences and their component S- and P-expressions.

The second stage is predication or significance. Here

1. Certain expressions have a property of being significant.
2. This property replaces, without being identical to, the unanalysed 'being a name'.
3. Expressions *qua* significant signify a kind or sort of nominatum.
4. But this kind or sort (the significatum) remains unanalysed.
5. The predicate expression in a sentence is an expression having such a significatum.
6. This significatum is the predicate term in a proposition.

This would provide the most charitable explanation why Philoponus, or his source, counted Porphyry among those who said that Aristotle's *Categories* was about concepts.

So far we have a clear distinction between things which are words or names and things which are objects or nominata. But what are the kinds (sorts), significata or terms? This is answered in a third stage: they are thoughts of common properties abstracted from the nominata.

But if we understood the imposition of names, there is a good sense in which we could be said to have known what a 'kind' or 'sort' of object was, for most of the names which it concerned were general names like 'pale' and 'man'. The third stage therefore seems explanatory in a different way from that of the first two stages. It is extra-logical by importing elements (thought and abstraction) which are not involved in the description of sentences, their components and, at least prima facie, nominata. The propositions and terms effectively introduced by the second stage could, it seems, have been explained as *logical* operations on (constructions out of etc.) the sentences, expressions, and nominata. This would have left Porphyry still within the framework of the imposition

theory. It would have been neutral with respect to the conceptualism which is entailed by the third stage; and it is what I meant by
the pure logicians' programme.

It is certainly anachronistic in so far as no ancient philosopher
completed such a programme. But the basic notion seems to me to
occur in Stoic logic; and, while detracting from Porphyry's originality, this implies that it would not be unhistorical to suppose that
he possessed the notion. For Stoics the expressions were physical
objects (or movements), and what they denoted was physical
objects, while the significata of the expressions—what these
connoted—were incorporeal. But since Stoics held that to be is to
be a body or physical object, it follows that, at the least, one
meaning they attached to 'incorporeal' was 'non-existent'. In fact
I am not sure what else it could have meant.[15] In a logico-
metaphysical context the most likely implication of something
being 'non-existent', but permanently there to be spoken of, is that
it is a 'construction'. With one proviso, the sense of this would be
illustrated approximately by Russell's calling the average man a
logical construction out of a range of sentences which do not
mention such a man. The proviso is that Stoic references to incorporeals including *lekta* were *reducible* to expressions and hence to
sounds; otherwise (as has been pointed out to me) the analogy with
logical constructions would be more than incomplete: it would
disappear. But, lacking sufficient evidence from Stoics themselves,
we might plausibly infer such a reducibility; for Russell did not
mean the average man to be reduced to actual men but to sentences
mentioning only actual men. Thus time, which was also an incorporeal, might plausibly be described in their system as a logical
construction out of expressions or sentences containing tensed
verbs. Another reason why this interpretation of a *lekton* is resisted
by modern writers is that they sometimes confuse such an interpretation with a philosophical position in which temporal statements are false *sub specie aeternitatis* or in some 'last analysis'.
Stoics did not believe that nothing has really happened in the past.
Something can be 'unreal' or 'non-existent' in the sense which
implies that no statements about it (barring opaque reference) can

---

[15] Except perhaps 'body-less', i.e. abstracted from a body (Long–Sedley, 1988,
I. 200). But what sort of abstraction? The relation is more like that of the knight or
the deuce to the appropriate wooden or cardboard object than that of the colour and
shape of the objects to the objects.

be true (e.g. the man in the moon), but something can be 'unreal' or 'non-existent' in a sense from which that does not follow (e.g. the average man). Stoic time was unreal or non-existent only in the second sense.

It is not an accident that in the Porphyrian semantics of Dexippus (whose terminology may or may not be taken from Porphyry) the significata are 'the things said'. This term is, of course, Aristotle's: but in Dexippus' version it can still be seen to play the same *logical* role—that is, ignoring its ontological interpretation as concepts—as is played by 'the things said' (*lekta*) in Stoic semantics. Neither class of things said can be physical things, for both are the results of a logical (semantic) operation on the class of sentences containing common nouns, adjectives, or verbs. What is lacking in the Porphyrian semantics, but less so in the Stoic, is a systematic handling of the distinction between connoting and referring. For this reason, if (as I have been speculating) the Porphyrians had their eye on a road which in fact leads to modern syntactic-semantic systems, they were not so far down it as the Stoics.

When is a proposition one proposition?

More can be learnt of Porphyry's semantics from a comparatively neglected topic in it: What makes a proposition one proposition and not two or more?[16] To be exact, the topic discussed was the singleness of a *logos* (*oratio* in Boethius), defined by Aristotle as a significant expression containing an expression significant in its own right (*De interpretatione*, 4); and this covered not only a declarative sentence or proposition but the definiens of a definition.

The particular crux for commentators had been at *De interpretatione*, 17ª15–17, where Aristotle had said,

A single declarative expression (sentence) is either one which indicates a single thing or one which is single by means of a connective; it is not single but several if it indicates several things, or if it is without a connective.

According to Boethius, Porphyry was the first to see the point of

---

[16] That Porphyry's criterion is to be found in Boethius is confirmed by its appearance also in Ammonius, much of whose exposition is identical with that of Boethius (*In De int.*[2], 101 ff. and *In De int.*, 70–5 respectively).

this, which is that it is not about criteria for distinguishing what in modern sentential calculus are simple and compound propositions. That is just a question of counting terms—where there are more than two a proposition is compound—and concerns *dictio*, that is expressions. The question of the singleness of propositions and definitions (since the crucial passage is in fact applicable to a *logos* which is not declarative) concerns *significatio*. For a *logos* to be single he accepted Theophrastus' formula: it must designate a single substance. Here it is essential to interpose a caveat. The ancient writers on this topic made no terminological distinction between connoting and denoting/referring. Boethius uses 'designativa substantiae' to report Theophrastus, and I have generally translated δηλόω as 'indicate' and σημαίνω as 'signify'.[17] But in the present context Ammonius uses δηλωτικός and σημαντικός interchangeably. This is not, of course, to say that they did not recognize the distinction at all, only that little or nothing is to be inferred mechanically from their vocabulary. It must not be forgotten too how, according to the commentator's (i.e. the Porphyrian) theory of meaning, any noun or noun-phrase would 'signify' both a significatum normally identified with a thought/concept *and* an object in the external world.

Theophrastus had a second condition, repeated from Aristotle, that it must be spoken without a break: but this seems later to have been tacitly left aside, probably as not interesting the logicians. 'Two-footed walking animal' is a single *oratio* because it signifies man. 'Socrates philosophus calvus senex' is not: but the explanation (which in the context may or may not be Porphyry's) leaves some unanswered questions. The attributes, we are told, do not indicate a single substance, since they are accidents and extrinsic; later it is added that it is not necessary for every bald elderly philosopher to be Socrates. Would anything count as a necessary identification of Socrates?

The individuation of compound propositions is surprising. One might have expected a conjunction or a disjunction, say, to be one proposition if it has identical terms in the subject positions: 'Socrates is walking and thinking', even when put into the form 'Socrates is walking and Socrates is thinking', refers to a single

---

[17] 'Designativus' almost certainly 'σημαντικός' in his Greek source; cf. Boeth., *In Cat.*, 176 D and 177 A (designant).

substance. But the question of applying the criterion for singularity does not even arise, for in this logic it is not even a compound proposition but simply two propositions. This is because 'and' was not recognized as a logical connective but only as a grammatical one, again concerning diction, not meaning. The proposition in question is therefore no better a candidate than 'Socrates is walking and Alcibiades is walking'. In fact it turns out that the grounds for calling a genuine compound proposition one proposition have nothing to do with 'signifying one substance'. Genuine compound propositions are either conditional or disjunctive, for here the connectives affect both the diction and the significance. Assume that they are in the form representing the minimum complexity, i.e. '$p \rightarrow q$' and '$p \vee q$', not $p \vee q \vee r$, and we can see from Ammonius' examples that it makes no difference whether the subject-terms of the antecedent and consequent, or of the disjuncts, are identical or not. 'If God is good, the world is eternal', 'Either the world is eternal or it is created'; each of these two is called one proposition because what it signifies is 'the implication or the disjunction of the several objects'.[18] So, while not signifying a single substance, it falls under Aristotle's rubric by signifying 'a single thing', namely 'the relation which holds between two states of affairs and which is the meaning of the connective that has the force in question' (Ammonius, 74. 2–3, Boethius, 105).

How can a proper name be ambiguous?

It was accepted that no sentence could express a single proposition if its subject term was the proper name of so-called homonymous objects. For, according to Aristotle's definition, such a name would designate at least two objects which would not be identifiable by the same description. As every schoolboy familiar with Homer's *Iliad* or Offenbach's *Belle Hélène* knows, Ajax, King of Salamis is not Ajax, King of the Locrians. Therefore 'Ajax is filled with valour' will signify one state of affairs if it refers to the one king, another if it refers to the other. Equally, it will not designate one substance. So it does not express a single proposition.

No doubt this does not conflict with the individuation of pro-

---

[18] Amm., *In De int.*, 73. 31–2; cf. 66. 31–67. 19 and Boeth., *In De int.*², 110. 6.

positions as Theophrastus, or at least Porphyry, had treated it. For the essence of that was for it to be a question not of sentences and their grammar but of sentences and their meaning. It does, however, require the possibility of disambiguation. Porphyry and his followers pointed to the device of adding definite descriptions to ambiguous names (as we may call them): 'Ajax the son of Oileus', 'Ajax the son of Telamon', or 'Ajax, King of Salamis', and so on. But the commentators found theoretical problems in disambiguating names; and if they are at first sight sophistical these probably deserve rather to be called sophisticated. Without trying to justify this, I shall give one example of a debate which was taken up by Neoplatonists and which the reader must judge for himself.

A second-century commentator had objected to the very notion of ambiguous names. His objection was treated by Dexippus (19–20) and by Simplicius (*In Categorias*, 27), whom I shall follow, for the less said about Dexippus' treatment the better for the reputation of the Neoplatonists. Until disambiguated, the objection ran, an alleged name is not a name; and since this is not restricted to proper names it will follow that there are no homonyms—they would not be 'significant'. For, when disambiguated, the addition of the disambiguating expression makes it a description not a name.

One suggestion was that the word 'name' was used in three different ways:

1. of a name from a morphological and grammatical point of view, even if it was not assigned to anything signified by it: e.g. βλίτυρι;
2. of a name assigned to something but without the morphological and grammatical character of a name: e.g. 'Admittedly' as the name given to a slave by Diodorus to make fun of linguistic theory;
3. of a name assigned and with the morphological and grammatical character of a name: e.g. 'Socrates', 'Plato'. Ambiguous names would fall in class (1). For a name can be 'common' independently of its being assigned.

Unless I am mistaken, what we have to bear in mind is the assumption that 'assigning' a name (κατάταξις) is not like 'christening'—and so not as in Kripke's and Mill's theories—since it is only indirectly a matter of giving it a reference. It is assigned to a meaning or, as we should say, has a meaning assigned to it. This might be *son of Oileus, of Locrian descent* or *fermented juice of the grape*, so that proper names and common nouns are on all fours, as in Stoic and Porphyrian semantics. So perhaps the puzzling claim that a name can be common independently of being assigned means that a name can have bearers just as well as one bearer without having a meaning—as does hold for Mill with 'Johnson' and 'Dartmouth'.

Anyway, Simplicius reported the following reply (op. cit., 27). A name falling into class (1) cannot be among the ambiguous names which are identified by the *Categories*' account of homonyms. For either (*a*) it is unassigned, in which case it is not connected with a description or definition, or (*b*) it is assigned, in which case it is not common; for there is no such thing as a common assignment—that would imply that the different definitions entailed by the assignment of different names did not in fact differ.

Thirdly, we have Simplicius' counter-reply, which is contained in a suggestion of his own (or which he adopts). To present it perhaps more clearly than he does we can present it in an applied case. We start by postulating three names. Let 'Ajax', 'Ajax¹', and 'Ajax²' be examples. 'Ajax¹' will name Ajax, son of Oileus and king of Locris; 'Ajax²' will name Ajax, son of Telamon and king of Salamis. 'Ajax' is the ambiguous or indefinite name, which has not been assigned a meaning (been assigned to a meaning, in the Greek terminology) that identifies a bearer. To assign such a meaning, i.e. disambiguate it, it must have a definition added to it. This defines the meaning and, through that, identifies the bearer; and it may be either 'son of Oileus and king of Locris' or 'son of Telamon and king of Salamis'. Neither of these is the disambiguated name: the disambiguated name is either 'Ajax, son of Oileus and king of Locris' or 'Ajax, son of Telamon and king of Salamis'. So 'Ajax¹' is identical with, or, if one prefers, an abbreviation of, the first of these, and 'Ajax²' an abbreviation of the second.

As for 'Ajax', this is the 'common name' or 'name in common' required by the definition of homonyms. It is better called 'undifferentiatedly assigned' (to a meaning) than 'unassigned'. For it 'signifies the . . . name assigned in common or undifferentiatedly' which belongs to everything called 'Ajax', i.e. to Ajax¹ and Ajax²; and, 'when it has a definition added to it, it produces the selected individual instance of the common name' (28. 4–6). Thus a common, that is ambiguous, name does have a meaning and can also be assigned, that is disambiguated, while still common or shared.

But what is this meaning? One suggestion might be the disjunction Ajax^1 ∨ Ajax^2, i.e. son of Oileus . . . or son of Telamon . . . But if that is what Simplicius had in mind it is odd that he should not have said so. He has described the meaning as 'that which is assigned in common and undifferentiatedly in the case of all homonyms'. What is *assigned* is a name, and the property which homonyms have in common is bearing the same name. I think therefore that his proposal must amount to turning a so-called ambiguous name 'Ajax' into the non-ambiguous predicate, 'named "Ajax"'. This may be thought no better a solution than the disjunction. But we can anticipate one objection. It had been argued long ago that all homonyms were synonyms, on the ground that they had both the name and definition in common, viz. those of homonym. To this particular argument Dexippus had replied not unintelligently that there was nothing to prevent things from being homonymous in one respect, synonymous in another: *qua* Ajaxes, the Ajaxes had nothing in common and were therefore homonymous, *qua* homonymous, they had the definition of homonym in common and were therefore synonymous (20. 32–21. 10). Dexippus no doubt had in mind that Aristotle had required the common definition to be 'in respect of the name', that is, what the homonym was being called, so that the relevant consideration would in fact be '*qua* Ajaxes'.

But when he states that *qua* Ajaxes they have nothing in common, he must be presupposing an Aristotelian logic which is able to demarcate essential or defining properties from non-essential. '*Qua*' Ajaxes' means possessed as essential properties by Ajaxes as such. Aristotle did not, of course, have to take into account individuals and their definitions. But once we presuppose a Porphyrian logic in which singular terms signify collections of attributes, who can say which of such attributes are essential to a given individual, unless it is to be the whole set? Consequently anyone who relies on Dexippus' argument must answer the question why, *qua* Ajaxes, Ajaxes do not have in common being kings, and, if being kings, why not being named Ajax? More generally, these Leibnizian considerations simply express the doubt whether the theory of homonymy and synonymy is applicable to singular terms.

Porphyry had grafted singular terms as predicates on to Aristotle's *Categories*, as one might say with the minimum of surgical shock. But, with the exception of Boethius, his successors seem to have been averse from repeating the operation. This may have been due to a desire to follow Aristotle, or to the belief that their audience would not understand Porphyry, or—what is not the most unlikely—to the fact that they did not understand him themselves. But the conventional comment to make was that 'the man approaching is Socrates' is an 'unnatural' predication inasmuch as it predicates a substance of accidents (e.g. Philoponus, or a scholium from his milieu, *In Categorias*, 37). That, of course, was a return to Aristotle.

Which animal *is predicated?*

Students of philosophy were taught throughout the Imperial era that there were two kinds of predication, and that Aristotle called them 'in a subject' and '(said) of a subject', the first being exactly equivalent to 'essentially' or 'in the category of substance', the second to 'accidentally' or 'in a non-substantial category'. As well as the transitivity rule of the *Categories*, which was threatened by paralogisms, the proviso that what is predicated essentially is 'one thing of another' ($1^b 10$) prompted regular comment. When *animal* is predicated of *man*, which *animal* is it? This startling question assumes that it might be answered by 'the animal as pure genus' or by 'the animal in the species'.

Let us approach it obliquely. Some Peripatetics had the laudable intention of explaining the non-transitive predication of accidents in a way that did not entail two kinds of syllogism with distinct formal rules.

If the body is white, and white (τὸ λευκόν) is a colour, the body too will be a colour. But perhaps we should say that 'white' (τὸ λευκόν) signifies two things, the quality (ποιότης) and the coloured object, and that the coloured object is predicated of the body (for the body is not whiteness) and colour predicated of the quality. (Simplicius, *In Categorias*, 54. 16–21)

Someone—it is unclear who—seems to have profited by the ambiguity of Aristotle's ποιόν, and perhaps the influence of the Stoic category ποιός (which was really ὁ ποιός), to interpret an adjective used as a predicate as standing for the subject qualified. This has two consequences. It would make the copula an identity sign; and secondly it would, barring some addition or adjustment, make what a statement means identical with what would make the statement true.

It is the line taken by the *Sophistici elenchi* commentary under Alexander's name (*CAG* II/3) to resolve the paralogism 'Socrates is white, white is a colour, so Socrates is a colour'. For, we read, in the first premiss the sophist 'takes the attribute together with what it is an attribute of as one thing' (37). At first sight one might suppose that the author is describing the proposition, or the force of a copula: but what is taken as one thing is in fact the predicate term, *white*. Secondly, one might reflect that he leaves it unclear whether this predicate should be expressed by 'the white body', 'a white body', or 'something white'. (In the last two cases he would be thinking of the subject of the attribute as whatever substrate is required by the attribute). In fact he means 'the white body'. Both doubts are settled by a second paralogism which he lumps together with the other (38. 11–16),

> Coriscus is a man
> Man is other than Coriscus
> Therefore Coriscus is other than himself

The middle term *man* predicated of Coriscus, is, he says, 'the man who is classed with/allocated to Coriscus', in short 'the composite'; the *man* which is subject of the major (second) premiss is 'the unclassed/unassigned man', in other words 'the universal'. So 'the body is white' comes out as 'the body is the white body' and 'Coriscus is a man' as 'Coriscus is the man Coriscus', meaning '. . . the man who is classed with/allocated to Coriscus'.

In either case identity is introduced into the proposition: but the predicative propositions are not reduced to identity propositions of the form $x = y$. For they must contain conjuncts of the form fy since the original predicate still contains a predicate. On the other hand, someone who takes *expressions* of the form 'the white x' for primitive and canonical as they stand can validly take the *proposition* for an identity proposition.

To interpret the copula in this way as a sign of identity really amounts to equating the proposition that S is white with the state of affairs that makes it true when it is true. In a variety of forms this extensional interpretation turns up in the fourteenth century as the Western theory of *suppositio*. For both are a semantic interpretation of predication, not a syntactic analysis of the proposition. And I still think it not unlikely that the Schoolmen were led to their theory by what they found in the Greek Aristotelian commentators, particularly Simplicius.[19]

So much for the oblique approach. When we turn to predication in the category of substance, the reaction of readers, ancient and modern alike, can be expected to be rather different. Students of Aristotle have long suspected that he believed propositions attributing essence to a subject to be identical propositions like definitions. And it is to this kind of predication that the Neoplatonists' questions of 'which *animal*?' and 'which *man*?' belong. (The question we have been looking at, and which might be called 'which *white*?', was recognized as bearing on theirs, and they went on to consider it: but because of a historical convention about the lemmata in the *Categories* they did not start from it.) We can expect to find an ambivalent attitude to answers which imply identity of subject and predicate. There will be the feeling that in Aristotelian logic a predicate ought to be identical with its subject if it seems to be its essence, and there will be an aversion from making important propositions apparently trifling or trivial.

The question 'Which *animal/man*?' was supposed to arise from combining Aristotle's proviso about essential predication with the anti-Platonic ontology of the *Categories*. The proviso, which we have already mentioned, was that essential predication predicated 'one thing of another'. But, as the ontology required, the genera exist only in the species, and the species only in the individuals; so, when the genus animal is predicated of man or the species man of Socrates, the generic *animal* is not something additional to and other than the specific *man*, and the specific *man* is not something additional to and other than the individual Socrates or Plato. Porphyry's solution was to say that in all three cases the predicate was not the *animal* or the *man* 'classed with' or 'allocated to' (κατατεταγμένος) the species or the individual but the 'unclassed' or 'unallocated' (ἀκατάτακτος) *animal* or *man*. So the *animal* which is

---

[19] I suggested this in Lloyd (1971a). But the Neoplatonists' discussion of the question, which *animal* is predicated of *man*, was wrongly represented there in several respects. The main point is the precise meaning of ἀκατάτακτον and κατατεταγμένον, and I hope that that will be put right in what follows.

said of *man* is distinct from the *animal* which *man* is, and one thing is being predicated of another. (See Dexippus' commentary, 26. 3–9, with that of Simplicius, 53. 6–12.)

The 'unallocated': Transcendent genus or concept? Multiplication of the universal

What are the 'unclassed/unallocated' and 'classed/allocated' terms? I hope that answering this question will explain why I have had recourse to such an opaque translation. First they were jargon abbreviations for 'the unallocated animal/man' and so on; and these stood neither for physical objects nor for expressions but for terms, which as we have seen are significata. (I continue to italicize *'animal'* and *'man'* so as to be non-committal about any possible reduction to another status.)

Whether or not this application of the word κατατεταγμένος was initiated by him, it was understood in the same way by Porphyry and all his Neoplatonic successors. It indicates the universal, that is the genus or the species as it is 'in' the species or individual respectively. This really means with the differentia. But, in the Aristotelian logic which is presupposed, the genus 'with' the differentia *is* the species, and in the neo-Aristotelian, Porphyrian logic the species 'with' an appropriate set of accidents *is* the individual. Consequently it can be described, as we have seen, as 'the attribute taken with what it is an attribute of'. As for the word κατατάττω, it is regularly applied by these same writers, as well as grammarians, to someone allocating some term to, or classing it in, this or that category. The technical use of it to distinguish a type of predicate is an extension in Imperial Greek to an impersonal use— for example, shape 'has been allocated in a material form to the individual'. But, although sometimes associated with subordination, that is not its meaning.[20]

---

[20] κατατάττω κατάταξις: the reference to shape is at Simpl., *In Cat.*, 262. 15 (possibly a quotation from Iamblichus, who uses it at *De myst.*, I. 8 *ad init.*). Proclus (*In Tim.*, I. 89. 15) associates it with 'descents': but other occurrences in *In Tim.* mentioned by Festugière (*Procl., Comm. sur le Timée*, III. 83 n. 2) confirm the technical meaning 'in a subject', not κατα- = 'down', pace Festugière. Examples of application to genera or species in their respective subjects: Syrian, *In Met.*, 7. 12, 28. 19–20, 36. 27–28; Dexipp., *In Cat.*, 45. 22, 56. 4–6, 95. 10–13; Procl., *PT*, III. 8. 30. 26; syn. ἐγκατατεταγμένος Elias, *In Cat.*, 154. 18 and 19. Notice κατάταξις coupled with Porphyry's favourite σχέσις; e.g. Amelius *ap.* Iambl., *De an.*, Stob., I. 376. 4 W.; Procl., *In Tim.*, I. 50. 1–3.

What is of more interest is the 'unallocated' *animal, man,* or *white*. For this is what Porphyry said was predicated. What can this be? An answer is not difficult for a Platonist, and for that reason most of his successors did not find it difficult. But in this context Porphyry was not writing as a Platonist. We suggested earlier that he had an uncompleted programme for a semantics that would eschew extra-logical explications of its terms. If we go back to this suggestion, we too shall not find it difficult to say what the un-allocated terms are. They *are* the predicates. The predicates are the common terms (κοινά), and the common terms, as the Platonists themselves sometimes acknowledged, were the *unqualified* (ἁπλῶς) terms.[21] An uncomplicated syntactic account of this, such as we find in P. F. Strawson's *Introduction to logic*, is feasible for Porphyry. In reality, or rather Aristotelian reality, we have the allocated animal and man—in other words human (i.e. two-footed rational mortal) animal, bovine (i.e. four-footed cud-chewing) animal, and so on, and Socratic, Platonic man, and so on. In logic we have simply *animal* and *man*.

Some Platonists objected to Aristotle's denial that secondary substances are the individuals; they asked how, if a particular man is *not* man and animal, and rational and mortal, we can call him all these things. Dexippus and Simplicius have word for word the same reply (*In Categorias,* 51–14 and 104. 21 respectively), which is almost certainly Porphyry's: 'it is the allocated species which we call individuals, but the denial [that species were individuals] was about the terms thought of by themselves'.

Of course the *animal* predicated of *man* must be the genus: but that is unimportant, because it can be understood as a tautology. In the Peripatetic logic, from which Porphyry started, a genus was simply a predicate which had a certain range of subjects. In Neoplatonic logic, which was even less free of extra-logical elements, the fact was not unimportant; and Porphyry's successors, who did not share and did not understand his ideal of a neutral and autonomous logic, commonly explained the unallocated term as the 'transcendent' (ἐξῃρημένον) genus. This is the non-Aristotelian genus which Neoplatonists believed co-existed with, though prior to, the Aristotelian genus in every generic class. Unlike the Aristotelian, its existence was not in the species; so it was natural for them to

---

[21] Cf. 'the man simpliciter' that is predicated of Socrates (Philop., *In Cat.,* 34. 24–8), 'the body simpliciter' of particular bodies (ib., 57. 29–30).

identify Porphyry's unallocated and allocated with these transcendent and the immanent genera respectively. (Its identity with the
imparticipable is well attested.) Syrianus provides a clear example
of this (99. 1); and his pupil Proclus correlates the unallocated with
'the whole', which has the same implication (*In Timaeum*, 1. 49.
27). In a characteristic extension of the logic to theology,
Ps.-Dionysius states that the participant in the One must necessarily
be 'unrelated and unallocated in all the divisions which follow the
One' (*De ecclesiastica hierarchia*, 2. 5, 401 A Migne). No matter that
he is describing the ideal bishop.

But we also find the unallocated term explained as the concept.
This was 'the universal in the soul' of Neoplatonic theory. I have
described (Lloyd, 1956) how a 'multiplication of the universal' had
established itself in the Middle Academy. Here, I can summarize
the result by reproducing a résumé of it in a form which became a
common feature of Neoplatonists' lectures (here from Simplicius
on the *Categories*, 82. 35–83. 20). There were three kinds of universal (κοινόν): (1) the transcendent or separate from the particulars,
e.g. 'the first *animal*' which makes animality for animals; (2) the
product of this, the *animal* which exists only in each specific and
individual animal; (3) the universal which is 'posterior' because it
exists only in our conceptions and which we form by subtracting
all differentiae that modify animality in the external world.[22] (3)
alone is a genuine universal, for (1) is 'a common cause rather than
a common nature' and (2) is not really the same in different
species.[23]

It is (3), that is to say the concept, with which many identified

---

[22] It is ὑστερογενές (posterior), the regular term in Imperial philosophy taken
from Aristotle's description of the genus as οὐδὲν ἢ ὕστερον at *De an.*, 402[b]7.

[23] *The threefold universal*: Syrianus' pupil Hermias had made four universals by
adding the form in the intellect (i.e. what others called the demiurgic *logos*), of
which the concept (3) is the copy in discursive thought (*In Phaedr.*, 171–2). But
readers alert to external motives will expect such divergencies. Here the motive is
to assimilate Plat., *Phaedr.*, 249. But he belongs to our first group, which has parted
from Porphyry; for, like Syrianus, he counts only (1) as 'unallocated'. For a
summary of Proclus' position, see Lloyd (1971a), 360.

A major influence in favour of the threefold universal was its equation with the
triad of wholes (for which the *locus classicus* was Procl., *ET*, 67), the whole before
the parts (or many), of the parts (or many), in the part. For the third member was
often replaced by 'after the many' or ἐπὶ τοῖς πολλοῖς (e.g. Amm., *In Isag.*, 42. 13;
Jo. Ital., *Quaest.* 71.3–4); see especially Eustrat., *In EN*, 41.

the unallocated.[24] But some of these are the same writers who in other contexts made the alternative identification, that is, with the transcendent genus. Among several reasons for their choosing the concept, the chief one is that they believed, and believed correctly, that they were following Alexander and Aristotle rather than Plato. But equally they could choose the transcendent genus because they rejected, or more often forgot, the connection between the unallocated and predication.

Where Porphyry stood I have already suggested. He certainly can be numbered among those who regarded predicates as thoughts in the soul. But his lack of explicitness about this in the *Isagoge* may be due to his including it in the status of universals, which is a topic not merely unsuitable for beginners (*In Categorias* 75. 24–9) but perhaps superfluous for logic. This does not mean that a class of significata in addition to the nominata was not needed, and recognized as needed—or so, at least, I have argued.

Given that, whether under the auspices of logic or of metaphysics, this class is identified with concepts, what are the consequences for a theory of meaning? Take the implications of Porphyry's 'unallocated'. First, these block the reduction of predicative propositions to identical propositions. Secondly, what is more important for the interpretation of Aristotle, we have a distinction between the meaning of sentences, which is mental, and that which makes them true, which is not. The outcome is in fact the triangular model of meaning—'cat', thought/concept of cat, cat(s)—familiar from De Saussure and, in a much cruder form, from Ogden and Richards (1930).

The myth of a Neoplatonic nominalism

In the traditional topic of the status of universals Porphyry is

---

[24] '*Lekton*' *as concept*: In the Empire, Neoplatonists equated the Stoic *lekton* with their own and Aristotle's thought/concept. This was not, as writers on Stoicism sometimes suppose, due simply to ignorance of the Stoics or, what amounts to the same thing, to inferring 'mental' from 'incorporeal'. For the more sophisticated of them it was a case of taking for granted a *philosophical* maxim, namely that what an expression immediately signifies is a thought. If someone chose to describe this significatum as a *lekton*, '*lekton*' was a description/name of a thought. This applies to Amm., *In De int.*, 17. 24–8, but not, it must be admitted, to Simpl., *In Cat.*, 10. 3–4.

clearly a conceptualist. The term 'nominalism' which has often
been assigned to him and other Neoplatonists is ambiguous. In a
broad sense it is merely the contrary of 'realism' and so applicable
to any denial of the reality or separate existence of universals that
is associated with Platonists. In this sense Porphyry and most
Neoplatonists were nominalists; for their universals, represented
in logic by general expressions, had no existence separate from
thought. In a narrow sense it identifies the universals with the
expressions. This no Neoplatonist did. If he did have a programme
of explicating significata by reference to the nominata, Porphyry
may be said to have hankered after this identification. But it would
have been peculiar to Porphyry, and he did not carry it out. As for
the conceptualism, it is in no way an invention of the Neoplatonists, but simply Aristotle's position as it was seen by all schools,
including the authoritative Alexander. Despite some ambiguities
which we shall see shortly, it included the doctrine that forms, as
opposed to universals, existed as particular instances. (Both these
points were, I hope, established in c. 4 of Lloyd, 1981.) So, harmonizing Aristotle and Plato, this was how, with few exceptions, Neoplatonists expounded those few books of the *Organon* which
amounted to the early, and for many the sole, stage of the
philosophical curriculum.

Nor was this conceptualism just a deduction from the chain of
being. To judge by Proclus, Neoplatonists objected to universal
attributes even in subjects, not on the metaphysical ground that
they would be inappropriate in the physical world, but on logical
objections from the Sail Cloth argument. This argument was used
to reject a comfortable compromise whereby only participants
and participated entities were called for. Once the need for imparticipables was shown, the participated entities, which were
attributes of the participants, were no longer 'common natures'.[25]

Plotinus too had denied that a quality possessed by several
physical objects, or even by parts of one physical object, was
numerically one.[26] But these particular qualities could be specifically identical (VI. 4. 1. 23–4); so the question may be asked whether

---

[25] Procl., *ET*, 23. For a strict account of 'participant' and participated', see Lloyd
(1982), 26–7, 44.
[26] IV. 2. 1. 47–53; VI. 4. 1. 17–29. (IV. 3. 2. 16–19, though doubtfully compatible
with the τοσοῦτον of VI. 4. 1. 22, denies only that the quality has parts.) That this
correction was needed to Lloyd (1956), 62 was noticed by E. Emilsson (1988), 156
n. 31.

the species was reducible to the logical sum (disjunction) of them, as it was in their interpretation of Aristotle. They would have said, 'It depends on the context: there are two kinds of species, the Platonic and the Aristotelian'. But in fact they left little room for a universal, or 'common nature'; for the Platonic species or genus turns out usually to be of the *ab uno* type which, as we shall see in the next chapter, cannot be predicated univocally of its subjects. Thus, much of the traditional 'problem of universals', though certainly not half-dead, was passed by on the other side. This is particularly noticeable in the *Enneads*.

The Aristotelianism of Byzantine Neoplatonists

Nominalism has been regarded as *specifically* Neoplatonic in Byzantium by many historians (e.g. Tatakis, 1949, 220–1). And let me repeat that it is only as specifically Neoplatonic that I am claiming it to be a myth. But the position was, and remained well into the Middle Ages, the same as that which I have described in Athens and Alexandria. The curriculum was the same and the programme of harmonization the same. As late as the twelfth century Philosophy was described in an address to the Emperor Isaac Comnenus as

first having been your guide through the Aristotelian mazes . . . and taught you to excel in such matters, but afterwards having, like some theurge, conjured up the divine for you in the Platonic writings . . . made you, to crown it all, a sublime, divinely inspired theologian.[27]

The whole succession of professors from Psellus onwards adhered to conceptualism. But there was always present a motive for weakening it that would have been much less felt in Alexandria. This was the theological attraction, for many a necessity, of the notion of a common nature. It was felt most obviously in the

[27] Theodoros Prodromos, Λόγος εἰς τὸν Πορφυρογεννητικὸν κυρὸν Ἰσαάκιον τὸν Κομνήου, ed. Kurtz, *BZ*, ll. 16 (1907), 112–17, 166–74; cf. Praechter (1910a). Early in the next century, Blemmydes' original Aristotelian curriculum was more restricted, and *theologia* apparently more based on biblical texts (*Curriculum vitae* I, §§ 5 and 10, Munitiz, *Corpus Christianorum*, ser. graec., 13 (= 2. 28–9 and 6. 9 ff. Heisenberg): but this does not mean Plato was dropped from the philosophical curriculum (cf. Praechter, loc. cit., 319–23). Lemerle (1971), 211 (Engl. fr., 244), noted that the publication of *CAG* 'has not provoked any major overall study of Aristotle in Byzantium'.

problem of the Trinity, where the Cappadocian Fathers were followed by the pre-eminently orthodox and philosophically respectable John Damascene.

They appealed to a universal—'the nature', considered synonymous with 'substance' and 'form'—in addition to particulars ('the persons').

Alexander's formula had been that the specific and generic forms had their existence (εἶναι) in thought but their 'subsistence' (ὑπόστασις, here meaning concrete or physical existence, possibly even 'substratum') in the particulars. And this is what Philoponus had in mind in his De anima commentary, although for him as for the other Alexandrians ὑπόστασις had become a straightforward synonym of εἶναι:

Universals have their existence (ὑπόστασις) in the particulars, but when they are understood as universals or general terms, they are found in the mind, for their being general consists in their being thought of as general, and thoughts are mental. (307. 33–5)

In fact he seems to have used it—defending what his opponents called tritheism—to have denied the single substance of the Trinity.[28] But it was sometimes claimed that these mental universals implied that there was also a common nature or 'generality' in the particular things of which they were predicated. This is also how Aristotle has been, and perhaps usually is, understood.[29] But it makes his position much less nominalist, in the broad and the narrow sense of 'nominalism', than Alexander and Porphyry after him had intended. For what they meant was that the universal, in effect the general term or predicate, depended for its existence on that of the particular forms in particular things because thought constructed it by abstraction from them. The Neoplatonist philosopher John Italos (eleventh century) perfectly understood this, having read his Aristotle through Ammonius' as well as John Damascene's spectacles. For he made it clear that the three properties of genera and species in the many, namely being inseparable, being particular, and not being predicable of many, are mutually implicative (Quaestiones quodlibetales, 8. 2–8). To have something common which is real (even if not on its own) as well as something

---

[28] R. Sorabji, in Sorabji (ed.) (1987), 31–2. In Op. monophys. (129 Sanda) Philoponus says that species and genus exist only mentally, 'sicut saepe ostendimus'.

[29] This is the version assumed and attributed to Alexandria and Byzantium by L. Benakis (1982).

common which is mental would have been seen by him as admitting Platonism—together with the Sail Cloth dilemma—by the back door. He mentions elsewhere this concession to realism because he finds it in the universally respected John Damascene, but he does not commit himself.[30]

Aristotle's own description of the mind's formation of universals by induction is one of the few texts which can be taken to commit him to universals in nature (*Posterior Analytics* II, 100ᵃ3–ᵇ5). For it suggests a process of recognition, and what is recognized must already be there. It is also one of the few texts from the *Posterior Analytics* II that was widely familiar. Philoponus' paraphrase of it, also known in Constantinople, had contained the same realist suggestion (437. 15 ff.). But it is possible to read both Aristotle and Philoponus in a conceptualist way. It is consistent with either text to suppose that a form exists as a set of particular forms in a set of particulars, and that when perception, thought, or the two combined, attend a sufficient number of times to a sufficient number of forms which in fact fall under one class-concept they become aware of the set (rather than recognize it) as being or containing one common attribute—in short they are aware of it as universal, not particular.

Ignoring the question of Aristotle's meaning, it is often impossible to be sure what an ancient or medieval expositor meant. (In the West the ambiguity we are concerned with is often concealed in the formula 'cum fundamento in re'.) In some cases it is more probable that he meant by the 'common' property in a set of particulars a property which was specifically, not numerically, one. Of course, as it stands, such a property would be a circular explanation of predicability: but it is consistent with a Porphyrian account of specific identity. In other cases we know that we cannot assume the expositor to be consistent. As for Philoponus, a realist interpretation of his words could be explained if we supposed that that was what he understood Aristotle to believe and that the context did not call for anyone else's belief. In Constantinople and the Eastern Empire John Damascene had great influence, and he took the realist line, apparently without finding it incompatible with the remaining properties of a conceptualist universal. It had already

---

[30] *Quaestiones*, 70. 34–71. 9. Psellus notoriously found Aristotle unsympathetic: but I cannot subscribe to Tatakis' judgement (1949, 212) that Italos was no more Aristotelian than his master.

been insisted on in more than one passage of Simplicius' *Categories* commentary.[31] At bottom the reason is that he did not accept the 'nominalist' interpretation of Aristotle and believed, contrary to Alexander, that *in re* forms were universals.

This realism was substantially supported by a practice for which Neoplatonists themselves were responsible. When they identified the form in matter with the whole in, or composed of, the parts, they could not help suggesting that it was a universal; for 'whole' was a systematic way of referring to a universal. As we shall see later, neither Plotinus nor Proclus accepted the suggestion, but it had been an original element in the project of harmonizing Plato with Aristotle. And if someone were to point out that the Sail Cloth argument must apply as much to an *in re* as to an *ante rem* universal, one could borrow Nicolas of Methone's reply that light and *logos* were two instances of things which were in two places at once without being divided. (*Refutatio . . . proeli platonici*, 70. 2–3 Angelou (91. 7–8 Vömel)).

From the standpoint of Porphyry's broad nominalism the false step which will have led to this position consists in having unwittingly crossed the boundary between logic and metaphysics. The harmonizing project went back to Porphyry himself: but it depended on distinguishing what it was proper for the logician to say from what it was proper for the metaphysician to say. That the three wholes belong to metaphysics, not logic, is shown by the presence of the whole before the parts; for this could not be used as a general term and, while it is exemplified by the Platonic Idea, Neoplatonists found it in Aristotle only in Book *Λ* of the *Metaphysics*. Furthermore when the form in matter is seen in the context of Neoplatonic metaphysics it will turn out not to have, except analogously, the properties of an Aristotelian universal. This will emerge in later chapters.

My own view, then, of their often ambiguous pronouncements is that their Byzantine authors had not sufficiently focused the question what exactly the *fundamentum in re* amounted to. Conse-

---

[31] e.g. in the first quarter of the treatment of substance, 75 ff. (Part of 84–5 is translated in Lloyd, 1981, 74–6.) Unlike the (other?) Alexandrian commentaries, his is evidently not written for beginners. But John Damascene is yet another example of a philosopher who suffered from having repeated and strung together excerpts from various handbooks and scholia, chiefly of Alexandrian origin. Cf. Hunger (1978), 48. For a more sympathetic and doubtless better-informed view of 'common natures' than mine cf. Owens (1957).

quently it is in a sense anachronistic to expect in each case to assess their commitment to nominalism. Still less should one expect each contributor to the controversy to have been conscious that he was protecting or dislodging a keystone of Porphyrian semantics, although that is what he was doing. In all this they were probably no different from most of the Alexandrians.

Confining ourselves, however, to the leading Neoplatonist philosophers, we find their broad nominalism confirmed by numerous applications to theology. Here are three examples from the eleventh and early twelfth centuries.

1. The unity or single God represented by the Trinity was regularly called ἕν. Italos argued that this implied a real, i.e. Platonic, notion of substance or nature (generally treated as synonyms in this context), which was nonsense; for universals were concepts, while the ἕν which signified a substantial universal was required to signify God himself. It should therefore be replaced by εἷς.

2. According to Porphyry's epistemological argument, there could not be mental essences before physical instances of them. Byzantine Aristotelianism went beyond that: the essence, as a specific form, existed only as individual instances which were the substances of individuals, so that essence and existence were inseparable. Consequently neither Italos nor Eustratius had any truck with the account of Creation whereby the world pre-existed so to speak, as essences in God's mind until they had existence added to them.[32]

3. Again, the reification was applied by Eustratius to existence or reality itself and rejected on the same grounds: there is no thing called reality which is prior to something which is real, i.e. exists—nothing is ὑπερόν. And this, he said, must apply to God. No doubt he would have had in mind Pseudo-Dionysius' claim that, like the Neoplatonic One, God was exempt from the rational constraints of categories because he was ὑπερών.[33] But Eustratius' argument is of more than historical interest. It implies that the *meaning* of 'exists' is the same in, say 'centaurs exist', 'frozen air exists', and 'God exists', for the difference

---

[32] The points about 1. the Trinity and 2. the Creation are both mentioned in Joannou (1954).

[33] Eustrat., Ὅρος καθολικὸς φιλοσοφίας Πλάτωνος, ed. Joannou, BZ 47 (1954), 365–8; Ps.-Dionys., De div. nom., 11. 6 (PG, 3. 953c). See further Lloyd (1987a), 346–7.

between the states of affairs which the sentences describe is to be looked for only in the differences between centaurs, frozen air, and God. One might add, Why should this not include 'qualities exist' and 'numbers exist'?

It should be evident that there was less formal division than in Alexandria between the spheres of influence of Aristotle and of Plato. Nor, among Byzantine theologians, are allegiances to philosophy schools to be relied on. Objectionable theses are refuted or abused because they are too Platonic or because they are too Aristotelian, depending on the opportunities they offer. This is not to be taken in general as discreditable. For much of it is to be explained by the relish with which these professionals, many of them at home in logic, all of them in rhetoric, indulged themselves in *ad hominem* argument.

3

QUASI-GENERA AND THE
COLLAPSE OF SUBSTANCE
AND ATTRIBUTE

P-series as quasi-genera

What can be counted as belonging to the logical structure of Neoplatonism? The most revealing element in it, if only because it pervades their logic, metaphysics, and psychology, is Neoplatonists' concept of the genus.

According to Aristotle, if the members of a class which might be said to differ specifically from one another are in an order of prior and posterior, the class is not a genus (*Metaphysics*, B 996^{a}6–14) and 'the universal predicate of the class is either non-existent or virtually so' (*Politics*, 1275^{a}35–8). He does not tell us why.[1] Certainly it is easy to see that if the first term of the ordered series is taken to be the universal common to all the terms, we shall have a contradiction; and it is not implausible for anyone influenced by Pythagoreanism to take the first term in this way. The paradigm case of what I call a P-series is the number series, and what was apparently common to all its members was the unit or monad. But this is also the first term of the series. If therefore it were a genuine or generic universal like animal there would be a contradiction like the contradiction of having animal both what is common to all kinds of animal and one of the kinds of animals themselves. Aristotle believed that some apparent cases of genus and species were just such quasi-genera because they formed P-series: for instance good, soul, constitution.

Platonists had plausible and familiar reasons for believing that all genera were quasi-genera in this sense, although the extent to

[1] The only plausible grounds among those suggested by the ancient commentators are found in Al. Aphr., *De an.*, 16. 18–17. 8, 28. 14–29. 1, and Simpl., *In De an.*, 107. They are discussed in Lloyd (1962), 79.

which they did so is not clear. The genus was for them a whole which was prior to its parts; and it was also in some way a member of whatever class it is the class concept of ('Is there anything more beautiful than beauty itself?'). In Aristotelian logic the standard genus is predicated 'synonymously' of all its species, that is, with the same name and the same definition or meaning. According to some modern idealists this is unreasonable;[2] for the species, say of birds, is animal *modified by* the form of being able to fly while the species of fishes is animal *modified by* being able to live in water, with the result that 'animal' no longer has the same meaning when it is attributed even to co-ordinate species. In the cases of super-ordinate and subordinate species this picture is clearly going to fit a Neoplatonic frame of procession and causation; for in this frame forms are not transmitted identically from agent to effect, as they are for Aristotle, but are altered qualitatively when received by the effect. But the underlying problem is the relation of the genus as matter to the differentia as form. The explanation that the generic substrate is individuated by the specific forms, as Socrates and Plato are by their 'peculiarities', while still being common to them, is no more than a statement of the problem (*pace* Elias, *In Categorias*, 155. 1–8). There is, however, no room, it would appear, for the application of Aristotle's deductive logic. As he says in the *Posterior Analytics*, there is no need of Platonic Ideas but we do need a ἕν or κοινόν since without it there is no middle term and therefore no proof (I. 77^{a}7–9). But the denial of a κοινόν, of whatever ontological status, is equivalent to the denial of a 'synonymous' generic predicate. Instead of demonstrating the propria of lowest species, syllogisms would systematically suffer from the fallacy of equivocation or quaternio terminorum. In short, class inclusion could no longer be counted on as a transitive relation.

On the other hand, although this would be the case according to the *Categories*, it was not to be inferred that a quasi-genus was said equivocally of the species (or of other series which derived from them): it was an instance of Aristotle's tertium quid between the synonymous and the homonymous, namely the *ab uno* (ἀφ᾽ ἑνός) or *ad unum* (πρός ἕν). This is the notion which he left notoriously unclear but illustrated by terms such as 'medical' and 'friendship', which, he says, depend on the 'first' or 'primary' terms (or objects)

---

[2] e.g. Joachim (1951), 39–40 and, by implication, Joseph (1916), 83–9.

doctor, i.e. medical man, and friendship for the good respectively.[3] In *Metaphysics* *Γ* and *E* Aristotle suggests that the notion is applicable to *being*, so that there will be what we may call a quasi-science of metaphysics. The quasi-generic term he describes as 'universal inasmuch as first' (*E* 1026ª30)—an epigram which could serve as the motto of Neoplatonism. It is recognized by all Neoplatonists, if not always by their expositors, re-appearing, for instance, in Marsilio Ficino as the 'primum in genere'.

How can they have a deductive logic? First thesis

It is obvious again that nothing could be more adapted to Neoplatonists' metaphysics than the notion of series ('chains' in their terminology) which were *ab uno*. But the fact that such a series is not homonymous is not enough to explain how the logic of a syllogism in Barbara, or its equivalent in the class-inclusion calculus is possible; and without this logic the Platonic dialectic was worthless. Moreover, this applies equally to the intelligible world and to the sensible world. What is needed is a positive thesis which will replace the synonymy which belongs to a standard genus. Three such theses can be found. They seem to have been treated as logically independent; so any combination of them might be accepted; and this in fact occurred.

First, whatever attribute is predicable of a species in virtue of its membership of the quasi-genus, that attribute is predicable synonymously of the co-ordinate species. Simplicius states this much more simply by saying just that the genus is predicated synonymously of co-ordinate, though not of subordinated, species.[4] But, while he doubtless means it in the form in which I have stated it, it will not quite do as it stands. For the generic property correctly attributed to a species is not to be defined as the genus itself is defined, but as it appears in the species. What does hold is that this,

---

[3] It will be recognized as 'focal meaning', the expression due to G. E. L. Owen. But I have avoided this expression because, even if the notion were a theory of *meaning* for Aristotle, which is questionable, it was not for the Neoplatonists.

Notice that things which are *ab uno* or *ad unum* were sometimes called neither homonymous nor synonymous, sometimes both. But they were often called homonymous, especially by Plotinus, to make only the negative point that they did not have the same definition (e.g. VI. 7. 18. 36; cf. VI. 3. 1. 6–7 and 21).

[4] *In Cat.*, 220. 29–221. 11. At 221.8 συνωνύμως is a slip for ὁμωνύμως.

as it were, specific definition of it is valid for all its co-ordinate species; and this can be generalized to cover attributes due to participation in any superordinate species. In whatever form fishes and oysters (assuming them to be co-ordinate) are water animals, they are synonymously that, while, given that we have to do with a quasi-genus not a standard genus, the 'water animal' attributable to trout and portuguaises, which are on a third level, is not synonymous with that attributable to fishes and oysters. The reasoning behind this is clear. All that might prevent a class such as animal— a 'division' as the Platonists would have called it—from being a standard genus is that it should be a P-series. But Simplicius' statement implies that while genus-species-subordinate species represents a P-series, the horizontal series, species-co-ordinate species does not; and it implies also that the only reason for denying a nominal, face value instance of standard or Aristotelian division to be such an instance is that it forms a P-series.

Thus it is rejecting the modern idealists' case for denying synonymy even among co-ordinate species. That case claimed that the shared or generic properties of *all* species were modified, i.e. made qualitatively different by the differentiae, independently of any order of prior and posterior. But Simplicius' is the official doctrine of the Alexandrian logicians. For them it was analytically true. They argued that if the predication of the genus were not synonymous, the division of the genus would have been incorrect in making the species in question co-ordinate (Ammonius, *In Isagogen*, 97). For the same reason, the lowest species is predicated synonymously of the individuals. And they used the argument again to defend Aristotle's dictum that there were no degrees of substance. The dictum, said Ammonius (loc. cit.) applied 'horizontally' (between say man and ox) but not 'vertically' (between say angels and celestial bodies).

This does not contradict the universal Neoplatonic rule that a form is altered by its recipient. For, according to the logicians, co-ordinate species did alter it, but altered it equally. But in metaphysics this position is often abandoned. The generation of nominally co-ordinate species is often counted as a procession of the genus as much as its vertical generation of nominally subordinate species or of lower hypostases; and procession implies an ordered series. The order can be accounted for by the order of value possessed independently by the differentiae. For example, several quasi-genera or diacosms, such as soul or intellect, divide conventionally into divine, angelic, and daemonic. These can be represented as the first division of a standard genus, that is, as the first line of co-ordinate species. But in fact they form a P-series in which a divine soul is more of a soul and a divine intellect more of an intellect than a daemonic soul or intellect, the angelic being intermediate instances. This occurs particularly in Proclus; and it can be understood as a super-imposition, bristling with difficulties, of the key concept of *procession* on the key concept of *division*.[5]

Second thesis

Even if we ignore horizontal procession, to have argued that 'co-ordinate' implied 'synonymous' is too close to begging the question and in any case concedes enough to enable only some of the ordinary inferences of a standard genus to be made. We must therefore turn to the second of the theses which go towards re-placing the synonymy. Unlike the first, it is accepted universally, in the context of logic and of metaphysics. The terms of a P-series, it runs, do not share an identical generic predicate, but the differ-ences between them in respect of this predicate are equivalent to different degrees of participation in its primary form, that is to say loosely, the first term of the series. To take a case which they and Aristotle agreed in counting as a P-series, the being or substance of the accidental categories was not synonymous: but the difference between its definition in the various categories was due to its varying degree of participation in being or substance, which, as it should be in a quasi-genus, is in fact the first member of the class or series of categories. Hence the attention which Neoplatonists devote to the question of the *order* of the categories.

This second thesis, reducing the recalcitrant series to degrees of participation in their first member, can be found quite explicit— random examples are Elias on the *Isagoge*, 71. 8–11 and Simplicius on the *Categories*, 32. But more often we find it by implication in the belief that the differing predicates are related by a continuous

---

[5] See Lloyd (1982), especially 29–32 and 39–40. In view of the context, it is unfortunate that Dodds should have chosen to translate Proclus' σύστοιχος syste-matically as 'co-ordinate' (particularly in *ET*, 108). It is synonymous with ὁμοταγής, which does mean 'belonging to the same order', but the order is commonly Dodds' *vertical* series.

analogy. In so far as the differences have been made quantitative, this can be considered valid. Its importance is that in so far as there are ratios of this kind there are inferences from one pair of terms to another and one term to another; and to this extent there is a calculus, or the possibility of one, for a quasi-genus, to replace that of a standard genus. To replace it by the same kind of inferences it would be necessary to translate quantities of a quality into qualities; and this would need a large contribution of intuition or dogma. But there are many indications that Proclus pictured an ideal Platonic dialectic of collection and division in which the 'lower' the species the more complex, and in which 'more complex' meant literally compounded of more forms.

Third thesis: Plotinian and Proclan versions

The third thesis is the most direct and adequate means of solving the problem. For it claims that the non-standard genus has in addition to, alongside as it were, the properties of a P-series, the logical properties of a standard genus.[6] According to Plotinus, the first, or quasi-genus, (1), is the whole which is prior to its parts, (2) 'remains' unaffected by any 'procession' of the genus and (3) is the 'power', the δύναμις of its species. But it is also, i.e. as a standard genus, (1) a whole which is in the parts and (2) potentially, δυνάμει, the species. As they are actually or *per se*, each single species is exactly 'what it is called', being defined, of course, by the addition of one or more differentiae to the genus. But the genus as it is actually or *per se* is not the standard genus, for, as we have just seen, it is not the potentiality of the species but the power of them. This means that it is a whole which *actually* contains the species—but the species as a whole, 'silently'. And if this means that it will embrace contradictory differentiae in actuality, not potentially, so be it.[7] It is one aspect or function (ἄλλως μὲν ... ἄλλως δὲ in Plotinus): in its other function it contains the species by being the universal

---

[6] The Plotinian version which follows is my understanding of *Enn.*, VI. 2. 20. But elements of it are confirmed by many scattered passages elsewhere. To give but two examples: the genus of being *qua/Nous* Living Creature is δυνάμει its species in VI. 8. 3, and this corresponds to 'wisdom' (knowledge of realities) which is δυνάμει the theorems in V. 8. 5. 4–7.

[7] Cf. Syrian., *In Met.*, 32. 5–6: 'how else could they come to make species?'

which is present in each of them singly and which (together with the differentia) completes their substance.

More difficult, but not strictly relevant to the thesis which concerns us, is the further claim that each single species is potentially the whole or genus. This is when it is taken as a member of the genus; for taken on its own, or actually, it is just what it is. And the ground given for the claim is that each has received the genus as a whole, not a part of it. Thus 'potentially' is here equivalent to 'if one abstracts the genus from the differentia in the definition, which represents the essence, of the species'. And an important, though not the most obvious, implication of 'received the genus as a whole' is that the abstraction would be valid, for the differentia will not have subtracted anything from the essence of the species. The same would be true in the Aristotelian semantics. But the difference is that it would be of no consequence there, since the genus has no existence over and above the species (or as a whole prior to its parts). It would be valid, but trivial to infer that man is animal, since this would mean 'an animal'. But in the Neoplatonic abstraction it would mean the whole itself. The validity of this inference is clearly open to question but can come under more scrutiny when we look at the radical criticism of Aristotelian semantics.

The conclusion, reminding us strongly of Leibniz, that substances contain all other substances, is a favourite with Plotinus and has other grounds which, again, do not need to be pursued here. Here, however, it rests on a premiss which seems to contradict the dogma that any transmitted form is altered by its recipient. All this leaves no obvious answer to the general objection that this version of the double aspect or function of the genus contains arguments which start from assuming one aspect, and in effect type, of genus but have conclusions which belong to the other type. But, as I have implied, the most likely case of this, the potentiality of the species, is one which need not affect the thesis that the two types co-exist.

Plotinus' version of this thesis is coloured by the context of *Ennead* VI. 2 which makes the genus he is describing that of Being or Intellect. This, however, makes it easier for us to understand the properties appropriate to the quasi-genus as belonging to the reified intension or class-concept and those appropriate to the standard genus as belonging to the extension. The distinction must not be ruled out as only modern. Damascius distinguishes two ways in which *animal* can be analysed, first into 'elements', i.e. of its definition, secondly into 'parts', i.e. its species. The first analyses animal *qua* animal, a genus (in intension) which is not composed of (ἐκ) *animals*; the second does analyse animal (in intension) so that it is composed of its parts, but is no longer, Damascius comments, animal *qua* animal, for it is analysed *qua* horse and man, etc. (*Dubitationes*), II. 74. 16–75. 10 R). Another writer offers what became a cliché of nineteenth-century textbooks of logic, the inverse variation of intension and extension, if we use 'intension' for 'meaning' without—and indeed contrary to—the Neoplatonic metaphysics (Elias on the *Isagoge*, 82. 12–14).

Must we infer that the Plotinian version does not apply to other genera, and more particularly to genera which are not categories? The Aristotelian commentaries regularly expound the distinction between our quasi-genus and the standard genus in order to explain the *Categories*. According to them, the term 'genus' is equivocal, for sometimes it means the categorial type, which is a P-series. They do not suggest that one and the same genus can be of both types, except to the extent that was implied by the second thesis. But it is probable that such an extension was regarded as out of place: it would go beyond what was needed to explain Aristotle.[8] As for Plotinus, he more than once implies that his thesis holds for any genus. And one could argue that logic dictates this. For (1) the genus and species, or whole and parts, described in the version we have taken from VI. 2. 20 must include sub-genera and their species; (2) these substances are also wholes with parts, and will therefore consist of wholes before the parts as well as wholes in the parts; (3) there is thus no reason why they should not have the same logical properties as the summum genus and its species; (4) but the sub-genera or their sub-genera will sooner or later include what are accepted by everyone as typically standard genera. In *Ennead*, VI. 2 these are, though not immediately, divine, winged, aquatic, and footed creatures, if only because Being is the Living Creature of the *Timaeus* (VI. 2. 21).

There is a Proclan version of the same thesis that represents the 'Athenian' system and certainly holds for all genera. Proclus summarizes it in a passage of his *Parmenides* commentary (707) which

---

[8] Nevertheless, tackling the difficult case of motion Simplicius makes the standard claim that Aristotle was speaking of sensible motion, Plato of intellectual or Ideal motion, but also argues that Aristotle did not realize that motion could still be a genus in the categorial sense, which is what it is in the *Sophist* (*In Cat.*, 402–6; cf. 66. 12–15; 20. 5).

is intended to answer the question how the 'many' of Zeno's first hypothesis (*Parmenides*, 127 ff.) are unified, but which is too long and repetitive to quote. It states that there is a double order of descent from the One: we can see how one order has the structure of quasi-genera and one that of standard genera. The first descends through imparticipables and the second through the participated entities. Proclus begins (l. 4) by distinguishing these as two types of monads or heads of series.[9] It will be enough here to abstract the properties which are attributed in the course of the passage to all imparticipables (I) and all participated entities (P) respectively:

I1.	prior to the many (14)	P1.	in the many (14, 25)
I2.	*per se* (17, 19)	P2.	in something else (17, 18)
I3.	binding the many *qua* cause of them (22)	P3.	binding the many *qua* universal (23)

Next, he says (28) that there is a corresponding distinction of the series or pluralities ('the wholes') engendered by the two types of monad; and he attributes the same or analogous properties to them.

Here, evidently, is a more structured form of the Plotinian version. What in Plotinus were two aspects or functions of an object re-appear in a typically Proclan manner as two objects. The clearest allusion to the two kinds of genus which they entail is in I3 and P3. For all later Neoplatonists every series contains the two kinds of entity, since every entity—usually a form—is both imparticipable and a participated entity. Consequently any series, in other words any putative genus, is, so to say, ambiguous. Read in terms of the participated entities, it is open to the ordinary calculus of class-inclusion and, if required, syllogistic.

Neoplatonists did not normally expound or even espouse any of our three theses for the conscious purpose of preserving inferences in P-series. Their interest was from the other point of view. They were constantly anxious to show how genera were P-series; and, not aspiring to the sophistication of the third thesis, they seem often content to assume that once the genus of being had been shown to be a P-series all genera could be regarded as P-series, because they were all by definition sub-genera of being. The self-

---

[9] A reader must not hastily suppose that the passage is about the henads with which he may be familiar from *ET*. Proclus (following Plat., *Phileb.*, 16C–17A) quite often uses ἐνάδες, a synonym of μονάδες, which will, of course, *include* the henads.

evident motive for so regarding them was, of course, that they would then display the chain of being in which all things depended on the One and each had its appropriate degree of reality.

Such a quasi-genus has also two purely logical advantages over the standard genus. Neoplatonists were well aware of them. First, it blocks the reduction of the genus to its species, that is, to the logical sum or disjunction of the species. By this reduction Aristotle believed that he had rebutted the Platonists' substantial universals, since genera were the prime instances of universals.

Secondly, it blocks the Third Man regress. For only if the form and its instances are ϕ in the same sense of 'ϕ' (i.e. synonymously) will they entail a further universal (a second form of ϕ). Of course the form must not share only the name 'ϕ' (i.e. homonymously) with its instances; otherwise we have no universal at all. This leaves the *ab uno* relation. Proclus, who states this argument, adds, 'And there is no need to hunt for any further kind of universal' (*In Parmenidem*, 880. 5–7). He is probably relying on the second thesis, which makes differences of rank differences of degree of participation on the part of the instances . . . Otherwise he will certainly need another kind of universal.

Plotinus' radical criticism of substance and attribute

Aristotle's world is one which reflects an ideal language of subject and predicate. His semantic objects, that is to say anything that we talk about, are not necessarily substances and their attributes, but when they are not they are usually reducible to them, like Socrates, or analogous to them, like actions. Shared attributes enable them to be classified under genera, sub-genera, and species. But a further stipulation prevents there being an indefinite number of alternative classifications. Only some attributes have the privileged status of defining the classes or kinds; they are the ones that are predicated 'in the category of substance'; and they are *par excellence* the specific (species-forming) differentiae. The remainder are accidents.

As for the subjects of attributes, they can be seen as matter stamped by the attributes as form. But the substantial attributes being logically prior to the accidental cannot correspond to predicates like the accidental attributes; otherwise their subjects would not be proper semantic objects divisible into matter and form, but

mere matter. Aristotle has to treat them as (grammatical) predicates of propositions which approximate to identical propositions.
But they are certainly distinct from their subjects. Indeed, when a
differentia is predicable of a species or an individual, say two-
footed of Man or Socrates, it cannot belong to the same genus as
that species or individual. If it did, the genus would be predicable
of it, but then it would not be a differentia but a species or
individual, for of these alone is the genus predicable (*Topics*,
122^{b}18–24; 144^{a}31–^{b}3; *Metaphysics B* 998^{b}24).

As well as matter to be stamped by form, the subjects of substantial attributes can be seen as potentially what they are when so
stamped. Such an attribute is one which completes the existence or
substance of some semantic object; and all Imperial philosophers
used the jargon-term 'completive' for them (συμπληρωτικός sc. τῆς
οὐσίας). Independently of metaphysical commitment, they spoke of
existence or substance produced in this way at each level of abstraction: generic, specific, and individual. Only at the level of
individual subjects do accidental attributes occur. These are primarily qualities and quantities; and for that very reason the Aristotelian model which we have been summarizing is ambiguous
whether differentiae can be counted as qualities, although it is clear
that they cannot be substances.

It is this logical model of substance and attribute which Plotinus,
like other Imperial philosophers, accepts for everyday purposes
but aims in the last resort to destroy root and branch.

His discussion of it arises from the topic of the Aristotelian
categories. But it is less clear than it might have been because he
has mixed together (in VI. 2) arguments that quality is not a
category with arguments that Plato's 'greatest kinds' are categories.
It is often said that he rejected the Aristotelian categories on the
grounds that they cannot have the same meaning when they are
applied to the intelligible world as they have in the sensible world:
but to the extent that this suggests that they have at least an
analogical application it is misleading. They have no place in the
intelligible world. In any case, as he regularly objects in VI. 2, they
cannot be among 'the first' or 'the first genera', since they are
compound, not simple. This flexible notion seems here to mean
that they are capable of analysis into subject and attribute. The five
greatest kinds of the *Sophist* are the only simple genera. They do not
form a P-series—otherwise they would not be summa genera—

although each is a P-series. But they form a whole, the name of which is 'substance' or 'being'. They are not attributes of substance/being—otherwise *it* would not be simple—but activities of it. For reasons which we shall see, it follows that each can be described as identical with it and therefore with each other; but the identity is in subject not concept—Plotinus uses the Aristotelian formula. Extensionally, therefore, there is one summum genus; and as a genus it is not simple in another sense, inasmuch as it contains sub-genera and species, which are the classes of all that is. By assuming this, Plotinus is enabled to make what I have alluded to as the radical criticism of the semantics of substance and attribute.

But first a remark about the terminology of 'substance'. Although the greatest kinds are usually called the first kinds/genera by Plotinus, I refer to them as summa genera, for they behave logically as that. Technically they are quasi-genera, but for our immediate purpose that is less relevant. Their totality is what Plotinus here usually calls *ousia*, though elsewhere more commonly τὸ ὄν. The reason is, of course, that he wants it to connote what the term connotes for Aristotle. Consequently it contains what to most post-medieval readers appears as an ambiguity: sometimes it is used as a common or count noun, in English 'a substance', sometimes as an abstract noun, in English 'the substance of x'. The abstract use is often translated 'essence'. But Plotinus, like Aristotle, is conscious that '*ousia*' is a nominal form of the verb 'to be', and primarily in its existential sense. There is no need to dissociate 'substance' from 'substance of'/'essence of' by asserting that the latter concerns only the predicative use of 'being'. For 'what it is to be x' can be, and I think commonly was, read by Aristotle and Plotinus as 'what it is for x to be, i.e. exist'. I shall therefore normally use the term 'substance' in translating the concrete and the abstract uses of *ousia*. This is not for the purpose of airing the justification I have just given, or even for the purpose of justifying Plotinus' argument against Aristotle, but in order to make that argument clearer. Most obviously, when the question is of a quality, say a specific differentia, which 'completes the *ousia*', it will not be helpful to have to decide whether 'the *ousia*' means 'the essence' or 'the substance'; for this would amount to deciding between ' the substance of' and 'the substance', and I do not think that Plotinus wanted to distinguish, even in meaning, between 'completing the substance of man' and 'completing the substance, man'. To return to the summum genus, we have to bear in mind that his contemporary readers, perhaps fortunately, did not have two words 'substance' and 'being'. I should add that, although it is irrelevant here, the division of substance into essence and existence does have its origin in Neoplatonism, and historically is another of the salient alterations made to the Aristotelian structure.

Plotinus' attack on Aristotle's semantics focuses, as we may expect, on the status of the completive differentia. Plotinus deals with it at three levels of reality, that is, Platonist reality. The highest, which is for the Aristotelian the most abstract, we have already seen. A summum genus or category must neither have nor be a differentia. Whether or not a differentia is a quality, it is an attribute of a subject, and motion and rest, for example, are not attributes of existence (substance). But he takes for granted that he is telling us about the nature of any genus, for Existence/Substance is the genus of genera. Certainly what holds of a superordinate genus can only be inferred to hold of a subordinate genus in the mode 'appropriate to' this subordinate genus. But in our case this means the following: just as existence is complete in the genus *per se* of Substance/Existence, so in a sub-genus of it *per se* the existence of the sub-genus is complete. In fact he takes the inference to hold also for the external procession of the generic monad. At this level this will be the procession of Existence to the next hypostasis, Soul, which, like a species, is also a particular kind or determination of it, since Existence is Intellect. The question is now whether what makes a particular kind of substance, rather than substance, what it is, is an attribute.

For in VI. 2. 5 he decides that to admit this in the case of soul would be to make these attributes no better than accidents. Suppose, he argues, that we take soul quite apart from its producing anything. Its existence/substance is not that of a stone. Consequently its existence is existence *qua* soul as well as existence. Must we then distinguish existence, which is substance, from that which completes the soul's substance and which is the differentia of soul? Plotinus replies,

Certainly soul is a particular (kind of) existence, not, however, in the same way that a man is white, but simply as a particular substance. And this is equivalent to its properties not having come from outside substance. (ll. 24–6)

Otherwise, he explains (c. 6 *ad init.*), only part of it will be substance/existence, namely its substance/existence, and the 'soul' of its being soul will not be substance. The substance of soul must be the source of all that it is—in fact identical with all that it is. To follow this, one needs to remember first the model which it is opposing. In Aristotle the differentia of a substance could not be a substance, for it had to qualify the genus; but the genus of a substance must be a substance. The Peripatetic rule expressing this in the jargon of the schools ran, 'the differentia must come from outside', meaning 'outside the genus': but it is obvious that it can be equally understood as 'outside the category', as it is by Plotinus, for whom the category is simply the summum genus. When he says that the substance of soul must be the source of all that it is, Plotinus means the substance of soul which it *already* possesses. He cannot mean that the differentia which supplements and qualifies the genus comes from the substance of soul, for the substance of soul *ex hypothesi* does not exist until the differentia has supplemented and qualified the genus. He means that the substance of soul is not brought into existence by anything supplementing or qualifying the genus. The reader might go on to infer that, unless all notion of genus has been thrown overboard with the notion of differentia as quality, Plotinus must mean the 'source' of particular substance (soul or stone) to be the genus. As we shall see, this inference would be correct.

What makes him think that a quality from outside substance cannot *become* part of something's substance once it qualifies it? Or, to put the same question in another way, what makes him complain, as he does in several passages, that a specific differentia of man like 'rational' is no better than an accident like 'pale'? In the first place, the Aristotelian position can be stated only if the notion of potentiality or some notion akin to it is involved. What is supposed to be 'completed' is not substance until it is completed, but unless it is capable of becoming a substance it cannot be completed: indeed this is what it is to be a genus. Certainly Plotinus is willing to take up this position when he needs to, for he believes that some of the consequences of it for the purely logical, syntactic not semantic, relations between genus and species are compatible with his radical criticism of it. But when he is dealing with this criticism, the semantic model, the thought that the higher, generic universal is the potentiality of the lower, is abhorrent to him: it would stand Plato on his head.

Secondly, he finds the notion of categories which divide qualities from substances unintelligible if they allow a quality to be an *integral* part of substance. This is the point of his eventually concluding that the only genuine qualities must be the non-essential 'affections', posterior to substances, such as a man's colour.

To go back to the 'source' of soul's substance. According to vi. 2. 6 this is Life, which as one of the greatest kinds is in fact identical with Substance itself. This fact does not help us immediately, for Substance must, of course, be the source of all substance. But, because he will not separate his negative criticism of Aristotle on genus from his positive case for the Platonic categories, Plotinus still attends only to the summa genera. So long as our interest (which may not have been primarily his) is in his attack on the notion of a differentia 'from outside', what we want is some mention of an intermediate genus, so that we may be able to see how that external differentia is to be replaced—what is to perform its supposed function. This mention we find in a later chapter. In a digression stating that he had not always held the position which I have described but does so now, Plotinus writes,

We now say that the properties which belong to [i.e. differentiate] particular substance are not what completes substance at all. Man *qua* man does not have an addition to his substance to make him a substance. His substance is from above, prior to the differentia—he is animal before he comes to be rational. (vi. 2. 14. 18–22)

Man is not, of course, man before he is rational, but his rationality, which makes him man, comes from the genus animal. Plotinus does not explain this in this passage. But Neoplatonists believed that the differentiae were contained in the genus 'occultly', that is, in a form which was distinct from their form in the species but could be inferred from it by analogy. This allows the general rule that 'all that comes later has an existence in what is first' (vi. 2. 13. 9). 'Occultly' does not mean potentially: otherwise we should be back in the Aristotelian position. Differentiae are activities (ἐνέργειαι) of the substance, whether at the generic or the specific level. For Neoplatonic commentators of the *Categories* it is a regular question whether the differentiae are contained by the genus potentially or actually. For although in Aristotle, and most would say in logic, it was impossible for them to be contained actually, Neoplatonists could not but be aware that a Platonic genus was a whole which was more real ('closer to the One') than its species.[10] In Alexandria,

---

[10] Objections to potential differentiae are made along these lines by Ammonius (*In Porph. Is.*, 103. 10–104. 26) and Elias (*In Porph. Is.*, 84. 19–86. 1).

Ammonius used the canonical formula to reconcile the two schools: the differentiae were actual in the generic whole, that is, prior to the many, and potential in the generic whole, that is, in the many.[11] As for the problem of self-contradiction, Plotinus has, I am afraid, only sophistical arguments. Rational and irrational, for example, are not opposites; alternatively, the co-existence of opposites is not a paradox in the case of incorporeals—the soul, since it makes judgements, contains the *logoi* of good and bad (III. 2. 16–17). The best exposition of this rejection of the Aristotelian differentia is to be found not in an Aristotelian commentary but, as we should expect, in a Platonic one (Proclus, *In Parmenidem*, 980. 29 ff).

But the rejection, I suggested, strikes deeper. It implies that a semantic object is not to be analysed into substance and attribute. So far we have seen this done at the level of generic terms and at the level of specific terms. For neither of these have accidental predicates, only substantial ones, and these do not stand for attributes but for activities.

Before we turn to the third and last level, that of individuals, we must answer an obvious objection. Are not activities attributes? The short answer is yes, but not in the sense of the terms, namely ἐνέργειαι and συμβεβηκότα, used by Neoplatonists and their opponents. Grammatically, of course, activities (ἐνέργειαι) can be predicated of subjects: but this does not make them attributes (συμβεβηκότα), for the semantic analysis of such a predication, or what would make it true, would be represented by a statement of identity. In the Neoplatonists' intelligible world everything is not merely ἐνεργείᾳ but ἐνέργεια; Aristotle called soul the place of forms, Plotinus calls the intelligible world the place of life.[12] There everything is by definition a substance: but the activity *of* substance is identical with the substance, as we have already noticed in the case of motion (*Enneads* V. 4. 2. 28–9, and for motion VI. 2. 15. 8–10). This identity is made easier by the fact that an activity does not, according to Plotinus, have any activities, and that he interprets this so as effectively to exclude from intelligible substances *per se*

---

[11] Loc. cit., 104. 27–105. 13.
[12] II. 5. 2. It is well known that Plotinus sometimes contradicts II. 5. 2 and other passages by referring to potentiality in the intelligible world (references in A. Smith, 'Potentiality and the problem of plurality in the intelligible world', in Blumenthal and Markus, 1981). Many of these references can be explained by the relativism of the notion or by Plotinus' own readiness to speak, as it were, merely *sub specie Aristotelis*.

what we should call activity. This activity he represents by the verb ἐνεργέω in contrast with the noun ἐνέργεια. The verb is applicable only when the ἐνέργεια 'stands in a relation', in other words has an object; and in this case there is also something to which we can attribute the activity. But when these conditions hold we have a case not of activity of the substance, but of activity *from* the substance, which will be explained in the next chapter. (This is what I take to be implied by the opening lines of *Enneads* v. 6. 6.) One of the functions, perhaps the basic function, of the Plotinian concept of life is to connote activity which has and is meant to have no effect.

On the other hand, the identity of the substance and the activity is not complete identity, so that it does not follow that the activities are completely identical, which would of course make nonsense. Subject and attribute are identical in subject, but they can be distinguished in thought; and when we think of them as distinct we are treating the activity as an attribute of the substance. Indeed, this is how the notion of quality will arise. But, like all distinguishing and abstracting within the second hypostasis, it is a departure from truth or reality, which is greater in the whole—the unity, not the plurality of the One-many.

When the search for qualities is extended to the level on which Platonists would be expected to find them, that of sensible substances, Plotinus finds that they too have lost the character of attributes. In the realm of ideas this was so because they were insufficiently distinct from their subjects: here it is because they have insufficiently identifiable subjects to be attributed to.[13] The *logoi* in the intelligible world, which are roughly the Ideas *qua* reproductive, proceed, and the products of their procession, which are inferior likenesses, are sensible qualities. Substances such as fire and water in that world are distinguishable from one another, but this is not by possessing a distinguishing quality but because each is uniquely what it is; as we have just seen, its peculiarity is identical, except in concept, with the substance or activity. But since it is not identical in concept it can be separated by the *logos*.

---

[13] VI. 2. 14. 14–22 distinguishes what 'we used to claim elsewhere' from what 'we now say', but, contrary to what scholars have understandably assumed, it cannot be made to correspond to a distinction between the doctrine of II. 6, although this is much earlier, and of VI. 4. The account I shall give is consistent with both tracts.

The *logos* separates it

without taking it out of the intelligible world but rather taking hold of it so as to generate something else—quality is generated as though it were a part of substance, taken hold of as it appears, to the *logos*, on the surface of substance. In this way heat can be intrinsic to fire and thus its specific form or activity and not a quality of it, but at the same time, in a different manner, a quality. As a quality it has been taken on its own and in something else where it is no longer a form or shape of substance but a mere trace or shadow or image: it can be a quality by abandoning its own substance, of which it was the activity. (II. 6. 3. 12–20)

The influence of the *Timaeus* is clear.

'The *logos*' which abstracts the quality is translated by Harder as 'das begriffliche Denken' and by Armstrong as 'the process of rational thinking'. It is more likely to be the Plotinian and semi-Stoic *logos* which a type of entity at one level has as its cause and archetype at the next higher level. (This tends to be obscured by a regular but narrower use of '*logos* of x' to describe an entity manifested at a *lower* level than x. In fact these *logoi* operate in chains like forms.) Its function here has been described by Plotinus in the previous chapter; and the present chapter is, I think, describing a metaphysical genesis similar to the more general accounts of genesis that bridge pairs of hypostases. 'Not taking it out of the intelligible world but taking hold of it so as to generate something else' will be the standard allusion to remaining and proceeding, and these belong to a metaphysical process rather than a process of human thought. That this is so will be confirmed by Proclus, whose version of it depends closely on Plotinus and who will not have misunderstood him. But Proclus' version will come later, when we ask how accidents are known.

If qualities depend on being abstracted from substances, they can sometimes be accidental attributes, sometimes essential (substantial)—but if they are essential they are not qualities but activities. Philosophers in the Empire were obsessed by the question how the same quality can be essential in one subject, say four-leggedness in a horse, and accidental in another, say four-leggedness in a table. Plotinus suggests it would have to 'change its nature'. In the tract *On Qualities* he can only propose that genuine qualities are confined to attributes which occur as accidents but never as specific differentiae.[14] (He does not deal with the question

---

[14] II. 6. 3 *ad fin.* He suggests here (1. 22) and elsewhere dispositions, such as virtues and vices.

of propria.) The problem regularly distracts attention from the treatment of genuine problems about substance which we have been pursuing. It was thought a problem only, I believe, because even Aristotle's commentators confused his doctrine of categories with his doctrine of predicables. The essential and accidental attributes are different classes of attribute only inasmuch as they are differently related to their subjects: in the Latin Aristotelian jargon they are different predicables. Only if they had been intrinsically different classes—in the Aristotelian jargon different categories—could one have taken exception to the same attribute's being sometimes essential, sometimes accidental. And it is hard to see how this distinction of predicables from categories is wrong. The claim is, of course, independent of Aristotle's own belief that certain attributes could be classed under more than one category.

The radical criticism has left sensible individuals as the only possible subjects of qualities which are properly called 'qualities'. What is the nature of a sensible individual? In the last of the three treatises *On the Kinds of Being*, Plotinus takes it for granted that as such it has no essential attributes—these belong to it *qua* species. Or rather, his position is less Aristotelian than that: such specific attributes as the individual possesses are not owing to its being a kind (a this such) but to its participating in one (VI. 3. 9). Consequently he is not left with the Aristotelian alternative to finding the individual's *substance* anywhere but in what it is as *subject* of its attributes. So he proceeds, like John Locke, to identify this substance with what is left when we think of it without qualities; and this can only be matter (VI. 3. 8. 14–17, a little corrected by 15. 23–7). Even this, as I shall mention in a moment, concedes less to his opponent than seems at first sight. The upshot is that the *actual* sensible individual is a 'bundle of qualities (including quantities) together with matter' (8. 19–23).

This is not the same as the standard position of Neoplatonists, such as the Alexandrians, who defined the individual as a bundle of properties. For (at least as I argued) they meant the definition to refer to the individual *qua* this rather than that individual. Their individual was in fact Aristotle's, because its properties included the specific ones, whereas in our context, Plotinus' bundle does not. Just because it was improbable that he would have been so un-Aristotelian I put Porphyry in their camp rather than Plotinus'; and we can add the fact that he omitted matter from his definition.

The matter which Plotinus includes cannot be the proximate

matter. Reflection will show that this would imply a distinction between essential, that is specific attributes, and accidents. But according to his radical criticism there is no such distinction.[15] So-called essential attributes are not attributes. Indeed, he only appears to be conceding anything that Aristotle would have counted as 'substrate'. He wanted *On the Kinds of Being* to be an *ad hominem* argument. But he is really following a good Neo-platonic principle. The individual is a pale shadow of a reality or substance; qualities are pale shadows of the realities that are *logoi* and ultimately activities; and, according to the principle, the reason is that they are not *per se* but 'in something else'. The abstraction of qualities was described in a way which was bound to remind us of the *Timaeus*. In this respect I agree with Rist (1967, ch. 8) that Plotinus' account of the individual marks a return from Aristotle to Plato. His matter is not the matter of the substance and attribute model from which we started. *Ennead* VI. 1–3 does not give us an individual constituted by mere compresence of qualities and such as we find in some versions of British empiricism. But it comes close to it.[16] In doing so it has made a much larger commitment for Plotinus: in the last analysis, substance and attributes coincide, either as substances and their activities or as imperfect projections of such activities.

Two structures, two levels of thought?

Plotinus' everyday use of the normal structure of substances and attributes requires a caveat.[17] It overlaps, but is not equivalent to, the 'speaking with the vulgar' which Berkeley contrasts with the 'thinking with the learned' (for we cannot say, we think and are clothed with ideas). That distinction must hold in any reductionist philosophy. But Neoplatonism is only half reductionist, since, while it is a philosophy of appearance and reality, the appearance

---

[15] Cf. Wurm (1973), 255.

[16] For example, a (so-called) substance is made by certain qualities' all being 'condensed (συμπαγέντα) in a single matter' or in 'the mixture of them' (VI. 3. 8. 21 and 26).

[17] Simplicius is constantly aware of Plotinus' criticism but more often than not takes the differentia to be (in his and Aristotle's terms) a quality of a substance. But it is likely that his motive is not to have Aristotle in the wrong. We have only his *Categories* commentary to go by.

cannot be dispensed with. Here (if I am right) we must see instead the distinction between discursive and non-discursive intellect. Thinking discursively involves abstracting subjects, attributes, accidents, essences, and so on. And although such thought is a departure from truth—or, to be more accurate, from the awareness which is above truth—it is inevitable. We must be careful not to think of it just as Aristotelian logic which had somehow to be 'harmonized' with Plato's. It is the Platonic dialectic of collection and division; and this is a necessary rung on the ladder to the One. More important, it is a necessary descent on the part of Existence or Thought itself. And the principle which validates the discursive description of reality is that there are degrees of truth or, again to be more accurate, degrees of awareness of reality. Such a description is therefore not false but misleading. In the language of Plato and Leibniz, the describer has not seen clearly. Nevertheless, to describe discursive thought of reality is to describe no less than the thinking of the human mind.

Plotinus does not tell us this about his radical criticism, and it must be speculative. He may, for example, have believed that the conventional account of differentiae was false even at the discursive level. This is the impression given by *Ennead*, VI. 2, but not at least to me by the tract *On Qualities*, which belongs to the criticism and which contains the striking account of the genesis of quality (II. 6. 11). Any reader accustomed to his method will be surprised if Plotinus was leaving a topic at the stage of *ad hominem* argument without presenting it in his own colours; and he will know that his usual method of doing that is to turn the reader's attention to the same subject at a higher ontological level. In a sense he cannot portray the logic of non-discursive Substance because it does not have one. But it is plausible to suppose that the upshot of the radical criticism represents a picture which we must have before we can realize the inadequacy of discursive thought and which is sufficiently logical for that purpose. For the same purpose, it describes quality in the language of a genesis in time which we associate with the procession of one hypostasis to another by self-determination. The higher intellect is not, of course, concerned with sensible qualities: but their immaterial origins are none the less there, and since it is from that point of view that Plotinus wants us to see them he rightly describes them as images of images.

Should the relation between Aristotelian genera and the quasi-genera be interpreted along the same lines? Do these structures represent a discursive and a non-discursive intellect? The answer must be that in some respects they do and in some respects they do not. The quasi-genera certainly represent imparticipables, for they are wholes before the parts; and participated entities represented by standard genera are images of the imparticipable. More to the point, the soul's ascent is through the participated forms to the imparticipable forms, and from them to the henads. Theoretically, then, it should be possible to correlate the two structures with the two intellects. But, while one hesitates to suggest that there was any avenue of systematization which escaped the notice of Athenian Neoplatonism, it should be said that the kinds of genera are accepted on the grounds that they obviate contradictions which would arise in it either from its Neoplatonic or from its Aristotelian constituents. Otherwise they are assumed and have to be inferred by the reader. We are given nothing which corresponds to Plotinus' demolition of a whole semantic system and which would suggest that one type of genus has to be replaced by another. Nor have we descriptions of the genesis or procession of the one from the other as part of the genesis or procession of one type of intellect from another. It is open to question whether Neoplatonists saw them from that point of view at all.

4

PROCESSION AND DECLINE

Emanation as external activity: The model in Aristotle's physics

We have to see whatever is real, or substances, as activities. If we do not, we shall not grasp how carefully constructed a theory lies in the concept of emanation or procession. The *Enneads* often make a crucial distinction between the activity *of* the substance and the activity *from* the substance. The first often appears as the division of a genus into species. In the all-embracing case of Being itself or Intellect, this can also be understood in a more Aristotelian manner as the actualization of thought; for, as the *Sophist* and *Parmenides* were supposed to have shown, thinking entails a complex object or, what comes to the same thing, a plurality of objects. The external activity (*from* the substance) usually appears as the production of a lower hypostasis, or at least a lower ontological type—Soul, for instance—as the external activity of Intellect. But a rigorous criterion for discriminating the two activities is difficult; and, if he has one, Plotinus for one does not apply it constantly. He certainly tends to assume that the external activity or its product is 'in something else'; and this implies the further distinction that the product will be only an imperfect likeness of the substance in question. But species are sometimes thought of as in matter and only likenesses of the genus, even if they are more often thought of as the standard case of its internal activity. One may suspect that the distinction is relative to the point of view. It was taken over by the Athenian School (see especially Proclus, *Platonic theology*, v. 18. 283.2–284.11 Portus).

As we saw in the previous chapter, the internal activity is ident-ical, save in concept, with the substance. But the external activity is not. It is, however, inevitable; the existence of every level of reality below the One is necessary, not contingent.[1] All freedom is Spinozistic freedom. When the internal activity occurs, in other

[1] e.g. VI. 6 *ad init.* (Intellect), IV. 8. 3 *ad fin.* (Soul), II. 9. 33. 7 (Nature).

words when the internal actualization is complete, it is necessarily accompanied by this second activity. It fails to be a permanent creation only inasmuch as it is not in time; Nature, for instance, proceeds eternally from the higher Soul (*Ennead*, III. 8. 5. 12). Nor is it the transmission of a property, even if we allow for the degradation of the property. For although a property is given—the regular Neoplatonic term—by the producer or agent to its product it is without loss to the producer, for it never leaves the producer. The doctrine will be repeated by Proclus. But he will make them images of the internal activities (as *Ennead*, IV. 5. 7 does) by identifying them with the *logoi* of the agents.

It is habitual, however, for all Neoplatonists to describe the two activities by referring to the heat or light which are intrinsic activities (ἐνέργειαι) of the sun and the heat or light which are diffused by it and warm or illuminate other objects. A. H. Armstrong pointed out that according to Stoics the ruling principle in man was an emanation from the sun's pneuma, which was not diminished thereby (1967, 240). Plotinian emanation, however, does not in my view have a Stoic source but takes over Aristotle's model of physical causation, transposing it, of course, to non-physical causation.[2] It is much easier to understand Plotinus' exposition if we recognize the many allusions in it to Aristotle's.

As is well known, *Physics*, VIII. 4 proposes to start from the ambiguous reference of 'potential and actual': (1) the learner potentially knows before he has been taught, (2) he is then in another way potentially knowing when he is not exercising the knowledge he has learnt. In (1) the potential (the scholastic *potentia prima*) becomes actual (*actus prior = potentia secunda*) whenever agent and patient are compresent. But in (2) the potential (*potentia secunda*) is always and necessarily actual (*actus secundus*) unless something prevents it. Aristotle takes this as applicable to the case of an activity which affects something else. Something cold which has been sufficiently heated is already fire (its *actus prior*) and has also the *potentia secunda* of heating or burning other things: but it is a contradiction of the nature of fire not to heat or burn things (*actus secundus*), just as something light goes upwards, unless it is stopped, since that is what it is to be light.

Physics, III. 3 had claimed that the actualized movement or

---

[2] This was recognized by C. Rutten (1956), 100–6. My next two paragraphs are reprinted with minor changes from Lloyd (1987*b*).

process in an agent was the same 'in subject/substrate' as the one
it caused in the patient but that they differed in 'being/essence'; in
other words, they are numerically the same event but conceptually
different. If A exercises his ability to teach, and B his ability to
learn, there is one fact expressed by 'A teaches B' and 'B learns
from A', but there are two descriptions of it, since 'teaching' does
not have the same meaning as 'learning'. The partial identity is
expressed by Aristotle in a terse formula: the agent's activity 'is not
cut off (separated)—it is *of* something *in* something else' (202^b7–8).

Turn now to Plotinus. The 'external activity' that follows from
something's 'repletion' or perfection is his version of the transmitted change or motion which is the *actus secundus* of any actualized
potentia prima. In VI. 3. 23 he broadly reproduces the doctrine of
Physics III. 3 and mentions that it applies as much to 'generation'
(of substances) as to qualitative change. The *necessity* of emanation
can be seen as the absence of need (according to Aristotle) for an
additional cause of this second actualization. Where his version
departs from Aristotle is over the inferiority, the lower degree of
reality, of the effect or product to that of the cause or agent. But he
does not admit this as a departure: he simply writes as though the
partial identity constituted by 'same in substrate but different in
essence' is the partial identity of his own pair, original and image
(V. 3. 49. 44–5; VI. 4. 9. 37–42). Plotinus regularly borrows the
metaphor from the formula of the *Physics*: the product is not cut off
from its origin—in V. 3. 12. 44, 'neither cut off nor identical'—and
commonly in connection with remaining.[3]

The diffusion of light, heat, cold, the power of drugs, and so on
are not mere analogies or metaphors: they are examples of the
physical model of emanation. *Ennead*, IV. 5. 7 tells us that light
should not be called a flux; it is not lost by the illuminating body,
nor does it have to return to it. It is an activity which reappears
($\pi\alpha\rho\alpha\gamma\iota\nu\rho\mu\acute{\epsilon}\nu\eta\varsigma$) if nothing prevents it, and is then a second actua-
lity/activity, an image of the first or internal actuality/activity and
not separated from that. This is the behaviour not just of light but
of everything. Plotinus adds however (so as to relate the matter to
his topic) that light, being incorporeal, more exactly illustrates the

---

[3] He quotes the term (which Plato had not used in this way) in his résumé of the
Physics chapter (VI. 3. 23. 19). So also of sunlight, corresponding to external activity
of the Good (I. 7. 1. 27; V. 3. 12. 44), of Being and its 'powers' (VI. 4. 3. 9; 9. 16),
of Nature as an image (VI. 2. 22. 34).

way in which the soul is an activity of another, higher soul, and its life the product of a higher activity. That the whole passage depends on the *Physics* model is evident. But it shows also how 'remaining' (μονή) can be derived from the model. For what remains is not something alongside the internal activity: it is that activity. Moreover, this aspect of emanation or procession is the same as the doctrine that what proceeds does not entail a loss for the original substance. Incidentally, it was part of accepted physical theory that supralunar causation did not involve constancy of motion or energy. In the sublunar world if a pot of water was heated by a stove so much less heat was left in the stove, but the sun and the stars, which were eternal bodies, transmitted their heat and light without losing any.[4] Not that Plotinus has given up a transmission theory of alteration and genesis. For what he presents as a paradox is that something of a certain kind can be the product of a substance of a different kind. He expresses it by saying that the donor does not need to have what he gives. But equally he repeats the dogma that the products of a higher reality are contained in it.

Later Neoplatonists made this dogma familiar by claiming that the products or their properties were contained 'occultly'. Although it is sometimes the case—for example in the henads—that such properties can only be inferred from the nature of the products, or at most understood by analogy, this cannot be what 'occultly' means. For if it did, each level of reality (except the highest and lowest) would consist of two mutually exclusive sets of properties/substances, the occult and the overt; the occult are those which cause the overt at the next lower level; but this would leave no causal function for the overt, which would contradict the universal principle that all properties/substances proceed to a lower level. It does not mean that the properties at the higher level which contain those below them are not overt: it means that the fact that they are manifestations of those below them is not overt. Indeed, the philosopher, aided by the experience of his interior life, does see the essential resemblance. The logic of the theory dictates that the properties will form chains. One such chain which is often appealed to is called life. It appears in the first stage of the genesis of Intellect—indeed it is what Plotinus calls that pre-intellectual stage. There, it is occultly thought, since its product, intellectual

4 Cf. Wallis (1972), 62, which suggested the point to me.

life, is overtly thought. Similarly at lower levels, where life is a hidden manifestation of something else which may or may not be called 'life'. Would it not then be just as correct to describe the product as, say, copying its cause occultly? Certainly, and this would be in the spirit of Neoplatonism. The term 'occultly' is relational and generally signifies 'not overtly resembling', which is a symmetric relation. But it so happens that as a technical term it was restricted to the containment of the effect by the cause.[5]

In any case, it can be concluded that Plotinus exaggerates the paradoxical character of 'undiminished giving' for rhetorical purposes. The essential point for him is something a little different, namely that the action of the higher realities in generating the lower should not be interaction.

The imperfect resemblance or degradation of the property transmitted depends on the rule that the reception of a property by a participant alters the property. We saw the rule presenting itself with some plausibility when it is used to justify the claim that 'animal' does not mean the same when it is qualified by 'land' or 'water' as when it is qualified by 'two-footed' or 'finned'. In a general form, Neoplatonists often represent the rule as stating that a property *per se* will not be the same 'in a subject'; and the Aristotelian expression is often replaced by the Platonic 'in another'.

If the intelligible is everywhere whole, why does everything not participate in the whole of the intelligible? How is it that one thing is placed first, another second, and others after that? Our reply is that what is present is present on account of the aptitude of something to receive it, and that being is present everywhere in being—it does not fail itself—but what is present to it is what is capable of being present and just in the degree, not in the place, in which it is capable of being present. (VI. 4. 11. 1–7)

This too we have met in connection with quasi-genera, where unequal participation was a regular palliative of non-synonymous predication.

But does not the rule imply the interaction between procession and its product that we have said Plotinus rejected? For a recipient is now said to alter the property it receives. The answer is that although Plotinus often writes as though this were the case it is not

---

[5] The *term*, at least as used by Proclus, was associated with, if it did not originate with, occultism itself, such as that of the Chaldaean Oracles (cf. P. Hadot, 1968, 1. 304 n. 4).

strictly so: the recipient will contain only an image of the property
in which it will participate. This is not a merely verbal point. It
would be that only if 'containing an image of x' were equivalent to
'possessing x in an altered form', but the two are not equivalent.
The gilt frame can be said to contain an image of the Lord Mayor,
but this is not because the Lord Mayor stepped into the frame but
lost his best features in doing so.

Ennead VI. 4–5 insist that being and the Ideas do not descend
into matter. This is a single treatise ambitiously designed to show
how in analogous, even identical, fashion, being is 'present', undivided, to the whole of sensible matter and soul to a whole body.
It is in fact a commentary of the unconstrained kind that is
Plotinus's own on *Parmenides*, 131 B–C, the problem represented by
the Sail Cloth. Too much of it is tediously pushing at an open door
(repeating, for instance, that 'being is everywhere' does not have a
spatial meaning). But readers who do not believe in a universal or
generic being must allow for the style of a metaphysician who can
happily spend pages on nothing but that and other categories, in
the full but unspoken knowledge that the properties he attributes
to them are to be attributed also to horses and colours. He has to
reject Aristotle's particular forms, because they cannot each be the
whole of the attribute (VI. 4. 8), and to rebut the other horn of the
Sail Cloth dilemma, it seems, by their having the attribute 'present
to', but not in, the particulars. In the end, his defence of the second
argument is not, perhaps, explicit but it is one with which we are
familiar, the *ab uno* universal (VI. 4. 9–10). The so-called parts of
Being—genera, species, and even individuals—are to be seen as its
powers. These can be taken as tantamount to its activities; for he
goes on to say that they could not exist if they were separated from
it, any more than a light, however far from its source, can exist if
it is cut off from it.

The inherence of an image or *logos* is usually described by
Neoplatonists as the reception of the form by matter. So Plotinus
follows Plato in explaining the degrees of participation and differences of rank in the scale of nature by different capacities of
matter to receive the form. This raises an immediate suspicion of
circularity. For one has to ask what explains these differences in
capacity. The problem will stand out in the case of the four
elements. (This can be seen in VI. 4. 8 and VI. 5. 8. 21 ff.,
despite the state of the text.) But, without pursuing this and other

difficulties, we can presume that none of Plotinus' interpretations of matter—extension, privation, and the like—will provide a *sufficient* condition for the degradation of the form.

Perhaps with such difficulties in mind, Proclus explained the imperfect reception of form and consequent degradation of being rather differently. His explanation is for the most part that of Plotinus, but more systematized. The whole before the parts which was Plotinus' theme is identified as it normally is after Iamblichus with the imparticipable; and this makes it readily applicable to the Sail Cloth dilemma.[6] At the same time, all procession is accomplished through likeness—a thesis which is equivalent to Plotinus' identification of causation with making something resemble the cause (*Elements of Theology*, 29; *Enneads*, IV. 3. 10). It is the automatic result of any entity's perfection; and this perfection is itself brought about by procession and reversion. But the cause 'remains' (op. cit., 26; cf. 30); and the proof given of this is that of Plotinus (V. 1. 6).

There is at the very least a difference of emphasis, which is not accidental. We are concerned here only with the datum of incomplete reception of the form, which it was quite logical to approach by looking, as Plotinus did, at the nature of a product or effect. In the *Elements of Theology* Proclus has, as it were, the motto, 'See what a *cause* implies'. The result will be that he finds it almost superfluous to mention matter.

He starts, like all Platonists, from a perhaps intuitive and certainly Aristotelian conception of causation which supposes that a cause transmits a property to its effect.[7] It underlies a principle which is familiar from one of Descartes' proofs of the existence of God and which requires a cause to be greater than or equal to its effects; for Descartes considers it logically equivalent to the principle that 'a nihilo nihil fit'. The reasoning is this. Suppose (and kindly ignore, for the sake of the example, factors known only to the scientifically educated) that a ramekin is standing in water, the water is heated to 50°, and the ramekin rises to 100°: the heat of the water cannot have been the cause of the heat of the ramekin, for half the effect would be unaccounted for ('would have come from

---

6 *ET*, 23. But 69 apparently contradicts the identification of the whole before the parts with the imparticipable.

7 e.g. *ET*, 12 (ll. 7–8); 18; cf. 7 (ll. 17–19).

nothing'). But the Neoplatonists see causes not as powers but as forces. We might imagine Proclus reasoning that if the ramekin's heat rose only to 25° it could not have been caused by the water at 50°, for that would leave half the *cause* unaccounted for. But a force can decrease; and the reason for its decrease in the case of forms we shall find also in the *Elements of Theology*.

The distinction of force from power is emphasized by Proclus' description of potentiality. This coincides with matter in Aristotle, as imperfect *dynamis*, while causal efficacy, which is 'active/productive *energeia*', is perfect *dynamis*.[8] As *energeia* it is distinct from whatever it is the activity of only as an abstraction, so that what we can say of it we can say of any substance which is a cause.

Here the most important fact is that these are values or perfections: e.g. *Elements*, 7 (ll. 22–5); 12 (ll. 15–16). 'A perfection' has the sense borrowed from this theory by Schoolmen and familiar again from Descartes. But something is a perfection in respect of some property; so the notion is evidently derived from that of a Platonic Idea, the Idea of beauty being what is perfectly or completely beautiful, the Idea of red what is completely red. We have already seen in Plotinus the universal rule of procession and 'generation' that the *energeia* 'from the substance' is triggered by the perfection of the substance. A perfection can also be called a value, because every entity 'desires' to possess (or to be) completely the property which makes it the substance it incompletely (or actually) is. It must not be thought a contradiction to apply this to the intelligible world, where the substances are already actual. For even these have a natural impetus to degenerate by 'proceeding', while their 'remaining' can be seen as the impetus to perfection. This impetus is described as the desire of everything for its own good: but it may help us to understand it if we realize that it is not just a familiar Platonic and Aristotelian rule but borrows from Stoicism. It is the instinct for self-preservation, the Stoic primary impulse—which survives in Spinoza as self-love.[9] 'The good' which is the power or rather force of emanation is thus not moral goodness, which is but one species of value.

---

[8] *ET* 78; *PT*, III. 8. 34.8–11; III. 10. 40. 12–23. See also Gersh (1973), 41–8.
[9] For Stoics, see Diogenes Laertius, 7. 85–6. Neoplatonists' use of the term συνεκτικός reflects this.

The Proclan rule

It follows that degrees of perfection are degrees of productive power. This shows itself in more than one way, but two are especially significant. The more perfect the cause, the greater the quantity of its effects.[10] Since we can take it for granted that the more perfect coincides with the higher in the hierarchy, it might correctly be supposed that this dogma follows analytically from envisaging the ontological hierarchy as a pyramid; for all the terms prior to a given term can count as its causes, or, as Proclus describes them, its co-causes (see *Elements*, 57). But this is not what Proclus has in mind. He means normally—and I do not myself know anywhere where he does not mean—that a greater degree of power implies a greater transmission of properties, that is, one reaching lower. Soul does not proceed beyond the animate, but Intellect, whose power is greater because it is closer to the source of all power, reaches the inanimate, for it provides form (ib.). This was called a 'Proclan rule' by Olympiodorus, who contrasts Iamblichus' rule that 'wherever something starts operating it will continue operating to the lowest level'.[11] And I shall refer to it often as 'the Proclan rule'.

The second way in which a superior cause manifests its greater power is by *operating first*, for the effects of a less powerful cause will depend on it, not it on them (ib. 70–2; cf. 108). We can see how important this is for Proclus' sense of structure or system. The task is to analyse a reality that is presented as a successive or serial genesis of its components, but one in which the terms are increasingly compound products of prior terms. This would have to be the case even if the series were a single line, for the causes of the terms would form an arithmetic progression. If we abstract bare hypostases of the Proclan system, we could say that the Dyad has one cause (the One), Henads have two causes (the One and the Dyad), Intelligible Intellect has three (the One, the Dyad, and Henads), Intelligible-and-Intellectual Intellect four, and so on.

---

[10] *ET*, 25. 28. 30–1; 57; 60; *In Parm*, 904. 18–24 (more clearly), and elsewhere. Dodds and others who refer the dogma to *ET* 57 seem to have missed its occurrence in 25.

[11] *In Alcib.*, 109. 18 Cr. (p. 72 Westerink) and 110. 13–15 for Iamblichus. According to Iamblichus, the higher causes were, however, 'more penetrating'.

But in fact we have a geometric progression; for every term contains prior ones in a triadic form and, in addition, proceeds to make species, and all of these extra terms contribute causally to corresponding terms later in the series. In all this compounding of causes, order is preserved by the theorem that degrees of perfection are degrees of productive power. For what I describe as the second manifestation of this theorem, the fact that the cause of greater power operates first, is interpreted by Proclus in *Elements*, 70–2 as meaning that the higher cause produces the generic element in a product, and the lower causes the specific elements or differentiae.[12] This is logical, for (1) the generic product must be prior so as to act as substrate for the specific differentiae, (2) to the prior effect will correspond the prior cause, and (3) the degree of power represents the order of priority among causes.[13]

Defective reception as weakness of the form. Proclus' aversion from dualism

What then of the degrees of receptiveness in participants of the forms? These, it seems, are no longer to *explain* degrees of participation in forms, for the two facts are identical. Defective reception can be put down to defective force or power which transmits the form: but it can equally be put down to lack of receptivity, because receptivity is itself power, some of which has been lost (*Elements*, 110. 98. 14–16). But in Proclus the power which the effect has lost is apparently nothing other than the power of the cause.[14] It is not just that they are correlative. For although we do not envisage the power in the effect in the same way in which we envisage it in the cause, namely as the power to transmit the form, both powers are fundamentally the power to *be* the form, or, what is the same thing, to be. Everything below the prototype (form 'itself') does this by copying it and participating in it. But the power to transmit it, i.e. to proceed, is a necessary part of being, a consequence, as we have seen, of the 'perfection' which *is* its being

---

[12] So also *PT*, III. 10. 41. 10–12; *ET* 108 is to be understood, I think, in this connection; cf. Lloyd, (1982), 29.

[13] When Proclus says of 2 that the order of effects is reversed, he is speaking from an Aristotelian point of view in which the generic effect is only the potentiality of the species.

[14] See *PT*, III. 10. 40. 20–41. 8, and for degrees of power *In Parm.*, 805. 35–41.

or existence—but existence *qua* having, and ideally being, a property, an essence.

Plotinus too was willing to summarize the differences in the degrees of being, and indeed its diversity, as differences of 'rank and power' (VI. 4. 11). And Simplicius is following him and Proclus alike in making the degradation equivalent to distance from the original form (*In Categorias*, 227. 4–5). But before we deny any theoretical disagreement we should notice that for his part Proclus will accept the Plotinian account of the receptiveness of matter only as it applies to the sensible world. I have described how his explanation was based on the manifestations of force: but at this point it will be best to place these in the more detailed context which we can find in *Platonic Theology*, III. 8–10.

It rests on the *Philebus*, where we learnt that all that is ('Existence' for short) has come into being by the mixture of Limit and the Unlimited, which are therefore prior to it. The true One—that of the *Parmenides'* first hypothesis—cannot be the cause of Existence for it transcends all causation, even unification. The Dyad is the first product of this One and the immediate cause by being equivalent to the one which can be predicated of Existence (cf. III. 8. 31. 2–5). But in order to generate Existence it must possess a generative force, that is, proceed. I translate *dynamis* for the time being as 'force', for it is an activity, while 'power' (which I shall also use where convenient) implies only a capacity to act. Force is procession because it is intermediate between every producer and its product—a procession, extension, or projection of the former, the anterior cause of the latter (loc. cit., ll. 20–3). The Dyad is, as it were, the representative of the One.

But prior to its force is its being. (Proclus continues his normal reification of functions.) And it is by virtue of its being that it has its occult unity, while its self-manifestation as a distinct unified entity ('the One that is') is by virtue of the Dyad's force (31. 23–32. 2). The 'occult unity' refers to the henads, which are by definition participable 'ones', hence between the Dyad and Existence and known only by their effects in the latter.[15] This representative of

---

[15] 'Being' and 'force' ('power') allude to the triad, ὕπαρξις, δύναμις, ἐνέργεια, which constitute every entity in the Athenian system. I mention this on account of an unfortunate lapse by Dodds, who translates ὕπαρξις and the corresponding verb in *ET* as though they signified the 'inhering' or 'belonging' of Aristotelian logic. I have had to call it 'being' in the triad only because I have used 'existence' for τὸ ὄν, which is thought, and the Dyad exists before that.

the One, says Proclus, is what the *Philebus* called Limit, and its generative force is the Unlimited. So we can attribute the uniformity of Existence to Limit and its occult plurality, which is tantamount to its own generative force, to the Unlimited. It is easy to see that these attributes correspond also to remaining and procession. And what can be said of Existence, or the whole of what exists, holds *eo ipso* for every existent: each existent, or substance, is nothing else than a unit (monad) consisting of many forces.[16]

In nature all phenomena resemble Limit in respect of their form, the Unlimited in respect of their matter.[17] Sensible matter is Aristotelian potentiality but, as we have seen, no passive principle but imperfect force. Derived from the original force it is everything, but imperfect as it is in nature it is only potentially everything.

Although the *Enneads* do not have the formula of imperfect power, it is only their acceptance of intelligible matter which Proclus openly attacks. Recognizing the presence of the Dyad, Plotinus' followers may be entitled to call the existent a compound of form and intelligible matter, where form corresponds to the one or being of the triad, matter to the power. But, he continues,

if they are crediting intelligible substance with something that has no shape or form or limit, then they seem to me to mistake Plato's meaning. The Unlimited is not the matter of Limit but its force, and Limit is not the form of the Unlimited but its being. (III. 9. 40. 2–6)

To leave no doubt how far he is from the conventional Pythagorean–Platonic interpretation, he even descibes the Unlimited as what defines or limits the perfect forces or powers of the intelligible world. Only in the world of becoming it is incomplete power. (His readers would recognize the Aristotelian definition of change or motion.) And only there is it, like Limit, a constituent rather than a transcendent cause of the mixture, and properly called matter (III. 10. 40–1).

How averse he is from dualism when he treats of matter as force, whether perfect or imperfect, is to be seen in a further point. His correction of Plotinus' followers on the relation of Limit and the Unlimited leaves it open to us to infer that the so-called Dyad is to

---

[16] III. 9. 39. For the application to every existent, Proclus naturally relies on the *Parm.*'s argument that 'one many' applies to every part of a whole, and for its being as force he naturally quotes *Sophist.*, 247 (III. 9. 39. 4–10; 21. 74. 11–18).

[17] Limit has here the consequences familiar in both Plato and Aristotle, viz. fixed identity and number of species, cyclical change (III. 8. 33. 24–6).

be reduced to Limit, the Unlimited being only its power (force) as opposed to its being/existence. Indeed, the inference is required by the statement that this power is the power *of* Limit. He could have avoided committing himself to a possessor of the unlimited power by saying that it was to Limit as power is to being. But, however valid, the inference is not really tenable. It is self-contradictory on account of Proclus' uncompromising realism, his reification of every property, from quality to activity. Since the expression 'power of' entails the concept of a subject (indicated by 'being/existence' in the triad) and a power, there must be power *per se*; and this is the Unlimited *per se*. Proclus often recognizes this: but his realism draws him towards one position, his aversion from dualism towards another. I do not know what means of reconciling them he had in mind.

Like the resistance of matter, the Unlimited cannot be a sufficient condition for the weakness of force by which Proclus accounts for failures in the transmission of forms. It is not even a sufficient condition of multiplication; for it represents infinity, and the difference between that and a plurality is provided by the iterated imposition of Limit. Perhaps he gives it an ambiguous function. For he does often present it more traditionally as the opposite of Limit and therefore as absence of order. But he does so particularly for the *Timaeus*, where one would expect him to follow Plato; and, as the principle of procession, the Unlimited cannot be a principle of disorder as such. (This seems to me insufficiently recognized by J. Trouillard, 1982, 247, in spite of interesting comments on the dualism of form and matter in Proclus.) Several other factors are commonly given today as explanations of decreasing participation. There is distance from the One, there is the 'Proclan rule', there is the dogma that an effect is an imperfect copy of its cause, and other features which may or may not be combined with these. Moreover, the same writer is often content to rely now on one factor now on another. There is nothing wrong with this. The task I am proposing will not produce any specially new or unfamiliar explanation: but among those which are familiar I hope to find some order of priority. To do so, we must start from the structure of chains or series, remembering that, prompted by the *Philebus*, Proclus commonly called them numbers. It can be gathered from 903. 6 ff. of his *Parmenides* commentary.

How monads descend. How transcendental triads function

Participation in a given universal essence, we learn, (1) becomes fainter as procession descends, and (i.e.?) (2) has varying degrees, and (i.e.?) (3) causes participants to resemble the given form in respect of one or more 'forces'. (These, we shall see, are usually found in well-known triads.) Consequently there are many chains from the same form. For instance, the form of moon appears in gods as a form of goodness, because that is the mode of its divine existence, in angels in the mode of intellect, in daemons in the mode of life.[18] The example may be less than riveting for the modern reader, but it will illustrate the structure. For each of these forms of moon has descended in respect of (in the mode of) a different member, called 'force', of the triad existence, life, and intellect, of which the original form, like every entity, is composed (cf. 904. 28–34). We shall see more exactly why later. Here, they are participated and completive forms which distinguish three sub-species of gods, angels, and daemons, namely lunar gods, lunar angels, and lunar daemons. In other cases, according to Proclus, a form can be found in one and the same participant in respect of all three modes: existence, life, and intellect (903. 14–16).

Although not all the properties or forces of the form are received by each of its participants, there is one universal property: this is its ἰδίωμα, which distinguishes it from all other forms (904. 1 ff.). It makes one chain of all the chains descending from a form. In this chain the order of its sections is accounted for by the order in the quantity of properties received (ll. 8–12). Participation ceases first in the case of properties already descended from some form or other, secondly in the case of properties superior to, i.e. more universal than these, while lastly those (the πρωτουργοί) which 'operate from the origins' and are '*par excellence* akin to the One' will be present in all effects. This can be seen in Figure 1 illustrating the descent of the form *moon* according to three triadic forces.

The last and most long-lasting properties will be Limit and the Unlimited, existence and unity. In the diagram, existence, life, and intellect are in this order of universality, not in that of the triad. For

---

[18] At l. 19 read probably κατὰ τὸ ὂν τοῦ εἴδους, on account of Plat., *Rep.*, 508d5. The MSS τὸ ἕν is, however, quite possible; it is sometimes used as an alternative first term of the triad (e.g. *PT*, III. 9. 39. 27).

FIGURE I Descent of monads

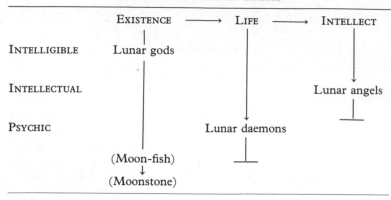

the same reason, the lunar species, save for gods, descend from right to left, angels having participated in three of the transcendental properties, daemons in only two because intellect (at least *per se* intellect) has ceased at that level.

To anyone at all acquainted with late Neoplatonism, several recurring triads are a familiar feature. But it must not be supposed that they are some additional and independent complication in an already complicated but more familiar scheme of descent through hypostases or diacosms. On the contrary, universal triads, that is to say those found in every entity, should be seen as a convenient way of summarizing a set of just such more familiar facts. These facts are (1) that there are reified properties of forms which constitute Existence (the one that is) and so are prior to these forms; (2) that in their function as powers/forces each of those more universal properties will necessarily be participated by each form; (3) that each will be altered by this participation (in other words the participant will possess a copy which only partially resembles it), but it will still be a force which must again proceed and be participated by entities below (less universal than) the form *per se*.

Ignoring the metaphysics, the logical effect so far has nothing peculiarly Neoplatonic, let alone Proclan, about it. We must not be misled by Aristotelian reflections on the relation of genus to species into protesting that the properties received by forms are not independent forces since they are absorbed into the substance of the form, and it is the form which is participated by whatever is logically subordinate to it. For even in Aristotelian logic every property of a generic form will be a property of its sub-genera, and every property of these a property of their species.

In the passage we have been considering, the properties which are more universal than any single form are three mentioned in *Sophist*, 249a: existence, life and intellect. In their inevitable procession or descent we can envisage them as funnelled through each form, only to emerge, as it were, spread out again by having necessarily differentiated the form into three types. Since these types will themselves proceed, the members of the triad can then be seen as monads of three chains or series. But alternatively we can, if we wish, see these series as three 'modes' of procession on the part of the form proceeding (in Proclus' language) existentially, vitally, or intellectually. Life, for example, can be said to proceed with Moon as a co-cause, to lunar daemons; or Moon can be said to proceed vitally or 'in respect of Life' to lunar daemons. The extensional equivalence of the two statements is reflected in, is due to, the fact that the Life which is proceeding or is operative here is not, except indirectly, the supra-essential, *per se* Life, but the life *in* Moon.[19]

For we are dealing permanently in abstractions from a complex reality. We are able to describe only one or a few elements of the structure at a time, even if the elements or laws which we omit contribute significant parts. The complexity which has been simplified here belongs both to the terms in the series and to the series themselves. First, the form Moon did not emerge as though from the head of Athena: it is already the compound of many other forms. Secondly, the 'transcendentals' or members of the triad are also compounds.

In our diagram the lines descending from each of the three run parallel until, one by one, they drop off; they represent what is really a composite chain, for a participant in intellect participates also in life and existence (and conversely too above the psychic level). The same structure of descent is found in the *Timaeus* commentary, I. 386–8, except that forms (such as the Moon) are omitted, because their place is taken by what is called 'the Demiurge' plus 'the Model'. The composition of transcendental properties is brought about by the fact that *each* member of the

---

[19] In the passage from *In Tim.* I mentioned below, the existence and life that were originally henads are *in* the Demiurge (386. 21 and 23–4), just as the good is (388. 11).

triad in the Demiurge participates in the corresponding triad which precedes it. The latter triad consists (as I take it) of unity (i.e. existence *qua* one, the ἓν ὄν), life, and intellect; and Proclus makes a point of mentioning that, when it descends, what is living is and is one, and that everything which has intellect shares in life, existence, and unity (386. 27–8).

But now, it seems, we are faced by the problem how the members of a triad can proceed to distinct types of substance (soul and intellect, for example), when each has the properties of the others as well as its own.

This comparative independence of processions 'in respect of' different transcendentals is usually explained by saying that each takes it in turn, as it were, to be 'predominant'. Aristotle had given an account of the way one or another ingredient such as an element can 'predominate' in a mixture. But this describes the facts rather than explaining them. In Aristotle there is an external, efficient cause to account for any case of such predominance. Nor do I find Proclus appealing to any such axiom of a predominance by turns, although he is willing to use the expressions 'predominant' and 'predominate'.[20] While not a sufficient explanation, we can of course point to the necessary truth, sometimes called 'plenitude', that every universal must be instantiated.

It is more plausible to suppose that for the transcendentals to operate independently, or even predominantly, they must be operating on participants which are already divided into appropriate and inappropriate—land animals already furnished with legs, aquatic with fins. When I mentioned earlier that Proclus could be found describing the failure to participate as due to the weakness of the recipient, I took him to be making a concession to the conventional expressions. For he is averse from a dualism of form and matter to a degree which Plotinus was not. But if we identify the weakness as inappropriateness, we may now be able to make this less dualistic by ascribing it to the working of two laws. They will make the participated or giver, and not the participant or recipient, responsible.[21] These laws will be the Proclan rule (which

---

[20] ἐπικρατέω, *ET*, 159, of Limit or the Unlimited as dividing types of god; *In Tim.*, I. 43. 10 and 312. 5, of transcendental triads. Aristotle: e.g. *De gen. et corr.*, 321ᵃ35; *Meteor.*, 347ᵇ25–8; cf. Simpl., *In De caelo*, 85.

[21] *ET*, 142–3 make the identification but emphasize that the weakness is to be attributed only to the participants. This is because it still belongs to the negative description of the facts. For the purpose of the theorems see Dodds on 140.

might be called that of 'first in, last out') and the composition of causes. The Proclan rule can clearly ensure that one property predominates simply by making another not available. But this needs to be ensured at levels above that at which the rule will operate. We shall have therefore to appeal also to the composition of causes, even though this too may be inapplicable at the highest levels of the transcendental triads. Its significance will be seen in two facts: it is forms which are compounded, and their composition amounts to dilution of force. Furthermore, there is a sense in which, as an explanation, it is prior to distance from the One, which readers may have been surprised to find ignored so far.

As for the Proclan rule, Life at an intermediate level will be able to produce Soul without interference from Intellect because the force of Intellect has dropped off from the causal chain. Similarly, Life in the form of Moon will produce lunar daemons not angels. It may be asked how Intellect in Moon produces angels rather than daemons when in this case Intellect and Life are both present. But this is not a problem at all. For angels are just what daemons are in the intellectual diacosm; and to show them schematically as caused by Intellect is to show just that fact. I do not think that a further factor of the 'predominance' of Intellect is needed.

There may, however, be a problem how the appropriateness of a participant is to be prior to the participation. For participation coincides with the action of the cause, and it may be held that it would not make sense for this to coincide with making the participant appropriate. It seems questionable whether this could be held about the intelligible world. For there, all the participant's attributes, including those which make it a possible participant, derive from properties contained in the cause. We saw in the last chapter how this step had already been taken by Plotinus. But we have also seen a corollary of the Proclan rule entailing that, when more than one cause operates, the higher operates first so that its product can be the recipient of less powerful causes—in effect be the substratum of their products (*Elements*, 70–2). So we can surmise that Proclus had our problem in mind.

The transcendental triads enable three distinct classes to contain all other classes. Every entity will have the same distinct three chains funnelled through it and will descend down each of them; it will spread itself into a 'variety beyond encompassing' of genera and species, but those which descend the same chain will display a common feature, however remote from its original attachment to the chain.

But triads generate triads, although not indefinitely. Proclus has three, in an order of subordination, for Existence (described in Lloyd, 1982, 20–2). His use of them is often excessively tiresome for the reader. In the first place, their members have more than one name, which are sometimes shared by the corresponding members of other triads, sometimes not; and secondly, it is not always clear whether a given triad is an alternative version of one already described or a second one subordinate to it. The trouble is that Book III of the *Platonic Theology* which describes them proposes to embrace what it takes to be different accounts of the same metaphysical structure in several Platonic Dialogues. But the scheme is not arbitrary. Like the triads, it is a selective cross-section of the descent of limit and Unlimited. The successive participation in the pair by, say, the form of the moon entailed the triad of the moon existentially, vitally, and intellectually, followed by its diacosmic images. The three triads of Existence are entailed by the successive participation by Existence itself in the pair plus the mixture. There are three such triads because Proclus envisages three stages in the self-creation of Existence; but equally he can point to its three causes in the *Philebus*, for each of these will have its own effect.

I have said nothing of triads which are, so to speak, second-order properties of monads. These are triads whose significance is formal, conveying no intrinsic content but only relations to other entities. They too have universal application. An outstanding example is unparticipated/imparticipable, participated, participant. They are of a quite different type, for they are properties which Neoplatonists do not reify. But there are also triads, such as whole before the parts, made of the parts and in the part, which are on the fringe of reification; for they are species of wholeness, which the Athenian School took as a *constituent* of their ontological system.

We may be led to ask, why triads? Has the number three a superstitious attraction for Neoplatonists?[22] First, it should be said that they are much less mesmerized by it than is often suggested.

---

[22] ‘“All things divided into three”, said the Paternal Intellect,’ he quotes from the *Chaldaean Oracles* (*In Parm.*, 1091. 6 = fr. 22 Des Places; cf. Procl., *In Tim.*, III. 243. 20). But Iamblichus was as recognizable there to Proclus as he is to us.

To give two illustrations of this fact: for no pressing reason, recognized triads are sometimes obliterated by the addition of a fourth term—the soul receives being, life, intellect, *logos*; the Demiurge is existence, life, unit, intellect.[23] More important, the categorial attributes which the *Parmenides* affirmed or denied of the One, and from which all others derive according to Syrianus and his successors, do not appear as triads. The rational ground which Neoplatonists gave for triadic patterns (and which was credited to Iamblichus) was the desire to show a continuity among all substances both for metaphysical and more commonly methodological reasons, the second term of a triad ideally sharing the character of the first and the second. If, in addition, the extreme terms are the result of a rigorous Division they will be complementary classes, and the triad A, A and not-A, not-A, will exhaust the possibilities, so that we can have omitted nothing under the heading of A. (For A and not-A may be exhaustive only at the cost of not-A being an indeterminate contrary rather than a contradictory.) A triad is, of course, only the simplest form of this type of progression, as *In Timaeum*, I. 373. 5–11, recognizes.

Matter replaced by composition of causes?

From this lengthy and, I am afraid, inevitably crabbed discussion of procession according to Proclus we can now gather together the factors which have been seen to affect the force of monads. (The term 'monads' will include henads and forms alike.) What, in the final analysis, causes their degradation, their loss of force, and the decreasing participation in them, these being three descriptions of the same phenomenon? The most striking thing to have emerged is the importance of the Proclan rule. But this cannot by itself account for the phenomenon (as Rosán, 1949, 78, might imply). For, if I am right, it is a rule which correlates the force of different monads throughout their descent with the levels from which they started, not the force of any single monad with the level which it is at; in other words, it compares series not positions in a series. What Proclus seemed to find significant was not the gradual weakening of forces and of participation but their causation at

---

[23] Procl., *PT*, III. 6. 25. 11–21; *In Tim.*, I. 386. 30–387. 3.

determinate levels. This is certainly a necessary condition of there being an 'ontological plenum' of the kind demanded by the *Timaeus* and the *Epinomis*; and the fact can therefore be counted as a transcendental proof, in the Kantian sense, of the Proclan rule. Proclus was more conscious than Plotinus of a desire to avoid interaction between agent and product. Where causation meant the production of an imperfect copy, the cause was wholly active. But what tends to make interaction unnecessary is the composition of causes. Proclus can describe it in terms which imply that the participant is one of the active forces, contributing its 'appropriate' power to that of the form received, but, as he says (like Mill), 'displaying a single effect from the pair' (*Decem dubitationes*, IV, § 22. 34–5 Isaac).

They say that the sun transmits to the moon light which leaves the moon to reach us, for it is neither hot and dry like sunlight nor thick and gloomy like the moon's own light, but being a mixture from the force of the participant and that of the participated it has changed both its colour and its previous activity. (ib., 35–40)

He is trying to account for degress of participation in providence without blaming providence, which is the One. Some things, he argues, participate in it in respect of existence only, some in respect of life, some thought, some all three, some, moreover, permanently, some impermanently, because their nature is unstable (ib., § 23).

Here too the Proclan rule is operating: but notice how the weakness of receptivity which is ascribed to the unstable nature of a recipient, and which is crucial for the place of human affairs in Neoplatonism, can be accounted for by composition of causes. For the correlative weakness which Proclus looked for in the form so as to avoid dualism does not need to be that of the form which fails to be received: it can be that of the forms which make up the remaining (or already existent) nature of the recipient. When it is a god who is rejected, Proclus eschews any idea of a failure of divine power and adds,

No more are we so bold as to accuse the sun of a lunar eclipse—instead of the fact that the moon has fallen into the cone of shadow. (ib., § 24. 29–31)

But as he knew quite well, the moon's entry into the cone of shadow consists in its participation in a conjunction of forms. (Witness for example *Platonic Theology*, III. 2. 8. 14–20.) Aristotle's matter was commonly treated as though it were a conjunction of accidents; and we have seen that Proclus raised no theoretical objection to the notion of matter in the sensible world. But even here it is at most, in my opinion, a name for the logical substrate and is reducible to co-causes. The 'essential' power of the soul, namely self-movement, includes (he says elsewhere) the ability to discover truth unaided. What appears to be a deficiency of this power is in fact the admixture of non-spontaneous movement from the body, but referred to twice by Proclus as effects of '(the) matter'.[24] So much for Proclan matter.

In the intelligible world it is more difficult to intrepret it as composition of causes because of Plotinus' argument that specific differences were transmitted from the generic monad, not from external chains. The logic behind the argument was thoroughly Neoplatonic; but I have to admit that I do not know of enough direct evidence to judge just how far Proclus accepted it. One may well believe that his attack on intelligible matter endorses it and indeed implies that Plotinus was in danger of being disloyal to himself. It is not certain that the dissolution of substance by that argument was seen to have much to do with the dissolution of matter into composition of causes. But we shall see in the following paragraphs how relevant to the *weakening* of a form this composition is. Nor did Proclus, any more than Plotinus, feel that it inhibited him from taking for granted more often than not the Aristotelian notion of 'receptiveness'.

Although Proclus is explicit about the decline of force, someone may wonder how the very notion could be applied to those monads which can be called principles and are by definition impassible. The question may be answered at two levels. First we must repeat that Neoplatonists claimed to preserve this impassibility and unchanging character of monads by the concept of *remaining*. But in so far as this only re-states the problem it will be necessary to consider philosophical interpretations, in terms which are not Neoplatonic, of remaining, procession, and reversion. These three activities are never independent of one another. We shall look at them as a complex in the next chapter. But for the present we can abstract procession in order to see how it involves multiplication in two distinct ways. This in turn connects it with another of the explanations of the form's decline; for, as we saw, there are several such explanations to choose from.

[24] *In Alcib.*, 225. 12–226. 7 (matter: 226. 4 and 6).

Decline of monad as distance from the One. Fundamental equations of force, value, and unity

If asked for a *sufficient* condition of decline, most readers of Plotinus, Porphyry, or Proclus would agree that it is proportionate to the monad's distance from the One.[25] Everything, of course, has to multiply in proceeding from the One, since it will no longer be simply a one, and, provided that the product of each step is also (though not simply) a one, this will hold throughout the procession. But as well as being similar to its cause, by virtue of the monadic property which is partially transmitted, the effect or product must also be dissimilar; otherwise, as Proclus points out, there will be no distinction between an effect and a cause (*Platonic Theology*, III. 2. 7. 2–8). This will be achieved and can only be achieved by multiplication. For one object differs qualitatively from another by the fact that one has more qualities than the other. It cannot be the cause which has more qualities than the effect; otherwise there will be one or more of them which are not transmitted, i.e. have not proceeded, which is not possible in Neoplatonism. So effects are necessarily multiplied by their causes—but 'multiplied' in a special sense. They will contain more constituents, which can be identified here as qualities. This is why Neoplatonists thought of the Platonic division and the Neoplatonic procession of a genus as two pictures of the same thing. Each represents the *de-unification* of a form by the successive addition to it of qualities which are other forms: say, terrestrial, footed, two-footed rational.

They also represent multiplication in the more natural sense of there being more instances of the monad. This takes place in the normal process from the universal to the less universal. It too is a form of diversification. Animal 'diversifies' into men and fishes, but only by becoming compounds of animal—terrestrial, footed, and so on, and animal—aquatic, finned, and so on; each of these is a qualified animal (Porphyry's 'allocated' animal) and hence, for a Platonist, to a lesser degree animal—less purely animal.

Because Neoplatonists were not so shocked by the thought of differentiae which were actually, not potentially, contained by the

---

[25] As Saffrey & Westerink notice ad loc., Procl., *PT*, III. 2 6.25–7. 1 makes descent equivalent to (καί as an *id est*) a decline in unity and at 7. 5 substitutes 'force'/'power' for 'unity'. Porphyry (*Sent.*, 11) calls the descent into particulars 'descent of power'.

genus, they found it less necessary than we should to distinguish the two kinds of multiplication.

We have still, however, to make explicit the logical connection between a decrease in similarity to a monad and a decrease in the force/power of the monad. Each monad represents a quality ϕ: but compounding ϕ with another quality entails a dilution of ϕ by non-ϕ and hence, according to Platonists, the diminution of ϕ. The one that is is to a lesser degree one than the One for the same reason that a bird is less animal than Animal. As for force, Proclus tells us that even unlimited force is both relative (*Elements*, 93–4) and has degrees (ib., 95); secondly, every force becomes feebler by becoming less unified and more particular (ib., 61; 94). But the connection between force and similarity to the monad lies in the relation of both to the concept of perfection, which we have already noticed as it concerned the Proclan rule. Force is the force of a reified quality to project itself so as to make other such things; it acts spontaneously whenever the quality has reached perfection, and it coincides with that perfection. But similarity to a monad consists in possessing or being, but to a lesser degree, the quality which that monad is; it is a lesser perfection and therefore coincides with a lesser force.

Perfection can, of course, be described as value; and then we find that all this is embraced by the further equation which characterizes Neoplatonism, namely that value is unity—the One is the Good, as it was expressed. For a Neoplatonist's own arguments for the equations, we could start from theorem 12 of Proclus' *Elements*, which states that the Good is the cause of everything that exists. Dodds objects to the question-begging nature of the main proof (ll. 3–17). He means that it contains an equivocation, $\kappa\rho\epsilon\acute{\iota}\tau\tau\omega\nu$, meaning first 'superior in the causal hierarchy' (loosely 'stronger') and then 'better' so that it may show that nothing can be $\kappa\rho\epsilon\hat{\iota}\tau\tau\sigma\nu$, stronger than, the Good because by definition nothing can be $\kappa\rho\epsilon\hat{\iota}\tau\tau\sigma\nu$, better than, the Good. But the reader who cares to examine the text will see that this interpretation makes ll. 4–10 redundant to Proclus' argument. In fact the argument is valid if we understand him to be thinking as follows: degree of goodness = degree of force; this is implied by a transmission theory of causation (referred to in l. 8); for *being best* is in respect of some ϕ and so = *being most* ϕ and causation (*qua* transmission) is in respect of some ϕ. Proposition 7, ll. 22–5 had already shown the relevance of the concept of perfection and its connection with that of force.

The first equation, that of value and unity is dealt with by the next theorem, 13. Value or goodness is what preserves anything that exists, as is witnessed by the fact that everything desires it. But it is unity which in fact preserves its existence, for to go out of existence is to disintegrate. So value implies unity. Conversely, by keeping something together unity can be said to complete it or make it perfect. So unity implies value.

As for the validity of the last theorem, I mention only historical antecedents. The concept of the συνεκτικὴ αἰτία that is necessary for existence is well known.[26] But, as I have mentioned before, Aristotle's doctrine of the convertibility of 'one' and 'being' was also constantly present to Neoplatonists.[27]

---

[26] e.g. *SVF*, ii. 440. For Platonic antecedents of *ET* 12 see Dodds ad loc.
[27] For its application here, see particularly Plot. vi. 9. 1–2. 16.

5

THE SPIRITUAL CIRCUIT

Only a particular soul can ascend

The world we live in is filled with things each kind of which is distinguishable from another by what it must do and what it can do. Grass must remain where it is and must die each year and it may make hay; sheep must eat it and must bleat and may be black; gods must live blessed lives, must not die, and must know everything and may fall in love. Humans, according to Platonists, are somewhere between gods and sheep, for the range of what they can do reaches from behaviour and life appropriate to gods' behaviour and life appropriate to beasts. Although doubtless Nebuchadnezzar is a more literal example than they had in mind, the later Neoplatonists, and particularly Platonizing theologians, took to describing human nature as 'inhabiting a borderland'.[1] This is the result of the procession and decline of triads and forms; and what we have been studying in the previous chapter is the logical mechanism by which this ensures the mixture of forms, which in turn produces the range of constraints and possibilities in each kind of object—their distinguishing attributes.

Inhabiting the borderland meant the possibility of further decline or a return, as it were, to a superior life. The superior life was sometimes understood to include physical characteristics: Christians, with the apparent authority of St Paul, and pagans alike sometimes claimed that under certain circumstances a man would exchange his human body for a 'vehicle' of fire or ether or pneuma. But generally, Neoplatonist philosophers meant that his life would be superior inasmuch as it would involve exercising certain faculties at the expense of others; and these in Greek classification were psychological faculties. Physical desires would be excluded by intellectual desires, the use of the senses by the use of the mind,

---

[1] μεθόριος: a borderland between the intelligible and sensible worlds according to Nemesius, 39. 7 Matthaei. Cf. Greg. Nyss., *In Ps.* VII, *PG*, 44. 457 B; *Or. cat.* VI, *PG*, 45. 25 C ff. Naturally angels were intermediate between God and men.

discursive thought by non-discursive. So we can describe the rise, or correspondingly the fall, as being in respect of the soul.

Since Neoplatonic metaphysicians are never tired of claiming that everything desires what is best for it, why should not sheep become humans in the right circumstances, or stones grass, since, according to Plotinus they possess life? As for the lower animals, they are prevented by the fact that they have no rational faculty to exercise. In the Athenian system this would be due to the Proclan rule. But that should not prevent stones from showing more life than they apparently do. In fact those philosophers, including Proclus, who believed in theurgy would point to the moonstone, which was sufficiently alive to respond to phases of the moon; and those, including Plotinus, who believed in the sympathies and antipathies derided by David Hume, would credit these with normal obedience to physical laws.[2] At the other extreme, angels, daemons, and heroes were presumably even better equipped for apotheosis.

It cannot be the universals, whether forms or hypostases, which are capable of leaving the life defined for them. First, this would be a logical impossibility and, secondly, if the life were a superior one, it would contradict the law of procession. We can imagine that Soul has been replaced by Intellect; we have to do so in order to understand the genesis, which the Neoplatonists described, of Intellect followed by that of Soul. But the only soul which can, actually, retrace the steps must be your soul or my soul. No doubt the salient point in which these differ from the universals is that they are in time. But, additionally, others such as the world soul or the most universal of all, imparticipable Soul, are perfect in their kind. And, as Proclus points out, that which possesses to perfection its proper character will have nothing to cause it to sink below or to rise above its existing condition (*Platonic Theology*, I. 19. 89). But it is difficult, perhaps impossible, to find a consistent theory of reversion in Neoplatonism. For instance, self-sufficiency does not rule out but actually implies the desire which is required for self-reversion according to the *Elements of Theology*, 42. But how often do we not find Plotinus arguing that desire implies imperfection?

---

[2] Cf. Iambl., *De myst.*, v. 7; Procl., *In Tim.* I. 210; Plot., IV. 4. 34.

Personal experience integral to Neoplatonism

What in fact makes the particular human soul have this apparently unique privilege? To this there is no complete answer in Neoplatonism, and I do not think Neoplatonists would have claimed one. Instead, however, we can ask what makes them believe that the particular soul has the privilege. This they did answer: personal experience.

It is a factor in Neoplatonism that we have ignored so far. Certainly there is an empirical element in the formation and ordering of concepts; to repeat our familiar example, that life descends beyond intellect has many consequences for the system, but it is a fact of observation. This empirical element is inevitable in any philosophy, and a rationalist epistemology will no doubt make it look less empirical. Moreover, its findings will have been absorbed into a comparatively deductive conceptual system. The fact of the soul's ascent is quite different. From the start to the finish of their reflections Neoplatonists appeal to what they claim to be their personal experiences of it. 'He who has seen knows' is the justification for a series of descriptions of diacosms with which they believe that from time to time their souls have been in contact. These diacosms or types of reality have objective characteristics which are required by the non-empirical system represented by the philosophical story of their genesis. Pure Intellect consists of thoughts which must form a *totum simul* and must be the life of eternity; both characteristics follow from its position between the One and Soul, which must live in time and must be conscious of its thoughts as a non-simultaneous plurality. But an individual who has exercised the faculty whose thoughts are those of Pure Intellect can give a phenomenological description of his experience. (It is assumed that he has correctly identified the experience by the same kind of criteria that identify objects of the real world in a remembered dream.) This will be a description primarily of the experience—what Intellect or the life of eternity feels like and looks like.

Speaking in a deliberately unsophisticated manner about mysticism, one could say that such a description will be in two respects mystical. It includes elements which at first sight are quite incidental to the object of the experience (Intellect, eternity), such as light, or purely subjective, such as joy, but which are common currency of records of religious mystics. *Ennead* III. 8. 8 is an instance of this. Secondly, it is a substitute for a direct description of what the experience is supposed to be *of*, for a direct description is inadequate. The inadequacy is a matter of degree: the nearer to the One and farther from discursive intellect, the more inadequate will be a description of it. But we must hestitate before calling it ineffable. The properties of Pure Intellect are stated at length in Proclus' *Elements*, and so are those even of the class of henads; the reason why he omits those of individual henads is that he does not know them. Furthermore, no Greek Neoplatonist wittingly countenanced propositions about anything real which were in breach of the law of contradiction.

What makes a non-phenomenological description of any hypostasis inadequate is Neoplatonic idealism. The hypostases *are* experiences; they are types of consciousness; while, therefore, they have abstract and objective properties, they have also what we call phenomenological properties.

It follows that the element of personal experience is needed to complement the non-empirical philosophical system. The two together constitute Neoplatonism. But the content of personal experience cannot be derived from the Neoplatonists' philosophical system. It is an unpredictable gift from their gods. Otherwise it would have applied to the universal soul, and the hypostases would have been 'telescoped' to a degree unacceptable to orthodox Neoplatonists. But this will not be the last word on the matter.

For the same reason, we can give no final reply about the uniqueness of particular humans. We know neither which angels, daemons, and heroes ascend to the One nor how often. They write no books.

Ambiguities of 'reversion'

Neoplatonists often—the later the more often—call the ascent of the soul 'reversion' (ἐπιστροφή). One of the first things that is learnt about them is their triad of remaining, proceeding, and reverting. But the term translated 'reversion'—*epistrophe*—is doubly ambiguous. First, we find it used sometimes with its strict meaning of 'being turned towards' something, in other words to refer to an inclination, sometimes with a much fuller meaning of 'returning' or 'having returned' to it; and there are times when the reader is unsure which is meant. Clearly a sunflower which turns its petals to the sun cannot be said in the ordinary sense to have returned to the sun. But when at higher levels of existence the only activity, or the relevant activity, of some subject is consciousness or thought, to be inclined towards something is to have the attention directed to it, and if this is necessarily accompanied by thought, then the subject must be thinking of that and nothing else. But at this level, say of Soul and Intellect, to 'return' is not to change location: it is to change the content of consciousness or thought, say from parts of a whole to the whole. So very often this ambiguity in *epistrophe* is of no consequence.[3]

In the second place, without changing the meaning, or rather two meanings, of *epistrophe*, it is taken sometimes to apply to a return/inclination to itself on the part of some subject, sometimes to a return/inclination to a higher source. In both cases it is commonly thought of as the third term of the triad, or at least to concern a subject which has proceeded. It has then a more or less technical meaning, since there is a theory of reversion. We find this for example in Proclus' *Elements*, 31 ff. Here, procession has caused the subject to exist, while reversion adds goodness, or what we preferred to call 'value', to its existence. Dodds' notes on these propositions are invaluable: but they do not to my mind put enough weight on the fundamental equation of value, unity, and reality. The theoretical function of reversion is to complete the reality of what has proceeded and so to give it an identity.[4] (The coinciding of essence and existence is prominent here.) It can be seen as the same function as that of the self-consciousness which according to Hegel has to be added to consciousness for a thought to be an object with an identity. Something like this is surely involved in the 'turning to the One' which establishes the original indeterminate thinking ('Pre-intellect') simultaneously as actual

---

[3] When it means 'inclination', it can sometimes be incompatible with 'return', for the direction of it is said to be upwards, downwards, or reflexive by Porphyry (*Sent.*, §§ 13 and 30) and Proclus (*In Alcib.*, 20. 1–5 Cr.) It re-appears in Pico della Mirandola's address by God to Adam, who, as in other Italian humanists, represents man *par excellence* (universal inasmuch as first!): 'poteris in inferiora quae sunt bruta degenerare. Poteris in superiora quae sunt divina ex tui animi sententia regenerari' (*De hom. dign.*, in *Op. omnia*, Basel, 1557, 314).

[4] Cf. Procl., *In Tim.*, I. 371. 20–5. For he correlates the first two terms of the triad—existence, power, and activity—with remaining and procession before stating that activity conveys completion.

thought and as its object or content, Existence. For in Plotinus' account (if Lloyd, 1987*b*, is right) the One which this Pre-intellect is regarding must be the first product of the One, which is nothing other than Pre-intellect seen as the thought rather than the thinking. So the process is a process of self-determination; and it is supposed to be repeated analogously in every case of the production of a novel entity. Proclus has a special type of reversion for things which have the appropriate faculty, 'epistemic reversion' (op. cit., 39); although nominally meaning 'consciousness of the goodness of their causes', this is, as again readers of Plotinus will know, awareness of the presence of an image of the Good and a form of self-awareness. The Proclan theory therefore brings self-reversion and reversion to higher causes under a single notion. But it does not avoid looking rather *ad hoc*.

We are in any case left with problems. Neoplatonists explicitly connect reversion to what is above it with establishing the identity of what reverts: but then will it not precisely have lost this identity—its newly won, if indeterminate identity which is due to its having proceeded from, and therefore *not* being, what is above it? They tend to blur this difficulty. They seem to rely on the normative concept of definition (i.e. one which is of the definiendum at its best) and the assumption that self-reversion leads naturally to reversion to causes, if it does not amount to the same thing. The best intellect, Plotinus writes, will be thinking of objects that are prior to it, 'for in turning to itself it turns to its origin' (VI. 9. 2. 33–6). Damascius is conscious of the problems, but his position is fundamentally the same: what had been taken as alternative kinds of reversion (as in *Elements*, 158) are involved in every act of reversion. Indeed, he points out that the same two factors occur in remaining and procession: when anything remains or proceeds, it can correctly be seen also as the remaining of, and procession from, its cause. So every case of reverting or remaining or proceeding is, in his formula, a single subject which stands in two relations (*Dubitationes*, I. 170. 16–171. 7 R). But for practical purposes writers often saw no need to distinguish reversion from the general notion of ascent to the One. To quote a post-Proclan example, the soul's circular motion

makes it revert and collect itself first into itself and then, having become uniform, by uniting itself to the singly unified powers [probably the angels] so as to guide it to the Beautiful and the Good. (Pseudo-Dionysius, *De divinis nominibus*, 4. 9, 705 A)

There is a second problem. How is reversion to the cause to be distinguished from remaining? Both are internal activities; and what has reverted has done so by being unified, multiplicity being the mark of its external activity. What *proceeded* was, or resulted in, the comparative multiplicity which *remained* only in its superior and comparatively unified form. Reversion to the cause seems thus to restore the status quo ante, but then what had proceeded will have lost its identity. So we have the first problem in another guise.

It seems clear that the function of reversion in fixing the identity of something otherwise indeterminate is incompatible with reversion to the cause and belongs only to self-reversion. This may have been insufficiently recognized by Neoplatonists, but they were not forced into a contradiction, so long as they recognized that the ascending reversion implied a prior self-reversion. They usually did. It is, of course, more promising to suppose that the problem was not there to be solved since, as a universal law, 'reversion' did not mean 'return', but only 'inclination'. For our concerns, this is certainly the case in Plotinus. At VI. 9. 2 he did not explain how 'in turning to itself' Intellect was 'turning to its origin'. But we can infer it, with some hesitation, from his accounts of its genesis. When it thinks of itself as Existence/Being it thinks of itself as one Existence/Being. (For the preceding passages have repeated at length Aristotle's argument that everything that is is one.) This is in effect a one that is, but to be conscious of that is indirectly to be conscious of the One. (A direct consciousness of the One is impossible.) Here, Plotinus calls this indirect consciousness 'looking in the direction of the One'. For this 'one' which is itself and which it does see directly is an effect and an image of its cause, which is 'the One'. So he can also say (ll. 41–2) that to be conscious of it is to be in the presence of the One. It is the nature of Intellect (l. 40) to be joined to the One in this way and to this extent, for if it were not 'the *one* that is' as well as the many that are (categories and forms), it would not be Intellect. A similar argument can be inferred from genesis accounts which substitute 'good', or 'object of desire', for 'one'. Either argument, we may surmise, explains proposition 15 of Proclus' *Elements*, which states that to revert implies being joined to that which is reverted to. It will apply, as in Plotinus, to everything above the level of Nature. For we notice that Proclus mentions 'being joined' or contiguity (σύναψις), not identity. Nor is it necessary to suppose that his 'reversion' is more than 'inclination': but I should have liked to be more confident of that.

If procession is thought of as the successful production of a new entity, it is easy to see that reversion can be thought of as a necessary condition of it; only when it is thought of as a process will it be prior to reversion. This was understood. Proclus describes the pair as forming a continuous motion which is circular and consequently excludes an order of priority (*Elements*, 33; *Platonic Theology*, II. 6. 41. 21 and 28). One may suspect that the simultaneity which was insisted on was often meant only to prevent people from taking the process of generation literally, that is temporally. But Plotinus' Pre-intellect suggests that he meant more. For in order to picture a process in which we have to make each of its 'moments' prior to another according to the function we have in mind for a given moment, the standard way to avoid a contradiction is to attribute to one or more of the moments an indeterminate or potential stage before it is determinate or actual. (Schoolboys used to learn to answer the question, 'Which came first, the hen or the egg?' with 'Neither', meaning something which could incomprehensibly be either.) Plotinus usually presented thinking as the first procession of the One, but since thinking requires an object the existent has also to be prior to thinking: Pre-intellect is indeterminately either.

Philosophical interpretations of the spiritual circuit

It is certain that, although they are distinct remaining, proceeding, and reverting cannot be separated. Because they are a timeless movement, this is represented as a circular movement of the universe and its contents. (Even the archetypal time which Proclus, in opposition to Plotinus, places above Soul and Nature is not 'temporal' in our sense.) This was found objectionable only when reversion was taken to mean return instead of inclination to a cause, and identification instead of continuity with it. Because it is in time, a particular soul can undergo the change which return and ascent entail, and these will doubtless contain in microcosm the cosmic changeless process. But the cosmic process cannot be just an allegory of the 'spiritual circuit'—to use a Renaissance term—which it is the hope of the purified soul to travel. That would be to reverse the order of reality in Neoplatonic metaphysics. Can it be given a philosophical interpretation?

P. Hadot has pointed out the similarity of the continuous centrifugal and centripetal movement of pneuma in Stoic physics and suggested that the Neoplatonists transposed this into their nonphysical procession and reversion.[5] It is certainly striking that this 'tensile movement' maintained dynamically the two features of their material universe which we can recognize in the Neoplatonic chain of being: continuity and stability. Incidentally, it had been given a non-spatial application to *logos* by Philo, two hundred years before Plotinus (*SVF*, II. 453). We are therefore tempted to describe the Neoplatonic motionless movement as a *tension* which holds every object, conceived or actual, between an inferior and a superior form. But of course this is a metaphor: the tension would be a logical tension, whatever that might be. For in a certain, highly qualified sense, the objects in question are reified concepts. As I shall suggest, the metaphor can be given a content only if it has an extra-logical aspect added to it and the concepts are not merely abstract. But ignoring tension, we must recognize the logical aspect of the movement; and there are some comments on it which ought to be made.

People often say that logical necessity does not belong to procession. Its necessity 'is not intelligible', according to Trouillard, 'but the principle of intelligibility. In fact we are here beyond necessity and contingency' (1965, ad 27). But they do not say what other kind of necessity is involved. For, as I mentioned in connection with the Aristotelian physical model, Plotinus expressly calls each of the hypostases—in other words the manifestations of procession—necessary. Or else they ignore this because they think that it compromises the freedom and the superiority to reasoning of the agents. But for Plotinus being free is not being able to do what one wants to do but wanting to do what one should do;[6] and what one should do includes what one must do. As for reasoning, if necessary propositions are ones which would be reached by reasoning, it does not follow that when they are not reached by reasoning they are not necessary.

However that may be, there is an important distinction to be

---

[5] (1968), I, 225–34. For Stoic 'tensile movement' see, e.g., *SVF*, II. 451; Long and Sedley (1988), 288; Sambursky (1959), ch. 2.

[6] Cf. Beierwaltes (1985), 192.

made. The fact that there is procession from an entity A must be distinguished from the fact that what proceeds from A is what it is, B rather than C. It is the latter—the contents of procession—which are open, by and large, to knowledge by dialectic or reasoning; and I can see no reason why this does not entail that they are logically necessary. That this too is how Neoplatonists saw it is shown beyond question by their appeal to the *Parmenides* as a deduction of principles. 'Logically', however, must be taken in a broad sense to mean the conceptually necessary, for it is this that is displayed by a Platonic division. In practice such classification is not entirely a priori. The order of its terms, corresponding to an order of procession, may be known, or at the least provisionally known, by observation. We saw how the priority of life to intellect could be determined by observing that not all living things are intelligent. Neoplatonist logicians rightly believed that this sort of question had been clarified by Aristotle in the *Posterior Analytics*. They appear to acknowledge two other sources of knowledge: states of self-awareness which tend to fall into an order, and inspired writings such as the Orphic hymns, the Chaldaean Oracles, and, above all, Plato. But of these at least the written authorities will be found being used to confirm what is acceptable on other grounds.

But I doubt that they envisaged even the fact of procession as a 'principle' of necessity, something which generated necessity—any more than they supposed that it generated freedom. They believed that the *Parmenides* founded what may be called the categories of existence on the procession of the One: but these did not include necessity, which was taken for granted.

A logical interpretation is perhaps easier when we take reversion into account.[7] Since an effect is only an image, it is other than, as well as the same as, its cause. So a Φ can be said to proceed to a not-Φ. But when it reverts to itself and its cause, the result is not to re-establish Φ, for the subject reverting is not Φ: it establishes itself as something which is Φ and not-Φ. (The subject which proceeded to not-Φ was likewise Φ: but procession is an overflowing which establishes nothing, while the stemming of it establishes it where it has stopped and consists in reversion.) The not One which has proceeded from the One tries, in reverting, to grasp the One but finds something else in its grasp (*Enneads*, v. 3. 11). It

---

[7] Cf. Beierwaltes (1979), p. xi, and more generally 34 ff., 91 ff.

reminds one of Hegel's famous simile of 'consciousness which can come only upon the grave of its own life', like the Crusaders who followed their Saviour. But the oscillation or cycle of procession and reversion could be seen as the intermediate position of the object which is neither A nor not-A but both; and this might be described as due to the tension of Φ and not-Φ on the grounds that if it were not for Φ the object would be not-Φ and if it were not for not-Φ it would be Φ. In Neoplatonic terms, grass is between sheep and stones inasmuch as the life (namely vegetable life) which is in grass is comparatively, i.e. in some respects, inanimate but still life.

But giving this logical fact a dynamic description such as 'oscillation' or 'tension' adds nothing, unless the description can be given some more literal sense. The positive term of this Hegelian-looking triad might be held to represent the more perfect, and therefore the more desirable, condition of an object. The Neoplatonic universe consists of parts and wholes, of which the greatest are commonly called hypostases, themselves containing parts which Proclus called diacosms and series. Every whole contains particulars, many of them perceptible. But the universal or intelligible wholes are already perfect in their kind; and I do not see how to avoid our earlier conclusion that inclination (or some form of *orexis*) towards a more perfect condition would be a contradiction. Of course it is the paradox of Neoplatonism that the best of all possible worlds should include what falls short of the best; and it could be suggested that the notions of procession and reversion, with their implication of desire and regret, stand for this paradox. They explain in cosmic terms what is meant by 'all things desire the good'. There is nothing wrong with this suggestion, except that it would be closer to aesthetic than to philosophical interpretation.

A more promising version of it is to recognize that the objects which enjoy the motionless movement are not reified concepts but 'living thoughts'. We can follow Aristotle in distinguishing a universal thought such as colour and a particular thought such as the colour of this tulip; we can also distinguish a thought which is the concrete act or content of some mind from a thought which is an abstraction and only the referent, or perhaps significatum, of the mental act or content. According to one picture, the universal thought can only be the thought which is an abstraction. But this was not the picture which the Neoplatonists accepted; pure Intellect, for example, was a mind whose content was universal but concrete thoughts; in other words, they were 'thinkings' or ἐνέρ-γειαι, which Plotinus called living thoughts. Since to be is to be a thought, all the elements in the Neoplatonic hierarchy are thoughts. All students of the subject know this, but they do not always bear it in mind. For instance, the *logoi* which are sometimes called the 'seminal' *logoi* have the task of conveying the proceeding forms to their recipients. Plotinus places them predominantly in the world soul, of which nature is a reflection or image; and in deference to their biological metaphor each might be described as his version of a genetic code. There is a *logos* which is the whole/universal of the particular *logoi*, and it both creates Nature and makes it intelligible. Both functions belong to thinking or consciousness (θεωρία). Plotinus' *logoi* are often mentioned as though they were a loan, and a slightly embarrassing one, from Stoicism. But, to the extent that they are Stoic at all, they are not a loan but a transposition. They too are living thoughts.[8]

This is no subjective idealism. The minds which the universal thoughts constitute are themselves both universal and individual or substantial after the manner of all 'wholes before the parts'. If we want to suppose a kind of 'Consciousness *überhaupt*' we need not be too afraid of anachronism. In the first place, the reduction of the thinker to the thought was already an Aristotelian commonplace. Secondly, the notion of a single universal intellect which is outside human intellects and in which the thinker is identical with the thought had been taken by the Neoplatonists from Alexander and the *De intellectu* attributed to him.

Suppose now that we can imagine thoughts which are actual 'thinkings', although not those of a person, instead of the abstract objects of thought or terms that we labelled 'Φ' and 'not-Φ'. They could be supposed, in the same way and for the same reason, to proceed and revert. For, as Plato claimed, being is pervaded by not-being. But there are differences. In the logical interpretation, to attribute dynamic, not to say anthropomorphic characteristics such as inclining and trying, tension and balance, to the objects was superfluous metaphor. In the case of thought which is actual thinking they could be claimed as more literal than metaphysical. One thought implies another, but rational thinking leads or tends to it. Secondly, there was the difficulty that a logical object is at any

---

[8] See especially III. 8. 2–3. For 'genetic code' (or blueprint?) cf. III. 2 and 3; VI. 7.7 ff.

stage what it is; in the context, this meant that it was perfectly what it was; consequently any desire to improve itself, even if possible, would have been irrational. It is true that the same can be said to apply in the case of thinking. But there is at least the partially satisfactory reply that thinking spontaneously explores itself. The Neoplatonic term 'self-knowledge' is confusing because ambiguous, but it included being aware of the nature of whatever one is aware of, and it is often described as a natural impulse of awareness. Thirdly, this would depend on extrapolation and analogy from our personal knowledge of our own thinking. That may or may not be considered valid, but it is thoroughly consistent with numerous texts which make it explicit or take it for granted. Such an interpretation of the cosmic movement is not thoroughly coherent, but it recognizes the essential contribution to Neoplatonism of the interior life.

Appearance and reality

Procession is caused by perfection and itself causes a departure from perfection; reversion is the impetus to return to it. But the ultimate key to the understanding of all Neoplatonism, whether paradoxical or not, must be its fundamental equations. One of these is that of perfection and reality, with its corollary that a departure from perfection is non-reality, or appearance. If we generalized this, we should have all procession as a multiplication of appearances. And this was a version which was in fact carried to one logical conclusion early in the history of Neoplatonism. The conclusion is that rather than composing the best of all possible worlds the apparently fixed hypostases are illusory.

In the anonymous (and fragmentary) *Commentary on the Parmenides*, preserved in a Turin palimpsest, we have a certain telescoping of the first two hypostases.[9] The second hypostasis is a one which is, but here the one 'by itself' is the logically simple One, i.e. the first hypostasis; and if the 'which is' of the second hypostasis is taken for the sake of argument as predicative, it is hard not to suppose that its subject is meant to be this 'one by itself'. This would explain why the author says that the second hypostasis is in

9 Text first edited W. Kroll in *Rh. Mus. f. Philol.* 47 (1892), 599–627, re-edited P. Hadot (1968).

one respect (viz. as existent) both in movement and at rest, but in another respect (viz. as the One) neither. So, instead of uniting itself with the One by means of reverting to itself, it turns out that what reverts is the One itself all along (fos. XIII–XIV). Nor, to enhance the 'telescoping', is it only the One which has, as it were, come down, but Being/Existence has, as it were, gone up: the One itself can be described as absolute Being or the Idea of Being (sc. of the second One, the second hypostasis) (XII. 29–34). The expression 'appearance', was not used by the commentator. But it is Plato's expression in *Parmenides*, 143 A, which has rightly been identified by P. Hadot as the text which the commentator was elaborating on. Nor, of course, is it a synonym of 'illusion'. But Porphyry, whether or not he is also the commentator, seems to me to come close to regarding the embodied soul as Intellect/Being seen through 'a screen of imagery'.[10] His refusal adequately to distinguish these two hypostases was a regular complaint of his successors. Certainly like any Neoplatonist he described an hypostasis as brought into existence by a higher one or, from another point of view, as self-created. But this is consistent with his having believed that this existence depended also on a dim sight or confused thought of the higher one, so that in a true light the hypostases would contract like a concertina into one.

Moreover, the question whether he believed this cannot be settled merely by appealing to such normal descriptions, for it is as much philosophical as philological. My meaning may be explained succinctly by a parallel problem facing the historian of modern philosophy. Does Berkeley's immaterialism imply that the external world is unreal? In the *Three Dialogues* Philonous (Berkeley) states categorically, 'I rob you of nothing in the world'. But who would take that to settle the question? Even when we are asking what an author *would* have said, Plotinus presents less of a problem than Porphyry, because he is writing from a much more constant standpoint: Porphyry ranges from Aristotelian semantics to protreptic and theosophy. Plotinus would not, I think, have accepted a monistic development of the kind suggested by the anonymous *Parmenides* commentary. Nevertheless, if Porphyry had, it would

---

[10] *Sent.*, § 40. 40. 4–7 Lamberz; cf. § 29. 18. 1–13, although Porphyry's well attested association of the soul's vehicle with φαντασία is obscure. *Sent.* § 40 otherwise largely repeats Plot., VI. 5. 12: but see my remarks in A. H. Armstrong (ed.), *Cambridge History of Later Greek and Early Medieval Philosophy* (Cambridge, 1967), 288–90.

have been because he believed that that was the way to make *philosophical* sense of the *Enneads*.

As for the contrast of appearance and reality, although the expression happens to be odd in English, 'an apparent cat' might mean an imaginary cat or the illusion of one, but in either case an unreal one; and an unreal cat is not a type of cat. In fact Neoplatonic metaphysicians do not normally speak of appearances of some *X*, but about traces and copies, or images of *X*. These too, it will be said, are not types of *X*. But that may be true, not because logic dictates it but because that is how we talk in the case of physical objects. Neoplatonism escapes this because it has a concept of reality which allows the more and the less real. Consequently a trace or copy of an *X* can also be an *X*. For it can possess sufficient *X*-like properties or similarities, in addition to dissimilarities; and, crucially, there is no property of reality, or existence, which is attributable to *X*'s but not to the *X* with which (on account of the similarities) the copy can be identified. When a copy of a form, henad, hypostasis is 'generated' by its perfection, original and copy are both existents (ὄντα), that is to say existing instances or types of what the originals are types of—not just existing instances of copies. To permit them both to be such existing types while still preserving a scale of nature, it is necessary for the copies to have less existence than the originals.

The reader must not complain that this is unnecessarily substituting degrees of existence for degrees of the type predicated. For Neoplatonists the two scales coincide, and, as we saw much earlier, 'existence', 'substance', and 'essence' must often be considered synonyms.[11] Many will follow Aristotle in finding degrees of substance as objectionable as degrees of reality or existence.

Nor must it be thought that the matter could have been dealt with by observing the ambiguity of 'copy'. A painting of the Lord Mayor is a copy, but not what its original is, a dignitary; but a copy of the painting, which we might distinguish by calling a replica of it, *is* what its original is, a work of art. And replicas can at least be better and worse replicas. But replicas are copies which preserve categories of their originals, such as that of being a person or of being an artefact, and which are not thought of as making only quantitative distinctions. And this will not serve the Neoplatonists. For it is an essential feature of their processions that a type or form

---

[11] This is excellently exemplified by *Enneads*, VI. 9. 1 and 2.

is continuous from one hypostasis to another, and 'hypostases' will imply the 'categories' whose identity is required by 'replicas'; Neoplatonists call the external world not only an image of Soul but a soul.

What could be seen primarily as degrees of existence showed itself in a number of ways. I will give one simple example, familiar throughout Greek philosophy: the difference between something which is always ϕ and something which is sometimes ϕ. But pervasive, 'transcendental' predicates such as life readily accustomed Neoplatonists to think of the scale as a scale of being rather than being ϕ; for a life is an existence, and a different existence a different life.

What was referred to as the monism suggested by the anonymous *Parmenides* commentary was not accepted for the whole hierarchy by other Neoplatonists. But we can conclude these speculations by asking whether it is not acceptable for the second hypostasis. (The signs in Plotinus that the third hypostasis might 'telescope' into it were noticed by his successors, who found it repugnant that Soul might not have an existence of its own.) It could be described as the mirror image of Stoic monism, the replacement of material components of a theory by immaterial; and to many historians this in itself will make it plausible to attribute it to the Neoplatonists. In Stoicism all events and substances are reducible to qualifications (themselves material or linguistic abstractions from what is material), but whose identities are preserved by the tension (expansion and contraction) of their elements. Can we not read the Neoplatonic Being/Existence as a system in which hypostases, processions, and the affairs of men are waves and ripples on, or rather of, a single substrate? We have seen how, if we attend to its other aspect, Thought, it may be possible to make the changeless ebb and flow of procession and reversion the mirror image of the Stoic expansion and contraction.

The universal subject is Existence or Thought. This is expounded in Plotinus' thesis that being is everywhere. But, for the reasons we have given, its appearances are not mere illusions, for they only possess the properties of existence (reality) to a lesser degree than the universal Existence. This fact is succinctly equivalent to their being parts of the whole instead of the whole itself.

The division of subjective and objective conveyed by the alternative aspects of thought and existence does not hold *sub specie aeternitatis*, and this fact puts us in mind of the monism of Spinoza. But as Plotinus' radical criticism of Aristotle showed, the universal Existence/Thought is not a *logical* subject. Nor is it God, for we had to conclude that, save for one or two uncertain exceptions, the telescoping of the first and second hypostases was not Neoplatonic.

6

THE LIMITS OF KNOWLEDGE

Knowledge as a P-series

Neoplatonists do not have a theory of knowledge which can offer a description of knowing in terms of fixed and familiar concepts like necessity and probability, justification and conviction. This follows chiefly from their belief that knowledge is both an ideal at all levels of thought and present in varying forms at all levels. For it will not be a single type of phenomenon like a Platonic Idea, but a Neoplatonic series whose terms are unified only by their depending partially on the same first term. We know the structure of such a P-series. Knowledge will be one of the chains of being whose links are not identical, but which manifest supposedly perfect knowledge ever less perfectly as they are seen at ever lower stages. These degrees of knowledge will necessarily involve qualitative differences, for the form decreases by being diluted by other forms. In the sensible, or, to be exact, the sublunar world, these contrary forms can be described, as we saw in an earlier chapter, as the constraints of matter. But, like terms of a mathematical series, the terms of adjacent pairs are identically related, so that the pairs are analogous. For example, the *process* of perception is itself a section of the ascending *scale* of knowledge. In this process, the sense organs, being parts of our body, can receive only 'impressions' of the qualities of physical objects, while thought can grasp them only as 'presentations' (φαντασίαι). But the impressions stand to sense perception as the presentations stand to thoughts (Porphyry *Sententiae*, § 15). Of course this could be said of any two pairs of objects in so far as some relation can always be found to hold between the components of both pairs. But the relations required, and in fact named, by Neoplatonists were ones which were relevant to the nature of the series, in other words essential relational properties of it. Favourite instances in the case of knowledge were *correcting* and *being a criterion of* the lower term; for it is a distinguishing mark of a known proposition that it can correct and judge (as they said) the truth of other propositions on the same subject. This suggests a similar difficulty over identifying the series or set of terms itself. By what class concept do we recognize it? A number of answers can be given. One is to use one or more of the analogical relations. For if, with Platonic Ideas in mind, we desire something more intrinsic, we meet an obstacle similar to that made familiar by Wittgenstein: where an apparently single concept is really a collection of concepts united only by a family resemblance, any definition purporting to state a sufficient and necessary condition will at best be abstract and uninformative. But the Neoplatonic series has a crucial difference from such a collection. Its terms are ordered both in priority and value; and, on the Neoplatonists' principle that x is defined by x at its best, 'knowledge' will be understood—or so they believed—as the identity of a *nous* with the content of its thought. The remaining forms of knowledge can in theory be extrapolated by appropriate 'dilutions' of the component concepts, *nous*, thought and identity. Plotinus had this in mind when he said that knowing was possessing, and rejected representative perception on the grounds that it did not allow the object to be possessed, but only the sensations or impressions caused by the object.

By the same reasoning, we could start at the other end and, using the name of the lowest form, 'sensation', extrapolate by appropriate purifications—which is just what Proclus did in commenting on *Timaeus*, 33 C. This purification is the meaning of the 'stripping away' or abstraction, that is, of material constraints, which was a watchword of Porphyry's *Sententiae*. These constraints are proportionate, if not equivalent, to the weakening of the form in question; for the form is substance and activity, and anything weakening this activity is extrinsic and incidental to it, technically an affection. Preoccupied with 'the will', modern readers often misunderstand the protreptic use of the division between 'active' and 'passive'. In the Neoplatonists' analysis of perception this division seems often to be applied to the components, where some might have expected them to be divided into incorporeal and corporeal. In fact it is 'extrinsic and incidental' that underlies what is often translated 'passive' but is misleading if it obscures the connection with πάθη; and this holds just as much for the protreptic passages of the *Enneads* and *Sententiae*, since moral progress and intellectural progress are not independent.

The process of perception

There is a second and more direct reason why we cannot usefully apply the terms of the Cartesian tradition to Neoplatonists' epistemology. This is that their account of sense perception stitches together materials from Plato, from Aristotle, and from the Stoa. There is a surprising consensus about the amalgam to be found in a number of writers not confined to Neoplatonists.[1] It was to be repeated by Bishop Berkeley—to the disgust of William Blake, repelled by its emphasis on reason.[2] Its Neoplatonic character lies in its insistence that perception, like the rest of knowledge, forms a process with stages, where each stage not only attains greater truth but does so by correcting the previous stage. But it is best presented in the fullest versions, where it is incorporated in the whole ascent to pure intellect. Here, there are usually five steps.

In the first, which is named 'perception' ($a\emph{l}\sigma\theta\eta\sigma\iota\varsigma$), the soul, or loosely the sense organs, receive impressions from a physical object. They are called affections, are sensible qualities of the object, and are communicated to the rest of the soul. But this soul is aware of them as presentations ($\phi a \nu \tau a \sigma \iota a \iota$); so its faculty (power or activity, also called $\phi a \nu \tau a \sigma \iota a$) of making presentations out of impressions can count as the next step. This, however, is still only knowledge of the object's sensible qualities, which are normally accidents. To identify the object for the kind of thing it is, to know its substance or to know the whole which its qualities represent— we find all three descriptions—is a further step. It is achieved by matching the presentations against concepts which the soul already possesses and for which it has names; and it is called belief, or judgement ($\delta \delta \xi a$).

Here, authors are found diverging. The order of presentation including belief/judgement which I have just given is Ptolemy's, Proclus', and that of the Alexandrian anonymous *Prolegomena*. But Albinus' *Isagoge* and Porphyry's commentary on Ptolemy's *Harmonics* put belief/judgement first. (In this he is not following

---

[1] These include Albinus (or the author of the *Didascalicus*). But Cicero's *Lucullus* has a more Stoic, less Platonic version. Otherwise one might have suspected that Antiochus was the originator of this portion of the epistemology. Further details about the consensus of writers on perception are summarized in a note at the end of this section; and several are referred to in Beierwaltes (1975), Blumenthal (1975) and (1982), and Moutsopoulos (1985).

[2] Berkeley, *Siris*, § 303; Blake, *Annotations to Berkeley's 'Siris'*.

Ptolemy.) Since Plotinus' less systematic account in *Ennead*, IV. 4 seems not to distinguish the two functions, one might suppose that Neoplatonists regarded them as simultaneous, so that it was arbitrary which was mentioned first. But they believed them to have an epistemological order, one actually correcting the other. According to Porphyry a 'doxastic judgement' (δοξαστικὴ ὑπόληψις) receives a form from sense perception, names it, and inscribes it in language on the tablet of the soul, where it is a concept (ἔννοια). This is mostly quotation on his part, but he means, I think, that recognition involves, or at least ought to involve, the capability of verbalizing it. But presentation is not satisfied with such judgement, calculates the whole form of the object, and makes a real likeness of it. Historically, he is very close to Albinus; but both are following *Philebus* 38–9, where the presentations are said to be after the beliefs or judgements (39 B 6). The philosophical justification for giving the function of recognizing the object to judgement is that, like many modern philosophers, they believe that recognizing (to quote Albinus) is saying to ourselves, 'Socrates', 'a horse', and the like, which are concealed predications. Nevertheless, if Porphyry is doing more than repeating Plato he seems to have confused himself by the ambiguity of *doxa*. To say that presentation is dissatisfied with it is to assume that it is contrasted with knowledge, as it is in the Divided Line and elsewhere in Plato, as well as in Alexander. He should have claimed no more than that presentation accompanied judgement. As for the Proclan version, the term *doxa*, as well as its function of recognizing substance or essence (οὐσία) in place of sensible qualities, evidently depends on the central argument of the *Theaetetus* (186 A–187 C). This version puts presentation at the top of the non-thinking soul.

But the problem what a presentation is is a philosophical one and belongs to both versions. It was, of course, essential to Stoic epistemology, where it was an impression in the soul (although that can hardly be what the term meant, *pace* Long and Sedley's translation). What did Platonists say that they were? According to Albinus, they are objects of our perceptual judgements which are like artists' representations of a physical object and which the soul looks at in thought as it looked literally at the physical object. (Would it be unphilosophical to wonder whether much can be added to this?) He, or some handbook, is certainly following Alexander of Aphrodisias. Alexander does not make it clear whether the presentations are achieved with the object still in front of one; and this unclarity would be enough to explain the divergence about their position in the cognitive process. However that may be, he did fairly clearly identify them with sensory images, which according to him were the 'residue' of the physical impacts of objects on the sense organs.[3] And it is hard to suppose that Plotinus did not do the same; for he suggests that the representation or 'image as it were' of a thought, which commonly accompanies the thought and is needed for us to remember it, is possibly what in the twentieth century we might call the auditory image of the thought's verbal expression (IV, 3. 30). He does not believe, as Aristotelians did, that an image always accompanied thinking, only that when it did not we were not conscious of the thinking (ib.; cf. I. 4. 10; IV. 8. 8. 1–13). The possibility of unconscious thought seems to be restricted to the non-discursive intellect. But it only partly depends on his well-known but idiosyncratic theory that this intellect had not descended into the human soul and was not a faculty which belonged to it. It is even more to be explained by the belief that thought consists in a process which will mirror that of sense perception (*locc. citt.*) The same belief allows Proclus to write of presentations produced by 'impressions from above' (*In Timaeum*, III. 286. 20–287. 4).

For Boethius the presentations were simply the forms without the matter in the Peripatetics' definition of perception (*Consolatio*, V. 4. 84–6). This is clearly inadequate for their dogma that there is no thinking without images/presentations; and save for Plotinus Neoplatonists too accepted the dogma at the psychic level. Still less was it adequate for the function attributed to the faculty of 'presentation' or imagination of providing the matter and substrate of mathematics. But I shall not pursue it.

After the three stages of sensation, representation, and belief/judgement all our writers put scientific knowledge (ἐπιστήμη) and, all save Ptolemy (whom it did not interest), intuitive knowledge (νοῦς). If the Divided Line was thought of, it had long been absorbed by an Aristotelian line in which scientific knowledge was demonstration. In Proclus' chain it is called 'the science of proof', for it provided the explanation or cause which was missing from

---

[3] Fotinis (1979), 257 ff. claims that they were representations of *common* sensibles. If so that would be relevant to the function which Porphyry gives them. But what is Fotinis' evidence?

the mere categorical assertions of the previous stage. It was still, however, inferior to the intuitive knowledge of Intellect, because it was discursive. But, true to the principle of the higher containing in appropriate guise the lower, knowledge of the *totum simul* incorporated knowledge of the cause. We saw earlier the logico-metaphysical structure of this whole which contained potentially or 'occultly' the genera and species; and we saw how the concealed intermediate subgenera or superordinate species were also the middle terms in the syllogisms that demonstrated, i.e. explained, the properties of species. Epistemological problems about it I leave until later.[4]

Natural science. Canons

It is only mildly paradoxical that the continuity of the universal and ideal, its descent to the lowest levels of nature, should seem to rule out a rationalist epistemology. For, if rationalism is taken as the claim that nothing which is in the intellect was previously in the senses, it might seem to rule out knowledge of the substantial and accidental attributes which were possessed by physical objects and which Neoplatonists thought of as wholes in, that is dependent on, the parts, that is the particulars. This 'knowledge' is, of course, ambiguous. To know what the attributes were *per se* was the task

---

[4] *Consensus of writers on perception*: The texts I have chiefly had in mind are the following, not forgetting Plat., *Phileb.*, 38–9 and Ar., *Met. Λ* 1074^{b}33–6, who, however, omits representation. Al., *De an.*, 66. 9 ff, which gives the 'standard' version. Alb., *Isag.*, c. 4 Plot., IV. 4. 13, 19, and 22–3; I. 6. 3 *ad init.*, although the texts are not as systematic as the others and do not go above representation. Porph., *In Ptol. Harm.*, 13. 15–14.28 his stages are explicitly 'judgements of objects'. Ptol., *Harm.*, 95. 21 ff. and *On the criterion*, cc. 2 and 10: his *doxa* means superficial conjecture, not belief/judgement, for which he uses *dianoia*. Anon., *Prolegomona to Platonic philosophy*, 10. 31–43 (21–3 Westerink); where, at 10. 36, presentation knows 'what it is which is white', not (*pace* Westerink) 'what white is'; cf. Ar., *De an.*, 428^{b}21, 'error does not occur in perceiving that an object is white but in perceiving that the white object is (a) so and so'. This author calls scientific knowledge *dianoia*, which corrects/adds to belief/judgement. Procl., *In Tim.*, I 248–9; 342. 25–343. 15; III. 286; cf. *De prov.*, c. 43. 18–19 and *In Alc.*, 250. 7–8 for stages as a hierarchy of *elenchus*; *In Parm.*, 956. 37–957. 9 for *doxa* and τὸ λευκόν (= 'the white thing').

There is some ambiguity over ἔννοια/ἐννόημα in perception. If it is the concept, as in Porphyrian semantics or in Aristotle's 'experience', Platonists continued to regard this as a posteriori (e.g. Procl., *In Parm.*, 893, believing he had the authority of *Phaedr.*, 249 B).

of science or dialectic, and was therefore a priori: but a faculty commonly called belief/judgement could know *that* a given attribute was possessed by a given object, not type of object, and this does not seem to be known a priori. It must be repeated, however, that Neoplatonists would not even pose the question of rationalism or empiricism in traditional terms inasmuch as they repudiate a single notion of knowing.

They do, however, present an ambivalence in their attitude to the knowledge of nature. To know Reason we must first see it in Soul, and nature is the visible image of Soul. Yet

> This Life's dim Window of the Soul
> Distorts the Heavens from Pole to Pole
> And leads you to Believe a Lie
> When you see with, not thro', the Eye.

But although the *Theaetetus* finds a place in the eclectic theory of perception which we have been looking at, that theory is so tinged with Aristotle and the Stoa that it will not repel empiricists. And, concerning perception, the earlier and far from superficial controversies about scepticism had ceased by Plotinus' time to interest Platonists.

At the level of general statements, which is the scientific knowledge of nature, the Pythagorean programme of Iamblichus looked in theory to be tailored to Neoplatonism.[5] Physics and astronomy were in effect to be reduced to geometry and arithmetic respectively, and could therefore be known a priori. The hierarchy of the chain of being would be matched by that of the chain of knowing: numbers and figures were intermediate between the Ideas and sensible particulars, just as the planets whose motions exemplified them *par excellence* were intermediate between the celestial and the terrestrial. More generally, the adequacy of the subject-matter to mathematical description was ensured by, so to say, the a priori constitution of a physical object: Platonists agreed that a solid or 'body' was matter on which quantities were superimposed before qualities. This is the significance of their altering the order of Aristotle's categories when they lectured on logic.

But despite the lip-service or rhetoric of Ptolemy, who was even more Cartesian than Iamblichus in claiming, in the proëm to the

---

[5] See particularly *De comm. math. sci.*, cc. 23, 32, and 44. Cf. Simpl., *In Cat.*, 128. 5–129. 7 for Iamblichus on weight as quantity.

Almagest, that mathematics was superior to the uncertainty not of physics but of metaphysics, Iamblichus' programme was not subscribed to by philosophers. Neoplatonists insisted, to be sure, that mathematical numbers and figures were not abstracted from physical objects. But the qualities we find in physical objects were not *reducible* to them. There is a passage in Simplicius which compares the geometrical figures of the *Timaeus* to the hypotheses designed by the astronomers to save the appearances (*In De caelo,* 641).

As for hypotheses, S. Sambursky (1962, 54) claimed that Simplicius understood those constructed by scientists and recommended by the *Republic* simply as models for calculation and prediction. Indeed, Duhem had attributed this instrumentalist interpretation to the Imperial philosophers and scientists alike. The controversy about the status of hypotheses was certainly familiar at the time. But, while in general most of the scientists' views on it are unknown to us, G. E. R. Lloyd has shown in an important article (1978) that Geminus, Ptolemy, Proclus, Simplicius, and, probably, Philoponus all took a realist stand. I mention this because, as Lloyd also showed, their grounds were that the hypotheses were in theory physical models. That of Iamblichus' would in theory have been mathematical. Our writers were following the spirit if not the letter of Aristotle's estimate of astronomy (*Physics,* II 1 *ad init.*).

We are accustomed to the Platonists' habit of seeing degrees of knowledge as degrees of reality possessed by different types of objects known. When they are expounding science in Imperial times they seem more ready to grade them as types of general statement which approximate to what we should call laws. Such laws are frequently called 'canons'—the term applied by Plato and his early followers to the Ideas. The less metaphysical, more neutral term 'canon' is appropriate to an age of handbooks, abridgements and other forms of digested information, which would satisfy readers of any or no philosophical persuasion. For after about AD 200 we have predominantly an age of the *preservation* of knowledge.[6]

A study of the texts I extracted on the process from sensation to knowledge will show how most parts of most of them could be read as Stoic, Peripatetic, or Platonic doctrine. This was not their

[6] Cf. G. E. R. Lloyd (1973), 165–6.

authors' intention—for the assimilation of Alexander's *nous* to the Neoplatonic has already been decided on by Plotinus—but comes partly from agreement on the facts and partly from agreement on terminology, which obscured disagreement on the facts. Here are a few instances. The Stoic doctrine that the soul had no parts, or faculties, contradicted Plato: but it would not have seemed foreign to Neoplatonists, whose own doctrine was not only more profoundly, but accurately expressed by the formula that defined perception as the soul's outward activity and thought as its inward activity. Everyone knew that the Stoics were materialists: but at the non-reductionist level of psychology the function of presentations could reasonably be understood by both schools as the same. While this would be debatable in the case of ἔννοια, the term, widely used in our texts, and still more Albinus' φυσικὴ ἔννοια were Stoic technical terms. At a higher cognitive level admirers of the *Meno* and the *Republic* would have been at home with the Peripatetic versions of scientific knowledge such as Alexander's, which gave knowledge of the 'cause'—Plato's *logos*, they would have said—as one of its definitions.

This feature, which would be more properly described as syncretism than as eclecticism, was due less to its appeal to a mixed audience than to the fact that it represented the actual practice of scientists. For it could be seen as judiciously blending a posteriori and a priori methods. This is particularly evident in Ptolemy's unoriginal but competent book *On the Criterion*.[7] At the stage in the cognitive process which is equivalent to belief/judgement he simply avoided the choice between rationalism and empiricism: he said that thought tested and corrected the data from the senses either by further use of its agents or instruments, the senses, or, more often, by appealing to its own rational knowledge of the classification of objects (c. 10; cf. p. 16. 19–20). It is unclear, however, whether this classification is not inductive so that, although it is counted as scientific knowledge, it would be a priori only relatively to the observations (see c. 12). But this, I think, is the point. What Ptolemy noticed, and restricted his epistemological interest to, was that theory can take precedence over observa-

---

[7] I agree so closely with A. A. Long's (1988) assessment that I would not care to estimate how much or perhaps how little of it I reached independently. I differ, however, over the a priori element in Ptolemy's epistemology that I have called only relative.

tion.[8] In fact more than one modern expert has argued that he allowed it to provide his readers with additional 'observations' which went beyond the bounds of professional ethics.

In the introduction to his *Harmonics* he compares the musical interval which the ear distinguishes with the circle which we see and whose exact nature is 'constructed by reason'. Reason is represented by the 'rational hypotheses' of the Harmonic Canon, which correspond to the astronomer's 'hypotheses about celestial movements'. But in both cases the hypotheses will agree with 'the sensory observations according to the judgement of the majority'; and the reason for this agreement is that they are derived from phenomena which are quite evident (ἐναργῶν)—but made more accurate by reason (5. 10 ff.). It is true that this work may be a compilation from Didymus, as Porphyry rather suggests (*In Ptolemaei Harmonica*, 3). But it is still worth noticing an implication here which has (I think) escaped notice: this is the identification of the scientist's task as that of saving the (rational) hypotheses not the (sensory) appearances (cf. *Harmonica*, 10).

All this is probably as reasonable a practical description of most scientific method as it is an inadequate philosophical contribution to the empiricist–rationalist quarrel. It owes its practicality to the shift from concepts, whether innate or inductive, to general law. Some of these laws were treated like axioms or very general rules, and it is these, or more often the set of them, that it became fashionable to call 'canons'. It is a normative term in so far as the members of the set determine the validity or invalidity of the scientist's inferences. Less attention was paid to distinguishing empirical and non-empirical sciences than in modern traditions; and the Aristotelian element in the syncretism diluted the distinction in the case of the laws themselves. A canon played the same part in music—where we have seen it represent reason—in logic, and in syntax.[9] Logic, in which the term had become technical for the Stoa, and syntax used the normative notion of 'consequentiality'

[8] As it did sometimes in his own optics. Cf. G. E. R. Lloyd (1973), 135.

[9] When they became increasingly associated with 'encyclopaedic' education, Platonists saw 'canons' as the methodology of a 'unified science': cf. Synes., *Ad Paeorium*, IV–V (*Opuscula* 140–1 Terzaghi); Psellus, 'Reply to Andronicus', in *De op. daem.* 159–61 Boissonade. In logic they used 'canons' as a jargon term for formal logic, i.e. 'terms without the things' (Olympiod?, *Prolegomena to Logical Theory*, 4, *CAG* XII/1, 14–18). The *word* is not of course new, especially in logic, where it had been used by Epicureans and Stoics.

(ἀκολουθία) to underlie the notions of validity and grammaticality respectively. But it is a notion which confirmed the syncretistic position, because it might be regarded either as a matter of value, when it corresponds to 'acceptable', or as a matter of observation, when it corresponds to 'accepted'. In Apollonius Dyscolus' syntax the Canon, again representing reason, is explained by analogy (καταλληλότης); and the later definition of this which became traditional was συμπλοκὴ λόγων ἀκολουθῶν. One grammarian reveals its function of justifying inference by calling it the 'demonstrative canon' (cf. Blank, 1982, 25 ff.). But the tautological character of *explanation* by such canons should not be played down: an 'analogous' construction commonly means a 'regular' construction, just as a conclusion which is 'consequential' is 'one which follows'.

In the process from perception to knowledge each stage represented a correction of the stage before it. But Neoplatonic theory dictated that, unlike entries in a scientist's record, the stages are not plain contradictions of the previous ones. If that were the case, one of them would not have been an instance or participant of knowledge; and they would not have been, as the theory assumed that they were, part of the P-series. Canons too were used to correct rather than deny judgements as they were propounded. We may therefore ask whether epistemological progress was not towards exactitude rather than truth. This is how Neoplatonists often described it. The point can be purely verbal, since we can use 'true' and 'exact' to mean 'corresponding to the state of affairs' and have the additional use of 'more exact' to mean 'more completely corresponding to the state of affairs' where 'more true' would be less acceptable. But while this fits the standard case of visible circles or straight lines, which Platonists called inexact copies of mathematical circles and straight lines, 'exact' had for them also the Cartesian connotation of 'clear and distinct', in effect the logician's 'well defined'. Again 'inexact' propositions included those which were not permanently true, on account of changing states of affairs, and those which were less explained (or explicable), because the state of affairs contained more brute fact.[10]

---

[10] Cf. A. E. Taylor (1926), 450, on the 'element of the given ... which Timaeus appears to be personifying in his language about Necessity'.

Ptolemy writes in his *Harmonica*:

Criteria of harmony are sound and reason (*logos*), sound by way of the matter and the affection, reason by way of the form and cause. For the senses discover what is approximate while receiving what is exact, and reason conversely. Form determines and completes matter, the causes of change and movement determine and complete the affections. It follows that the rational cognitions determine and complete the sensory cognitions, which receive the initial distinctions in a more rough and ready way and are then conducted by the rational to the exact and agreed distinctions. This is because reason is simple or unmixed, and therefore self-sufficient and identical in identical relations, while sensation is accompanied by matter and always in a state of flux, so that it cannot be guaranteed to be that of everyone or to be identical in the case of identical objects: it needs reason like a tutor's attendance.

Thus a circle constructed only by sight can often seem exact until the one constructed by reason conducts sight to the knowledge of the really exact one. And in the same way some determinate distinction [i.e. interval] of sounds may seem at first, if it is grasped only by hearing, to be neither less nor more than it should be: but if it is compared with the interval required by the appropriate 'reason' or theory (τὸν οἰκεῖον λόγον) it will often be exposed (ἀπελεγχθήσεται) as not the genuine one. (3. 1–47, slightly abbreviated)

He continues that the instrument corresponding to the ruler and compass is 'in the accepted nomenclature' the Harmonic Canon (5. 11–12).

Commenting on Plato's remark that exposition takes its character from what it is expounding, Proclus gives us the Neoplatonic version, in which the 'criteria' are not propositional canons but reified concepts and Ideas.

When we are content with an account which is not exact but approximate, are we not falling short of exactitude (it might be asked) owing to our weakness, not to the character of the subject? Rather, when we are not starting from perception but from universal propositions, in an account of perceptible objects propositions about the heavens will stand out as exact and incontrovertible, but in a context of scientific knowledge these too are subject to correction by means of the matterless forms . . .

Speaking generally, just as what we say about intelligible objects does not fit the objects of discursive thinking, so what we say about the objects of scientific knowledge does not fit perceptible objects. For the intelligible objects are the models of those of discursive thinking and these in turn of the perceptible. (*In Timaeum*, I. 349. 6–28)

But, as we shall find shortly, Proclus believes that our weakness does contribute to the shortcoming of our knowledge, and that our strength can overcome the shortcoming of the subject-matter.

Sensation as obscure thinking

Meanwhile, we can already see how he is committed to the rationalist thesis that sense perception is dim, or confused, thought. (The traditional 'confused' means the contrary of 'clear and distinct'.) Adding that thoughts were clear sensations, Plotinus had used the thesis to dismiss the question whether there was a faculty of sensation in Intellect (VI. 7. 7). Influenced by Stoicism and anxious to avoid any passive affection on the part of soul, he had said that perceptions were judgements, meaning not mere discriminations but propositions (e.g. III. 6. 1. ad init.). This might seem to be close to a modern anti-Cartesian theory which (roughly) makes seeing white a belief, resulting from using the eyes, that something is white. But it is no more than close; for, in spite of being anxious also to avoid representative perception, he maintained that the judgements were *about* the effects of the object on the body. The thesis of confused thinking implies and is implied by the account of perception which made thinking a stage of it: for one is prevented from saying 'the stage which completes or perfects it' only by having to add that the thinking has to be completed by scientific knowledge, and scientific knowledge by non-discursive awareness. Correlative with this psychological and epistemological reason for the thesis there is the metaphysical reason. What we perceive through the senses are first the qualities which physical objects possess and then the objects as types; but each of these are images, the first being images of the inseparable forms in matter, the second being these forms themselves, which are in turn images of the separate forms (or Platonic Ideas). And for Plotinus these images—which are, in one of his uses of the term, *logoi*—are thoughts.

We find his position in a nutshell when he states that it is impressions that we are aware of—'but by then they are intelligible objects' (1. 7. 11–12). Does not this imply that, since sensation is conceptually completed by belief, and belief by knowledge, perception of the physical world will result of itself in knowledge? Will not knowledge be the automatic end of a process, in the way that Aristotle and the Stoics thought of action as the automatic end of a process consisting of judgements, images, and desire or impulse? No, for the process which results in action is causal rather than conceptual; and, apart from that, what completes a conceptual process is (in the following sense) neither causally nor logically necessary. The conceptual completion of the process called 'growing up' from childhood to adolescence and from adolescence to adulthood is being an adult; but some children never become adolescents and some adolescents never become adults. On the other hand, calling a child a child usually implies that he is in process of growing up, so that although failing to reach adolescence is contrary neither to logical nor to causal laws it may be thought 'unnatural' and even undesirable. Different examples can easily be imagined in which the completion is not even usual, but still ideal. These will of course be the ones in which a complete x is valued more highly, or rather is more valuable than an incomplete x; and 'complete' is relative to a given process.

This is how Neoplatonists thought of the stages in the epistemological progress from sensation to non-discursive awareness.

In his *Timaeus* commentary Proclus said that the obscurity which is seen in the unreliability of descriptions of the sensible phenomena come only from the obscurity of the phenomena. But, still tied to the text, he abruptly changed tack and allowed that our weakness as humans restricts us to probabilities, because we are compelled to use our senses and instruments—living on earth, astronomers are a long way from the planets! 'We must be charitable to human nature' (I. 351. 15–352. 5; 352. 27–353. 29). The reader must not, however, be too romantic about this. Sambursky for one has exaggerated a pessimism which he attributes to Proclus because he quite mistakenly attributes to him a 'theological belief that matter is evil'.[11] Proclus in fact agreed with Ptolemy that the obstacle to a satisfactory explanation of the planetary phenomena was their complication; and by and large both denied that they contained irregularities. But it must not be forgotten that the difference between the supra-lunar and sublunar spheres was an integral part of Neoplatonism; it belonged to the great chain of

[11] 'As against Plato's qualified optimism, Proclus' doctrine displays a definite pessimism which is determined by the philosophy of his era and by the theological belief that matter is evil. On the scientific plane, this evil is identified with the irrational' (1965, 10).

being. In that part of his work which attacks the difference, Philoponus is no more a Neoplatonist than Epicurus or Chrysippus. As for the purely contingent sublunar world, Proclus recognizes only Aristotle's 'for the most part' (loc. cit. 353. 1–3). But he does not make it clear whether this imperfection is due to the intrinsic unreliability of the material world as well as to the limitations of the observer.

In short, the imperfection of his level of knowledge does not entail that the human observer will attain the more perfect ones, but it entails that he can attain them. In the *Timaeus* commentary Proclus avoids pursuing this capability, because it is not found in the *Timaeus*. After all, he implies, the man who did have *knowledge* of the sensible world would be transcending his *human* condition.

Iamblichus' principle of knowing. Future contingents

So much for limitations on our knowledge of the world about us. But divine knowledge of it was a traditional problem which was theoretically more pressing in a universe peopled with suprahuman entities. On this Proclus tells us that

the gods know the generated ungeneratedly, the extended unextendedly, the divided undividedly, the temporal eternally, and the contingent necessarily. For they generate all things by thinking alone, and what they generate they generate from the indivisible, eternal matterless forms; therefore they must think of them in that manner. We cannot suppose that in each case their knowing takes on the character of its object . . . (*In Timaeum*, I. 352. 5–12)

So we have an epistemological principle which is more general than a distinction between divine and human.

Instead, the differences between knowers alters the manner of their knowing: the same thing is known as one by God, as a whole by Intellect, as a universal by discursive thought, as a shape by representation, as an affection by sensation. Because what is known is a single thing it does not follow that there is single knowing of it[12]

In fact Proclus infers the principle from the more general law that everything acts according to its nature and grade in the scale

---

[12] Procl., loc. cit., ll. 15–19; so also *De prov.*, c. 64; *ET* 124; Boeth., *Cons.*, v. 6 *ad init.* (omne quod scitur non ex sua sed ex comprehendentium natura cognoscitur).

of being (*In Parmenidem*, 956); and this is virtually analytic, since the grades are not like houses which can be identified independently of their occupants. Its epistemological version which has just been quoted I shall refer to for brevity as Iamblichus' principle of knowing. (He is credited with it by Ammonius, *In De interpretatione*, 135. 14.) The reader will be aware that it was—and still is—used to allow human affairs to be known by God; for it was commonly, though not universally, assumed that knowledge of them was necessary for the exercise of his providence. But it has a quite distinct implication for the range of knowledge open to humans. For at whatever level the gods have this knowledge, provided that the human soul reaches that level in its ascent it will share their knowledge. This is significant, not just for the acquisition of new knowledge, but for a factor which has, I think, been neglected, namely the preservation of former knowledge.

The problem fell into two parts. How could gods be aware of particulars, whether events, things, or persons, when at the lowest their cognition was intellectual and its objects therefore universal? Secondly, how could they entertain future contingent propositions when divine knowledge is of timeless necessary truths? This second point can be dealt with summarily. Not that it is of minor importance, for it was believed that freedom of choice, and hence morality, depended on its solution. But the appeal that was made to Iamblichus' principle in solving it was for the most part superfluous or muddled; its connection with Neoplatonism is only historical.

As we can see in Ammonius' commentary on *De interpretatione* ch. 9, this problem of future contingents is complicated by the denial of the law of excluded middle in respect of them. Here, Iamblichus' principle is invoked in order to claim that such 'indeterminate' propositions can be known *sub specie aeternitatis* determinately, i.e. with a determinate truth-value. Ammonius has no argument for this unless he takes it to be an argument that the propositions are not then tensed (see his commentary p. 136). But given this, together with the unquestionable fact that an indeterminate proposition can be necessary, he is justified in claiming that (1) the gods' knowledge of the outcome of what is contingent does not make that outcome necessary; and (2) the case is rather that because the contingent will turn out this way or that it is necessary that the gods know which way it will turn out; so (3) the contingent remains the same in its own nature but no longer indeterminate in its knowledge by the gods (136. 25–137. 1). It is noticeable that he does not deal with the more familiar problem why being known does not make a contingent proposition necessary. Every student of logic is aware that it is solved by reading

if p is known, p must be true

not as

p is known $\rightarrow \Box p$

but only as a *necessitas consequentiae*:

$\Box$ (p is known $\rightarrow p$)

But we know that he taught very clearly the distinction between this kind of necessity and that of a proposition on its own, which he described as a *de re* necessity (*In Analytica priora*, 29. 30–4), and it is unlikely that he did not recognize its application here. Boethius did, though only under the Aristotelian names of 'simple' (or 'absolute') and 'conditional' (*Consolatio*, v. 6. 100–5 and 110 ff.). But, equally, he may have thought the distinction of doubtful use here, for he would certainly have held that

p is known by gods $\rightarrow \Box$ (p is known by gods)

since whatever gods do they do necessarily.[13]

That the future as such is contained in the eternal, and therefore accessible to gods was suggested in Ammonius' *De interpretatione* commentary, but it is explicit in Boethius (*Consolatio*, v. 6). It is, of course, believed by all Neoplatonists that eternity is the paradigm of time, and as such it contains it in an occult form. To complain that in an eternal now, 'will be' cannot have the character it has in a framework of time is legitimate and philosophically interesting.[14] But to the extent that Boethius is taking a Neoplatonist position it cuts no ice; there would be something more radically

---

[13] Prior (1962) and more specifically (1967), ch. 7 has examined some ancient and modern versions of the logic involved.

[14] Cf. W. Kneale (1961).

wrong with his position if it were not the case. I think that when it is realized what Iamblichus' principle does *not* mean, it will be realized that it would be better to complain that 'knowing' cannot have the character it has in time. I shall leave the subject of the future altogether, remarking only that the knowledge of it which is appropriate to eternal knowers follows in theory the same rationale as all applications of Iamblichus' principle.

Boethius relies on the principle (loc. cit., *ad init.*). But we can find the rationale best in Proclus, although his exposition is not one of his most perspicuous and assumes a good deal of technical knowledge on the part of his reader. He describes the objects of our awareness as things, whether concrete or abstract, not events or propositions . . . But let us first be clear what Iamblichus' principle means. At the cost of repetition we must recall the crucial notion of an immediate object of thought, regarded by Neoplatonists as itself mental, by means of which we think of something else, mental or non-mental; in semantic theory we saw it as the 'concept'. Greek philosophers could recognize it (or suppose they did) since it could be named by the grammatical object, in an 'internal accusative', of the verb 'to think', which is not possible in English. It is this object, which is more like the content than the object of thought, that I shall call the *internal object*. There is a scholastic terminology for all this, but it has largely fallen into disuse.

In Iamblichus' principle of knowing, knowing a sensible object (or objects) *X* intellectually does not mean knowing the intelligible object *X*, for *ex hypothesi X* is not an intelligible object but a sensible one. It means being directly aware of an intelligible object *Y*, i.e. having as an internal object of thinking an intelligible object *Y*, where being aware of *Y* is a means of, and entails, knowing *X*. Suppose that *X* is something white: I know it or—shall we say?—cognize it, intellectually when I judge that it is white, for I employ the concept white to do so. If I see it as white, I cognize it sensibly, for I employ the sense impression to do so. (The example, which was used by Neoplatonists for elementary exposition, may, of course, be an empty one if their theory of sense-perception required seeing something as white to include seeing that it is white, and so required the cognition to be at least half intellectual.) One could say that in one case the internal object is a thought and in the other case a sight, but that the thought is the thought *of* the same thing that the sight is *of*. To describe what either is of is to

describe what the other is of. But the descriptions are not necessarily the same: in fact the descriptions warranted by two cognitions in modes, or levels, farther removed from one another than
sight and judgement will be different, since the cognitions will be
coloured by different internal objects.

Thus the adverbs 'intellectually' and the like, which distinguish
the knowing as opposed to the known, indicate the type of internal
object, and this is equivalent to indicating the level of knowing.
'Everything thinks as it is, and it is as it thinks', says Proclus
(*Decem dubitationes*, 1 § 3. 24–6 Isaac). But that function in this
context is not to modify the knowing as an event in the way that
'painfully' does, not as a proposition in the way that 'necessarily'
does. For this reason it was misleading of Proclus to treat
Iamblichus' principle of knowing as just a principle of any activity.
It depends on the presence of the intentionality that is involved in
the notion of internal objects. It is only when these are left out that
readers of the Neoplatonists are liable to expect time or life or their
wives 'known eternally' to look like time or life or their wives
known temporally.

Some may be inclined to make the opposite mistake. Recognizing that every kind of thing differs qualitatively as an intelligible
object from what it is as an object of *logos*, or discursive thought,
and again from what it is as a sensible object, they may suppose that
knowing something intellectually is simply knowing its intelligible
form, and knowing it sensibly is knowing its sensible form. In one
respect it will be the same object, because that is how one kind of
thing manifests itself 'appropriately'; in another respect it will not
be the same, because as a kind or form descends, its resemblance
to its archetype becomes increasingly partial. It might therefore be
inferred that to know perceptible humans intellectually is to know
them, but with a significant qualification. This mistake is just what
Iamblichus' principle intended to deny. According to my analysis,
it confuses the internal object with the object, or what the knowledge is of. It might well have been shared by students of
Ammonius' *De interpretatione*. For, in spite of depending on
Proclan texts to expound the principle, he apparently includes
under it the rational knowledge of particular actions which consists
in bringing them under universals. This would not fit the requirement that to describe what the two internal objects are of should
identify the same object. The description of the general notion,

revenge, is not a description of the particular notion, Medea murdering her children, because it omits too much, and that of the notion, Medea murdering her children, is not that of the notion revenge, because it omits too little.

How henads, not intellects, know particulars. The accidental

So much for the meaning of the principle. Proclus' explanation how it enables gods to know particulars presupposes only the structure of Athenian Neoplatonism. He holds without prevarication that knowledge of universals does not entail even potential knowledge of the particulars under them. This is the case with the participated as well as with the unparticipated universals, while it would not be the case for knowledge of genera and knowledge of species, which is, of course entailed. But, whatever has sometimes been maintained about Aristotle or about the Tree of Porphyry, Proclus admits no analogous reduction of species to individuals. But he says that the demiurgic Ideas, which are only intelligible universals and their intellectual subordinates, have 'taken on' providence concerning human affairs. Does not that imply that the requirement of knowledge for providence has been dropped? No, it implies that their knowledge extends only as far as genera and species; at most their care is for the human race not for each person.[15] This restriction on knowledge can be invalidated only by postulating that there are Ideas of individuals; and Proclus will have none of them.[16] Does this imply that even the gods' omniscience does not extend to particulars? No, for the gods who need it because they exercise providence over particulars are above Intellect.

What makes it possible for henads to know sensible individuals when intellects cannot? Here, the elements of the answer are not new. Because of the structure of procession and participation, every entity is contained in the entity from which it proceeded and in which it participates, as the effect is contained in the cause. Only, since to descend is to be altered, it is not found there as it exists for itself ($\kappa\alpha\theta$' $\H{\upsilon}\pi\alpha\rho\xi\iota\nu$) but only as appropriate to the cause of itself ($\kappa\alpha\tau$'

---

[15] *In Parm.*, 951. 36–953. 1. Cf. 959. 11 ff., where the knowledge corresponding to the agency of the pure Intellect and of our intellect is described.

[16] *PT*, I. 21. 98. 16–19; *In Parm.*, 824. 12–825. 9. Cf. Trouillard (1982) 155–6.

αἰτίαν).[17] (To take a very simple Plotinian example, place in the sensible world is the product of the abstract 'being in something else' in Intellect. See v. 9. 10.) It is the product's occult existence. But when the causes are henads it will be occult in the additional, non-relative sense; it will be hidden from any knowledge save analogical inference from its effect, for it is beyond existence and consequently beyond anything that our minds can conceive (cf. *Platonic Theology*, III. 25 *ad init.*).

The only way in which to know such causes directly would be to be a henad. I say nothing yet about the possibility of that for a human soul. The reason why things—to be accurate, self-subsistent things—are aware of that which they contain is that they spontaneously revert or have reverted to themselves. For this reversion is activity directed towards themselves—the preservation of their real selves in fact—and the activity of intellects and souls, below which the question does not arise, is *par excellence* awareness.[18] It will be remembered how in fact it is their internal activity in contrast with the external activity of procession.[19] And now see its connection with our epistemological problem.

Reversion is two-fold, one towards the good, one towards existence; that which falls under life makes all things revert towards the good, that which falls under knowledge towards existence. Consequently the soul that has reverted in the one case is said to possess the good, in the other the existence to which it belonged; 'being truthful' is the apprehension of existence or what is, whether this is contained within that which has grasped it or is prior to it or posterior to it. (*In Tim.*, II. 287. 5–288. 11)

The important word is 'possess' (ἔχειν). For a Neoplatonist it represents not so much the limiting case of what he calls knowledge but the ideal case.

Finally, we come to the reason why henads' knowledge extends to sensible particulars and even to things 'contrary to nature', whose 'existence' is sometimes qualified by being called '*parhypostasis*'. Since the origin of *everything* is the One, its participated form, the henads, will contain occultly everything. (Similarly,

---

[17] See chiefly *ET* 65, where the ἔστιν of the theorem is existential as at l. 21. It is as unfortunate as it is surprising that Dodds was all at sea here because, failing throughout his edition to recognize that ὕπαρξις is in Imperial philosophy normal Greek for 'existence', he believed that it had to do with Aristotle's 'inherence'.

[18] Cf. *ET*, 83; *In Alcib.*, 20.

[19] *In Parm.*, 791. 17–18; *PT.*, v. 18. 283–4 Portus.

when the One is understood as the Good, the smaller its trace in some object the more evil by definition the object; but Proclus argues at length that the completely evil is not even a parahypostasis but an empty concept.) This represents a straightforward instance of the Proclan rule that the higher the starting point of a chain the greater its descent. 'The One is everywhere', as he puts it in our context, 'but the whole'—that is the genera and species of Intellect—'is not everywhere' (*Platonic Theology*, I. 21. 98. 25–6).[20] We saw in an earlier chapter how matter, in a complicated way, could be reduced not only to otherness but to positive factors, in particular the composition of causes. It is in keeping with this that Neoplatonists tend to distinguish sensible individuals by their accidents rather than by matter. So as to complete the picture of knowledge by causes, and fit accidents into the causal chains which descend from the henads, we ought to ask where accidents come from. Proclus' answer is to repeat Plotinus' account quite closely, although he does not mention him. It is part of his survey of things of which there are not Ideas—a survey obviously dependent on *Enneads*, v. 9. 9–12. He begins (*In Parmenidem*, 826. 27 ff.) by saying that the composition of bodies is an insufficient explanation of accidents, meaning, I think, a Stoic or Peripatetic reduction of accidents to combinations of the elements. (These would be the 'temperaments' used to explain differences of character in humans.) Being 'in a subject' they are, as I have repeatedly stressed, particular; so they cannot come from Intellect, which provides only the substantial and universal. Nevertheless, there is

---

[20] *Henadic knowledge: stumbling blocks for Proclus' readers*: (1) Many expressions (such as 'sensible objects') can refer to the individuals or to the species; e.g. 'last division' at *X dub.*, § 10. 20 does mean individuals, while the 'multiplicity' of *In Parm.*, 959. 16 does not. A key passage, *In Tim.*, I. 351. 20–353. 10, could be taken to imply divine knowledge of human affairs without knowledge of individual creatures or events: but N.B. 351. 24 and 27–9, 352. 8. Individuals are explicitly mentioned e.g. at *PT.*, I. 21. 98. 10–12 with S.–W. ad loc.; *X dub.*, § 5. 31–3; *In Parm.*, 958. (2) There is a providence in each diacosm. *In Tim.* for example is concerned with it at intellectual and intelligible levels, not henadic. (3) Similarly, 'gods' are normally henads at any level. 'The one' must not be expected to indicate the One, but more likely the relevant 'first' or *per se* henad. e.g. after solar light, (solar) intellect and soul have been rejected as the source of the series, Light, 'there is left only the one' (*In Parm.*, 1044. 26–7), which is 'the henad of henads' (i.e. of the rest of the series, 1045. 1). Cf. 1048 *ad init.*; *In Tim.*, III. 72. 29–30. (4) Proclus' nearly systematic names for the modes of knowing appropriate to each hypostasis are (i) ἑνιαίως ('henadically) ~ Henads, (ii) ὁλικῶς ('holistically', not 'universally') ~ Intellect, (iii) καθολικῶς ('universally') ~ *Logos*/discursive intellect.

a form that they have in physical bodies, and this 'comes from within Nature—not, however, in accordance with any distinct intellectual cause'. Nature has in fact received from Intellect the forms of physical attributes—but 'undivided' (into individuals, I take it). She has her own power of dividing and uses it to 'unfold' the forms by separating the substantial from the accidental among them. Proclus emphasizes that all this takes place 'according to the *logos* of descent' but at the lowest level of it.

On the surface, his account has not much philosophical significance. But what it implies has more. To understand it, one needs to have in mind Plotinus' version, which was integral to what I called his radical criticism of the Aristotelian notion of substance. As a comparison with *Enneads* II. 6. 3 will show, the separation which Proclus says Nature makes of the substantial and the accidental is the separation which Plotinus said the *logos* makes of substance and its activity so as to produce a so-called quality. To recall Plotinus' summary, the head (specific form) of fire is its activity; separated by Nature it is the quality (accident) of physical bodies, which are not substances at all—for these have been lost in the 'separation'—but matter and bundles of qualities.

As a quality it has been taken on its own and in something else where it is no longer form or shape of substance but a mere trace or shadow or image; it can be a quality by abandoning its own substance, of which it was the activity. (II. 6. 3. 16–20)

But his inferences concerning Aristotelian substance are not pursued in this context by Proclus.

According to Plotinus, accidents will have intellectual archetypes inasmuch as they derive from the substantial activities, although the derivation is not within Intellect; it is only things contrary to nature which do not have such paradigms (v. 9. 10 *ad init.*). According to Proclus, neither these nor accidents (save normative ones like health) have paradigms. But he too referred, as we have seen, to Nature separating accidents from or among the forms she received as they proceeded (827. 5–7). Even if 'proceeded' means only proceeded to species, there is clearly a problem. He assumes, one may suppose, that the power of Intellect fades out by the time that it reaches the numerically indefinite instances of accidents. On the other hand, the Proclan Rule leaves them participating in henads. That the henadic gods are their ultimate causes is entailed by the gods' knowing 'henadically' sensible individuals and therefore accidents.

This is a metaphysical problem about the generation of the accidental in general, and his solution must be considered uncertain. How a given individual is caused is a concrete question. And Proclus rightly gives a concrete answer. It confirms our description of descent, and even of matter, as multiplication of causes. Proclus dismisses almost impatiently the question what replaces the generation of individuals by a paradigmatic cause:

If one is to name one cause, then the order of the universe; or if one is to name several, the movement of the heavens, particular types of nature, the properties of the seasons, climates, as well as those who superintend all these . . . (825. 13–17)

But it seems that we must accept a leap in the causal chain from Henads to Soul and Nature.

7

MYSTICISM AND
METAPHYSICS

Pure Intellect in Plotinus

There is a divergence between Proclus and Plotinus on the mode
of knowing which is found in pure or non-discursive intellect. It is
not immediately apparent, and it may cause difficulty for anyone
who comes to read the one philosopher through the spectacles of
the other. Nor does it belong solely to the history of Neoplatonism:
it will bring us to the question of the value of knowledge and the
question of the limits of mystical knowledge in Neoplatonism.

In his tract *On Dialectic* Plotinus envisages three cognitive stages
for the soul: (1) its reception and judgement of sense percepts, (2)
collection and division of universals, or 'intelligible objects', (3)
simple 'seeing' and tranquility, when it has reached its origin and
become a unity (1. 3. 4). (2) can be recognized as the activity of the
intellect in the soul, commonly called 'scientific knowledge' (cf. v.
9. 7. 5–6), while in (3) the soul has identified itself with the undescended and non-discursive intellect. So far so good. But he now
puts himself in a certain muddle about the place of dialectic in the
education and ascent of the philosopher's soul. For, if it is not
philosophy, it is, as Plato taught, the most valuable part (not
instrument) of philosophy. It is also logic, but formal logic as
practised by Peripatetics and Stoics concerned only with propositions and words. To avoid this (by the standard move which we saw
in the logical commentaries), he says that his logic will move from
the theorems and terms to the real things that they are about, in
other words the values of the variables (1. 3. 5). On the other hand,
to be the most valuable part of philosophy it will have to be the
'wisdom' which can belong only to another intellect, the undescended intellect which sees all that is as a *totum simul*. This we read in the
tract *On Intelligible Beauty*; and its immediate sequel v. 5. 1 shows
that we are dealing with the same scheme of the philosophical

ascent, when it tells us that this wisdom dispenses with propositions. Elsewhere he calls it 'true science', so as to distinguish it from the 'science' which is the discursive knowledge or classification of the Ideas. The upshot is that the two meanings of 'dialectic' will apply one to the collection and division of the Ideas usually named 'scientific knowledge' and the other to their apprehension as a *totum simul*.

This second type of dialectic is non-discursive by ruling out not just inference but the transition from subject to predicate and definiendum to definiens. Indeed, it rules out langauge itself; it consists of the Ideas, which are, of course, thoughts, not the Ideas *and* knowledge of them. This is already implied by the thesis that they are not outside Intellect, for it implies that as they really are they are not prior to knowledge, and it is as they really are that the undescended Intellect presents them.[1]

To be non-propositional, this whole has to be undifferentiated, but to be Existence and to be thought, it has to be differentiated. This is possible on two suppositions: first, that it occupies the place of the genus of existence or being; and secondly, that its non-complexity belongs to it as a phenomenological or intentional object while its complexity belongs to it as an extensional object or *in fact*. *Enneads*, VI. 5. 5 provides good evidence that it is generic Existence. It is regularly called 'the all' in this tract, and it is not really distinguished from the Living Creature (which Plotinus says 'is all things because complete Existence/Being belongs to it, VI. 7. 12. 3–4; so too VI. 7. 36. 12). He compares it there to a circle whose spatial dimensions are infinitely diminished, so that its radii, standing for the 'parts' of Existence, contract to a single point, the centre, standing for Existence as an 'intelligible nature', or form. And its function as a Platonic universal appears when he compares it to the Idea of man by virtue of which all men share humanity. To think of the species of a generic form, even simultaneously, is to diminish oneself (VI. 7. 33. 8–9). But undivided into species it must be an internal object in the narrower sense of being only an intentional object. It is what the soul sees when it is united to the pure Intellect, but what it is looking at is divided (cf. V. 17. 36. 12). The division is a property of Existence which no amount of dialectical or mystical ascent can make it lose. Does not this imply a

---

[1] I have aimed at a fuller justification of the paragraphs on the nature of non-discursive Intellect in my article (1986).

certain subjectivity, even illusion, about the non-discursive thinking? No, for it is not the soul's thinking that makes it thus, but that of pure Intellect. Or rather, it is the self-thinking of Intellect and the self-thinking of Existence, which is more really what they are than when they are divided. But their division is also a fact because procession is real: but what it proceeds to, the parts of the whole, are less real. If this implies a paradox, we are by now at home with it, for it is simply the claim that it is the nature of reality to contain the less real.

We can thus, I hope, understand Plotinus' remark that when our knowledge is that of pure Intellect, 'we feel as if we know nothing' when really we are 'most of all in a state of knowing' (v. 8. 11. 33–4). For the extensional view, with which we are more familiar, of the whole together with its parts, he also recognizes—not as false, but as how an observer sees it from the outside instead of becoming (*sic*) what he sees (vi. 7. 15 *ad fin.*).

Certainly the (Neoplatonic) genus which contains its species only latently—still more the genus of all genera—cannot possibly be covered by a phenomenological description. It can at most be a mystical experience with the addition of an inference to identify the experience. *How There Is a Multiplicity of Ideas* (vi. 7) goes the closest to a concrete description. The contents of pure Intellect, it tells us in a famous passage, are like a single breath or warmth, or rather it is as though there were only one quality, which possessed all qualities—all tastes, all colours, and the rest (ch. 12 *ad fin.*). And if Plotinus' recollection is not dismissed out of hand, it may be worth considering not just how the logical structure requires this mystical support, but how the mysticism would lose its philosophical interest were it not for the logical structure.

Pure Intellect and Henads in Proclus

For Proclus, the non-discursive intellect and the henads (the diacosm of 'first henads', that is) are each a 'simultaneous whole', but the henads are closer to the One. How then do they differ as wholes? He mentions cursorily three such differences of the henads from Intellect. First, among them there is an unqualified identity of knower and known, which in Intellect coincide but are not identical in essence (*Platonic Theology*), I. 21. 97. 22–98. 1).

Secondly, although each one is distinct, they are 'all in all': the contents of Intellect, the Ideas, are not 'all in all' but instead participate in one another (*Parmenides Commentary*, 1048. 11–12). 'All in all' means the relation which Plotinus found among the categories and which implied that motion is at rest, rest is in motion, being is at rest, in motion, other, and so on with all the categories. There is a third difference between henads and Intellect: although both know 'all things together' and the henads know, for example, the temporal as well as the non-existent, Intellect knows the particulars only through the universal and the non-existent through the existent (*Platonic Theology*, loc. cit., 98. 7–12). This must not be misunderstood. 'Through the universal' means 'so far as it is a universal', and similarly with the non-existent. In other words, the closest that Intellect comes to knowledge of particulars is knowledge of their species. To confuse it with knowledge of particulars would be one of the mistakes we mentioned that Iamblichus' principle of knowing was meant to contradict.

If we compare this non-discursive Intellect with that of Plotinus, we find a divergence between the two. That of Plotinus is more of a unity, that of Proclus is nearer to the conventional scientific knowledge which belongs to the lower Intellect. In fact the *totum simul* which Plotinus attributes to Intellect is virtually the *totum simul* of the henads. Nor shall we be surprised; for the Athenian Neoplatonists have postulated a type of entities—not normally or overtly recognized by Plotinus—which are more like the One than are the thoughts of Intellect, whose kinship is with Being. But the accepted logic did not provide them with a type of whole which was more like the One than was Plotinus' Intellect. The result is that in this respect, but not in others, his intellectual *totum simul* can be seen as promoted to the position of the henadic *totum simul* and that of Proclus demoted to a half-way position between Plotinus' two Intellects.

To specify the relevant characteristics, the substantial identity of knower and known, which Proclus allowed only to henads, holds in non-discursive Intellect according to Plotinus, for whom they were distinct only in definition. Similarly, the relation of 'all in all' must hold for its extensional contents, since it holds for the classes in which they are included, namely the so-called greatest kinds. More important is the non-propositional character of the non-discursive knowledge. Whether this belongs to the henads Proclus does not say. He had barred himself from all but an analogical speculation about the first henads. In Plotinus the soul which is united to pure Intellect has always potential knowledge of the latent genera and species. Not that he would allow that they were known only potentially. But *ex hypothesi* the soul can at this level say, indeed think, nothing about them, and this is incompatible with our ordinary notion of knowing, which is also the everyday notion of Neoplatonists. According to this notion, to have knowledge of them actually, the soul has to pay the price of descending to its discursive intellect. There it will find the set of propositions which it had already learnt there and which Plotinus had once called 'science' as opposed to 'true science'. They are not, of course, entertained simultaneously. Proclus, on the contrary, supposed that just this set of propositions when entertained simultaneously constituted non-discursive Intellect. It is for this reason that we can describe his non-discursive Intellect as half-way between Plotinus' non-discursive Intellect and conventional scientific knowledge. It is exactly what R. Sorabji (1982; 1983, 152–6) attributed mistakenly (as I have argued) to Plotinus instead of Proclus, and R. Norman (1969) to Aristotle's God.

The reader will not, however, have missed an inevitable distinction between henadic and intellectual knowledge; Proclus mentioned it in his own list of distinctions, and it must apply to Plotinus. Intellectual knowledge leaves no room for knowledge of particulars, at any rate until someone explains how Ideas of individuals, other than those without accidents, can find room in Plotinus' system.

Proclus' use of a famous metaphor may be thought to confirm our comparison between the two philosophers. But a closer look may suggest also that we should modify an assumption which we made when comparing them. We assumed that on Plotinus' side there was no intermediate state between Intellect and the One. To start from the metaphor, he had said that the Intellect has two powers, one of thinking by looking into itself, one of looking beyond itself to the Good; having reified these as a 'thinking intellect' and a 'loving intellect', he had put together two Platonic themes by describing the second intellect as 'the intellect drunk with nectar' (VI. 7. 35). Proclus borrows the description for the *henad* of Intellect, identified as 'the divine Intellect' or 'the god in the Intellect', whose thought is 'motionless in the now'. He calls it 'the whole as henad', 'the whole' being the regular designation of Intellect/Existence. Similarly, he explains, the soul, by virtue of its own 'summit', which is beyond soul, is intellect, just as the body by the power which is prior to body is soul.[2] That the summit of each hypostasis overlaps the hypostasis above it has always been noticed in the *Enneads*; and it can be seen here as a feature not simply of Plotinus but of Neoplatonism. Only, Proclus often uses the term 'summit of' to mean 'henad of', and is certainly doing so in the present case. Here the quotation from *Enneads*, VI. 7 shows that he means what takes place in Plotinus' loving intellect to be taking place in the Proclan henad of Intellect. If we take both at the universal level, this makes an additional correlation to the one we made previously between the diacosm of Henads and the Plotinian hypostasis of Intellect. The previous correlation was in respect of the types of whole they represented, and the present one cannot directly confirm that, for we are no longer comparing the whole which is formed by Intellect with the whole which is formed by all the henads but only with that of the henad of Intellect. Nevertheless the henad of Intellect can well be supposed to stand towards the diacosm of henads as the genus of Being stands towards the hypostasis of Being/Intellect—i.e. for most purposes identical.

Since he knew very well that Plotinus had refused to admit a diacosm or hypostasis between Intellect and the One, Proclus' use of the description 'drunk with nectar' can be seen as intending to correct him. But he must have thought that the absolute beauty of the *Phaedrus* vision which Plotinus had been trying to assimilate in *Ennead* VI. 7 cried out for an intermediate diacosm. That tract called it 'the flower of beauty' (32. 31), and he would surely have inferred that Plotinus was recognizing a henad in spite of himself.

The loving intellect = pre-intellect

Let us return to Plotinus' 'loving intellect', and we shall see that he did himself patently place it between Intellect and the One. For he

[2] Proclus, *PT* I. 66. 23–67. 6, and *In Parm.*, 1047. 18–24; cf. *In Parm.*, VII. 58. 13–16 Klibansky.

identifies it with a pre-intellect which he posited for the genesis account.[3] From a number of such accounts we gather that this Pre-intellect is the external activity of the One, which (1) will make it possible for Pre-intellect to make itself Intellect by (2) making determinate its indeterminate activity; (3) this indeterminate activity is described as just sight rather than seeing, since (4) it lacks an object; (5) in the genesis of Intellect it can even be identified with the ability to see or potential seeing, since if seeing stands for thinking, it is imperfect Intellect, not yet actualized. For this is a process, which is often alluded to, and pieces of which are more than once described in *Ennead* VI. 7: but it has the goal of Thought/Existence.

The process which belongs to the theme of the tract as a whole runs in the reverse direction, since it is the ascent of the soul to union with the One/Good. So what was not quite Thought, namely Pre-intellect, now appears as what is not quite the Good, namely the loving intellect. (For in the ascending process the particular soul has first to become an intellect and then the universal Intellect.) That the two are one and the same for Plotinus is confirmed by the way in which the properties of the loving intellect match one by one those of Pre-intellect which I have just summarized. (1) The intellect is a thinking intellect when it sees what it contains and itself generated, but when it (the loving intellect) sees what is beyond it, it does so 'by the same power by which it *was going* to think' (VI. 7. 35. 30–3); (2) the *love* of this intellect for the Good is unlimited because its object is unlimited, while the thought/existence which is generated is limited or determinate (ib., 32. 10–12, 24–8); (3) the loving intellect exercises the power by which it 'just saw' (35. 22); (4) for while light is normally what makes an object visible, there is in this case no such object, only the light itself from the Good (36. 19–22); (5) just as Pre-intellect was sight which did

---

[3] This was mentioned in Lloyd (1987*b*), 182. The evidence of the identification which is now described ought perhaps to qualify the suggestion there that Plotinus did not undertake detailed matching of steps within the genesis and the ascent. Nor is such an undertaking a sign that the genesis is to be treated as a fable. It is a sign of the interlocking of the contributions from personal experience and from philosophical reasoning. This book was virtually completed when P. Hadot's admirable (1988) commentary on VI. 7 was published. He makes, as I believe he had done earlier, the same identification of the loving intellect with Pre-intellect (l'Esprit 'naissant').

not see, the loving intellect is an intellect, i.e. thinking, which does not think (35. 30)—although of course in the ascending process, which reverses the order of potential and actual, this is no longer an imperfection. Proclus recognizes the deliberate paradox of the expression 'it possesses not-thinking'. When in the *Parmenides* commentary he is transmuting the loving intellect into the henad of Intellect he writes,

By its own not-intellect, Intellect is a god, and by its own not-god, the god within it is an intellect. (1047. 16–18)

A constructive interpretation of the motionless movement

Among the many loose threads which have been exposed, there remain some which threaten to undo the fabric of Neoplatonism. Even allowing that the reversion does not take place in time, we suggested that for universals to abandon their own rank, or at least their hypostasis, would be to abandon their proper identity and to contradict their perfection. Particular souls could ascend through the hypostases because their identity is not fixed and they are not perfect. In their case reversion is a *change* because what they do takes place in time. Many Neoplatonists believed that this universal law of reversion applied to every object in the universe, animate and inanimate. It is part of Proclus' theory of henads (*In Timaeum*, I. 210. 14–16). But, it may be objected, the ascent of each particular takes place by means of its union with a universal, usually an hypostasis in the *Enneads*, the monad of a series for the Athenian school. For instance, it is 'pure Intellect', not the particular psychic intellect, which has the power to see the One; there is only one pure Intellect—the same for every individual—and only by 'becoming it' has a particular soul seen the One. But, like any such universal, it is outside time; indeed Intellect *is* eternity. It follows that either there is no ascent that entails change and time for the particular soul, or there is ascent beyond their hypostatic rank on the part of the universals.

To this objection most Neoplatonists would reply that as a consciousness (if I may so put it) the particular soul will have been annihilated by its union with Intellect or one of the diacosms of Intellect, but the 'union' is not an identity that implies that the soul is not there during the union.[4] The same thing can be thought of, and therefore exist, *sub specie aeternitatis* and in time. What evidence of its continued existence can there be? Plotinus appeals to personal experience: we can recall a unique kind of joy which we believe that we experienced (VI. 7. 34). This is only partly satisfactory; but it can be compared with someone's ordinary evidence for having had a dream; and I am not pursuing it here.

As for the universals which, as it were, carry the soul beyond their borders, none of them has to travel so far as to abandon its identity and contradict its perfection. Each crosses one border, where its task is continued by the next universal or diacosm. This is made possible by the familiar overlap between the highest level of one diacosm or hypostasis and the lowest level of the one above it. Syrianus and his followers are more explicit than Plotinus in making the reverting particular retrace the steps in the order of procession, and there are more steps. Moreover, it has to do so in order to purify itself, for as the *Phaedo* said, it is not lawful for the impure to touch the pure. But impurities are going to include ignorance; and without forgetting that the ascent of persons is not automatic but due to their efforts, we know how to translate 'impure' into 'diluted by non-essential forms'. Quoting the *Phaedo*, Proclus replaces the moral and religious 'impure' with the still normative, but non-moral 'incomplete' or 'imperfect'; he is referring precisely to the increasing degrees of imperfection or perfection of a property which are represented by the terms of a proceeding or reverting series, and whose logic we have discussed in detail.[5] It follows too that a particular soul or physical object cannot miss or bypass any major step in its reversion. In case the ascent is 'in respect of the property of unity' (rather than for instance, goodness) the terms of the series will be henads, but, contrary to what has often been supposed, this is no royal road:

---

[4] The problem had been debated since the second century but usually against a background of esotericism and theurgy, where (in the Emperor Julian's words) faith not proof is to be looked for. Iamblichus seems to imply that angelic souls retain their specific identity or rank, i.e. remain angelic even when they join the gods in their supra-celestial revolutions (ap. Stob., I. 458 W.; *De myst.*, II. 2. 79. 16–19 Des P.) I take this to account for Proclus' unexpected claim that in reverting nothing rises out of its rank (*PT*, I. 19).

[5] Plat., *Phaedo*, 67 B; Procl., *In Tim.*, I. 301. 20–2, Cf. in general loc. cit., 301–2, and *In Alcib.*, 242 ff. Cr.

there are as many henads as there are forms.

Tardi ama il cuor quel che l'occhio non vede.

For the present, however, we can take it that the relay system (if the expression will be pardoned) of the universals explains the restriction that we found required by reversion. This was that the universals and hypostases cannot revert, in the sense of returning, rather than inclining, to levels which would make them what they are not and telescope them in a way which is inconsistent with the procession of their causes. What reverts in the sense of returning either to the One or to the first Henads will be particulars whose reversion is change.[6] Finally this is the view of Neoplatonists in general.

We have been considering the union with the One or first Henads as the final stage of an upward movement or change; and Neoplatonists rarely consider it in any other way. But, in a chapter of the *Platonic Theology* devoted to correlating the names 'One' with procession from it, and 'Good' with reversion to it, Proclus conventionally attributes these movements to everything but also describes them as simultaneous (II. 6. 41. 21). He proceeds to infer that there is a permanent union of everything with the One (ib., 41. 29). It comes about because (1) the One is omnipresent, that is to say, everything participates in unity (or a henad), just as it does in goodness (42. 2–3), (2) what is participated in is the principle, i.e. cause, of the participant, and (3) contains it occultly. (3) is equivalent, we are told, to the third term of the triad, remaining, and in effect to union with the first principle.[7] Finally, union is not a matter of knowledge or activity on the part of the objects concerned, for it includes objects which are not endowed with either.

The passage (41. 18–42. 16) would seem to be describing the connection of everything with the One rather than claiming that everything enjoys the mystical union with the One, for (3) can be taken only to mean that the causes of everything remain occultly in

---

[6] I write 'One or first Henads' because there is a good case, which I shall not make here, for Proclus' having believed that nothing came closer to the One than by union with first Henads.

[7] The equivalences in (3) can be derived from the expression τὴν δὲ μονιμὸν αὐτῷ ἐν τῷ πρώτῳ περιοχήν, εἰ θέμις εἰπεῖν, καὶ τὴν ἕνωσιν τὴν πρὸς τὸ ἄρρητον (42.4–6)— 'mais l'embrassement, si l'on peut dire, qui les fait demeurer au sein du premier principe et leur union avec cet ineffable . . . ' (Saffrey–Westerink). The 'and' could be taken as an '*id est*'.

the One—or more likely in its representatives, the first henads. This connection is nothing other than what is constituted by the chain of being. It is the same thing too as the overlap of diacosms which is afforded by the occult remaining of each monad which accompanies its procession and is the focus of its reversion. Viewed statically as they are in the present passage, these phenomena can be translated into the language of participation and the partial transmission of properties—the Neoplatonic substructure in fact which we have been studying in the greater part of this book. So (3) suggests the possibility that, with one proviso, the spiritual circuit *is* just this substructure. The proviso is that the motionless reversion in it is confined to the universals and excludes the ascent of particulars.

I should not wish to commit myself to this interpretation as having been intended by Proclus. But it is a possible one, and possible interpretations of a theory throw light on the structure of the theory. It is also in keeping with the increasing 'logicizing' of the spiritual circuit which we find carried further by Damascius.

We can picture the particulars passing through the overlaps until they reach the One or a first henad; taking on the character of each appropriate monad (whether or not a henad) successively, their ascent and return involves change and probably takes time. Their reversions and processions can be repeated. But they can, of course, be partial, for, although they are all connected to the One, even the most likely candidates, it seems, do not necessarily achieve union with it. The two 'movements' of the universals coincide and involve neither change nor time, but if they had been movements the paths they were taking would have been those taken by the movements of the particulars—or rather those they provided for the particulars. Instead of movements, therefore, they can be pictured as lines. The universals do eternally what the particulars do in time. But the Greeks envisaged an eternal activity as an archetype and perfection of one in time; the notion was reached mainly by excluding that of cessation and succession, and the consequence was that something eternal was logically something temporal minus certain properties. But this priority of the notion of time is only epistemological: no one doubted that eternity was naturally and normatively prior.

If we accept this picture, we must correct a detail of the account we gave of the soul's being carried by one diacosm to the next. It is not a vehicle but a connection—or, to be exact, its overlap with the next diacosm is the connection. For each diacosm is the *logos* of the one above it, according to Plotinus, or has its imparticipable illuminated by one in the diacosm above it, according to Iamblichus and his successors. The particular soul in the *Enneads* would have to travel to pure Intellect, but pure Intellect would not need to travel, because it is already in contact with the One, having never wholly left it. But this is an attribute of Intellect, and even if not as a vehicle the soul is still 'using' it. We can recall that Plotinus had accepted the theory of *De intellectu* that when our thought was the matterless forms the thinking was done for us by the 'intellect from outside', in the way that an instrument can be used to handle things. But this does not mean that the universals are connected just for the sake of the particulars, for that would reverse the normative order. They compose what is already a whole: the particulars have to become that.

What I have called the universal 'connection' and *Platonic Theology*, II. 6, calls 'union' was the 'sympathy' of religious language. In the excursus on prayer, sympathy was exactly the 'connection' between objects and the powers of various gods to which they revert—the sunflower to Helios and so on. Like reversion, it is based on resemblance. The objects contain hidden signs (συνθήματα) which are equivalent to (or at least cause) the 'correspondences' of traditional occultism and magic literature.[8] Historically, Proclus' combined theory of reversion and henads is a philosophical rationalization, first suggested by Iamblichus, of the theory of sympathy.

Our constructive interpretation of the eternal procession and reversion concerned a problem which immediately recalls the two powers of Intellect in Plotinus. These are the 'power', described as the thinking intellect, which looks within it and sees its own creations, and the 'power', described as the non-thinking or loving intellect, which sees what is beyond it. But in a cryptic but important couple of sentences we are told that Intellect does not see these two kinds of thing 'by turns': 'it possesses uninterruptedly thinking and non-thinking' (VI. 7. 35. 27–30). This cannot, of course, refer to the mere capacity to think and not to think, for that

---

[8] See Procl., *In Tim.*, I. 210, probably following Iamblichus; *ET*, 34. 36. 26; Iambl., *De myst.*, v. 23; Bidez (1928), 145. Proclus' use of sympathy depends mostly on the hermetic use, Plotinus' in my opinion on the Stoic.

would be compatible with its doing both alternately. So we have a position which is very close to that described by Proclus, for an activity at least similar to procession is simultaneous with one which is plainly reversion, and both are eternal.

But the sort of interpretation that might fit passages in Proclus should not be tried on *Enneads*, VI. 7. 35. In the first place, Plotinus does not have a systematic theory of reversion, although he does of procession. Secondly, what he says is said only of Intellect; and thirdly, it is complicated by being really about Pre-intellect, which is—and is regularly called so by Plotinus—Intellect, but Intellect in an ambiguous, inchoate state. Instead, we can ask a question about the simultaneous movements which will have occurred to the logically minded reader as a pressing question.

Suppose that an ascending soul succeeds in being absorbed by pure Intellect, which contains, indeed comprises, two movements simultaneously, or, if it is preferred, two directions: what decides which 'movement' or direction it takes, or, if the non-thinking Intellect is by definition united with the One, what decides whether the soul has this mystic union? As far as the first question goes, other places in the *Enneads* make it reasonably clear that the particular soul is assumed to have preserved its ability as an individual sufficiently to eschew thinking.

For the road and the journey there is instruction, but the vision is the task of whoever wants to see. (VI. 9. 4. 15–16)

The vision, we know, is of the light itself, and

by attending to the nature of the things that are illuminated, it sees the light: but if it will abandon the things it sees and should look instead at that through which it sees them it would be looking at light and the source of light. (V. 5. 7. 18–21)

Plotinus says this of Pure Intellect, but the end of the chapter makes it clear that he is thinking of the soul (or its intellect) which it has absorbed.

It would be wrong to suppose that it rests with the One whether to appear or not. The reason is not that 'the One is already present to those who seek him', for, except in a tendentious or irrelevant sense, he is 'present' only in images.[9] It is rather that what happens

---

[9] 'The One is already present . . . ' Rist (1967), 225. The omnipresence is well described and compared with Malebranche's account by Moreau (1970), 189–95.

to sunflowers, human souls, or the Pure Intellect makes no difference to him whatever. But it seems to me exaggerated to make it depend just on effort and the recognition of our responsibility. Many of Plotinus' descriptions of the conditions under which the vision occurs can be read as such and not as oblique injunctions. There is a well known injunction

not to pursue it but to wait quietly for it to appear, and prepare to look at it just as the eye waits for the rising of the sun (v. 5. 8. 3–5).

But I do not think that astronomical necessity is part of the simile. He refers elsewhere, although casually, to the 'good fortune' of anyone who has seen the god (VI. 9. 11. 4; cf. P. Hadot, 1988, 337).

What is presupposed by thought and existence

Let us stay with Plotinus so as to advance a little towards placing his type of idealism. The last resting-place from which the fortunate individual will obtain his mystic vision is what we have been calling Pre-intellect. This is a stage below the One but above the hypostasis of Intellect and Ousia which we have regularly been calling Existence. We know from the logical structure of a Neoplatonic hierarchy that the properties of a prior term in the series are properties which are not identical with those of a succeeding term but implied or presupposed by it; indeed the fact that there is this prior term is implied or presupposed. Nature for example presupposes Soul. Plotinus commonly provides, as it were, a narrative of the generation of one hypostasis by another, and this will include intermediate terms, which share in the same logical structure. For he repeatedly conjures his reader not to take literally such a 'didactic story' as he calls it, but this is only on the ground that it represents facts which are eternal and simultaneous as though they were events in time. Pre-intellect must be one such fact.

What is the nature of it which will be presupposed by the second hypostasis? It is indeterminate thinking which Plotinus treats like Aristotle's potential thinking—but, unlike Aristotle's, as a real activity, although not of 'complete' thinking. He describes it sometimes as 'living'. It is complete thinking or Intellect proper only when it has a determinate object. But, equally, it is the indeterminate object—or better, content—of thinking, since thinking and its content are identical save conceptually. To be a determinate object is to be something that is. So that when in the next stage of the narrative the indeterminate object is made something that is, the result will be both the creation of what is, or Existence (the completed content of thinking) and the creation of Thought (the completed act of thinking *qua* thinking). But this does not mean that it is existence which can be said to be making both, and therefore to be prior to thought. For thinking can be said to be required for making an indeterminate object into a determinate one. Like indeterminate or pre-thinking, the indeterminate or pre-existent object is only potentially existent, but is for Plotinus something actual, although not 'completely' existent. (We might think of what we are sometimes aware of when we begin to wake from sleep and what we are aware of has not quite turned into a place, a room, walls.) To make it an existent object is to make it a something, one thing that is this rather than that, which implies that there are others from which it is distinct. To do this can be said to require thinking. But this thinking is inseparable from the fact that it has an object (or content): and, in Plotinus' narrative, there can be no answer to the question whether it is making or discovering. The result is the creation of an hypostasis which is both Intellect and Existence, and the manner of whose creation has shown neither to be prior to the other.

This is the first of two implications for anyone who is concerned to ask what kind of idealism he should attribute to Plotinus.

Pre-intellect must now be understood as Pre-existence too. In the *Enneads* they are two aspects of the external activity of the One. Consequently it is something that is neither just thought nor just existence nor both. What it creates is both, and the two are distinguishable only by later, discursive thought—that of philosophers for example. But while, with some wavering, he prefers to count it as the internal activity of Pre-intellect/Intellect, Plotinus presents the Intellect/Existence which it creates as a lower stage in the procession of the One; and this is clearly confirmed by its being an earlier stage, as we have seen, in the ascent to the One. In logical terms, therefore, it implies or presupposes Pre-intellect. And because of the meaning and structure of procession, which have constantly been emphasized in our study of it, this tells us about the properties of thought and of existence in general. Since Intellect is what is thought as well as the thinking, we can infer that what is thought and what exists presuppose something which is neither thought nor exists.

This is the second fact which has a bearing on Plotinus' idealism. For 'existence'—more commonly translated as 'being'—has here the connotation which is appropriate to idealism, namely of being a distinct object of thought. But so far from exhausting the *realist's* notion of 'existence' this has turned out to require there to be something which does not, in Plotinus' and the idealist's terms, exist. At any rate, this something can have no fixed and concrete properties (for otherwise it would be an object of thought) but is *there*.

There is another and modern way (which I mention without approving or disapproving) of characterizing this Neoplatonic world of existence or being—for what we are now taking from Plotinus holds for all Neoplatonists, whether they have pre-intellects or henads. It can be characterized as a world full of meanings, for it is in a literal sense conceptualized. Philosophers who believe that things do not require meanings ('significance' for those who want 'meaning' confined to words) in order to exist, or that the meanings are imposed on them by users, often look for brute facts, that is facts which are independent of concepts and meanings, among things which are only observed through the senses and are perhaps identifiable by demonstratives without connotation. But it is just this possibility which Neoplatonists were rejecting when they adhered to the syncretistic scheme of sense perception, which contained presentation and judgement at early points in the process. That enabled them to have perception as confused thinking. Other philosophers who in one way or another posit a world of meanings have claimed that they are rebutting the dilemma of realism and idealism by positing objects which have two faces, one which endows them with meaning and one which is independent of it. This might suggest one half of Plotinus' position. To complete it, one would have to posit a kind of substrate or stuff which had neither character unless it stood in one or another relation, like the substrate of neutral monism.

Plotinus was entirely confident that philosophy could demonstrate that thought and existence depended on there being a supraexistent One. To make the same case for a Pre-intellect he relied on the model of Aristotle's account of sight as a capacity and sight as seeing. But his own ambiguities and obscurities suggest that his 'narrative' was not even claiming to be a demonstration. To make up for that, we fall back on the non-philosophical but integral component of Neoplatonism, personal experience. In this case, he does not say so. But in fact the mystical experience (assuming its authenticity) of the soul's resting-place there is the evidence for the crucial point. Even in Aristotle's model a potential seeing has to be the actuality of something else, say the sense organ, and this is describable. Philosophical reasoning can give no inkling of what the actuality would be in the Neoplatonists' case of potential thought and existence. Certainly we can know that it will not contain things or meanings. But reasoning cannot say what *that* would be like, and it cannot infer it from what it would be the actuality of; for all it can deduce is that it would be the actuality of the One's external activity; and that is uninformative. It is the mystical acquaintance with it which tells us what this actuality is like—or rather tells anyone who has had that good fortune.

Pre-intellect and Intellect have to be distinguished in order to make sense of Plotinus' 'didactic story', although he makes little effort to do so for us. But they are not to be separated; and nothing rules out the transition's being a gradual one. His sketches of the mystical experience do not demarcate them in any way that obviously matches that of the reasoning.

What is so valuable about knowledge?

This enquiry into the realm of Pre-intellect and first Henads began from problems about the limits of knowledge. A loose thread to be gathered about knowledge is this. Neoplatonists speak repeatedly of the need for it; but what is so valuable about it? This will be answered very concisely here, for the materials of the answer are all to hand from previous chapters. We can ignore the religious and quasi-religious influences. These are needed to explain why it was thought valuable. But we are concerned not with historical explanation of beliefs but with analysis. For this, the key to understanding is to remember that Neoplatonists' 'knowledge' is a P-series, so that it has two groups of meanings. The first, which is prominent when the topic is levels of thought below that of pure Intellect, corresponds to our traditional and everyday 'knowledge' and 'science'. Here, it obviously and commonly refers to the processes leading to knowledge of things natural and divine which constitutes theoretical wisdom. That this is a virtue and consequently valuable is a commonplace of ethics. For instance, Hierocles argues in the *Carmen aureum* commentary that it is the imitation of God (cf. 468–9 Mullach). But it is also made to refer particularly to self-knowledge. For as Plato's much-read *Alcibiades* had said, within ourselves we shall find a god, or as Plotinus explained, our selves are products of God (v. 3. 7). 'Return to yourself and look' (in the tract *On Beauty*, v. 9. 6. 8) can be called the Neoplatonic 'Know thyself'. This too is a path to wisdom. But it has two other obvious features. It is incorporated into the ascent to absolute beauty or the neighbourhood of the Good which Neoplatonists found in the *Symposium*; and it is bound up with the doctrine that 'the intelligibles are inside Intellect'. Both these features are bound up with the deeper group of meanings of 'knowledge' which belong to the higher levels of the P-series while for that reason pervading all levels.

This is the notion of knowing as possessing, of which the limiting and ideal case is identification or union with the object. It is clearly found better in knowledge by introspection than knowledge by observation. The objects of knowledge, as we and the Neoplatonists use the term, are by definition the contents of the hypostasis Intellect, since this is also the whole of existence. But they will be known *par excellence* non-discursively, in other words, in the pure Intellect. Here, the knower (or his intellect), his knowing, and what he knows are identical. And this indicates the *Neoplatonic* answer to the question what is valuable about knowledge. For it leads us immediately into the fundamental equations. What is in pure Intellect is by definition what is *par excellence* real; and, as we have seen, reality is equivalent to perfection, and perfection to value. The individual who can pursue his science to that level has perfected himself or made his self, real. For there were differences over identifying what we might call the empirical self, but not over the fact that it could join itself to the universal Intellect. Satisfying a further term of the same equation, he has unified himself, according to Neoplatonists; for, while differing about the exact degree of unity, they concur in regarding the contents of non-discursive thought as a single object.

How consciousness creates

In the everyday notion, knowing is a form of consciousness. The Neoplatonists' notion can still maintain this, because their notion of consciousness matches it by stretching its upper and lower limits beyond those of the everyday notion. Some modern idealism has made this less strange; Neoplatonists tried to do so by stretching another notion, that of life, and assimilating the two. Following the traditional and literal translation, the term is rarely translated as anything but 'contemplation'. But all Greek philosophers would have known that Aristotle commonly used it and the corresponding verb for the actual exercise of knowledge which is possessed but not exercised. The man who θεωρεῖ geometry is not contemplating it but doing it. He can also be said to be conscious of it as he was not when it was not a θεωρία for him. I am anxious not to exaggerate the point: but there are contexts in our authors where there is much to be said for actually translating the term as 'consciousness'. At any rate, in the chapter of Plotinus' tract *On Nature, Theoria, and the One* (III. 8) to which I now turn it should, I suggest, be *interpreted* as 'consciousness'.[10] It will provide another indication of Plotinus' idealism.

The tract is about the creation in general of new forms by *theoria*, considering first the creations of Nature, then of Soul and of Intellect. Plotinus claims that all do so by *theoria*, although, as we could predict, by ascending degrees of it, according to the Neoplatonic notion. These will not be touched on here. It is intended only to suggest how the claim can be tied in with that part of the underlying web of Neoplatonism that has been selected in this book. The problem can be stated simply. How is the creation of forms by *theoria* not some new, enigmatic alternative to emanation or procession?

Procession was the necessary overflowing or external activity of any real or perfected type of thing, as a result of its perfection. But perfection coincides, and is even identical with consciousness. For except at the limits of thought consciousness is what Plotinus calls thinking; and every real thing *is* a thought. Secondly, a true

---

[10] It refers to knowledge in actuality at e.g. Ar., *De an.*, 417^{a}28–9; *De mem.*, 449^{b}17; *Phys.*, 255^{a}34; ^{b}23; and in *Met. B* 5 (cf. Lugarini, 1961, 47.) At *De mem.*, 450^{b}15 virtually ≡ 'be conscious of' (memory images).

thought is not just an object of thought but the thinking of it; and thirdly, in order to be a complete or perfect thinking, it must be a self-thinking. This is equivalent to a thought without a thinking subject (cf. 8. 8 *ad init.*); and if this is a strange idea, it has been made less so by the history of philosophy, where it is often attributed to eighteenth-century idealists. It is what, in chapters 6 and 7 of the tract, Plotinus refers to, and probably means by, *theoria*, which I have called consciousness. This is in keeping with his description of a 'living theoria' in chapter 8. And that it is the perfection which corresponds to the perfection which triggers procession is confirmed by its being the condition to which everything aspires (7. 15 ff.). Even among plants and animals, to reproduce is

to fill all things with *logoi* and to maintain, as it were, an unbroken consciousness—for to create is to create a form, and that is filling all things with consciousness. (7. 20–2)

For we are explicitly reminded that the *logoi*, which perform the part of the Stoic 'seminal principles' and are aspects of forms, are acts of thinking (8. 16).

Since consciousness at its best does not have a thinker who is distinct from it, we cannot ask whose consciousness creates what exists. We can repeat what we saw earlier. Consciousness *überhaupt* is not an anachronism in Greek philosophy; and Imperial philosophers had been taught by Alexander of Aphrodisias (or his milieu) that our own higher thoughts were really the activity of a single, non-human *nous*. But the fact that this consciousness was 'absolute' did not imply that it and its content were abstractions, the mere universal or attribute of consciousness and the concepts which comprised it. While not particulars, they are better described as concrete, and closer therefore to Hegelian than to Kantian idealism.

At the same time, Plotinus does believe that we as particulars are creative, in respect both of things and of actions, and that both of these are the proper result of our *theoria*. It contributes to our philosophical knowledge because it mirrors the structure of Neoplatonic reality. This feature it shares with the mystical and theurgic experiences which, as we saw, were integral to our knowledge of the chain of being. But such a process is a pale reflection in time of the timeless creation of existence as such, which is the whole that has, or rather is, not merely an intension but an extension. And, unless the drift of the earlier chapters has been quite wrong, timeless creation stands for analysis into elements, and the order of the creative stages for the order of logical, or at least conceptual, dependence of those elements.

All creation involves procession, and everything which proceeds has proceeded from the One or a form of it. Since this is also the Good, the creation of Nature and even works of art are cases of spontaneous multiplication of what is good, that is to say, has value or is capable of perfection. Equally, when *Nous* creates it can be seen as the spontaneous multiplication of reality. None of these alternative but not synonymous descriptions can be wrong, for each is guaranteed by the fundamental equations. But in *Ennead* III. 8 Plotinus is considering existence and its degrees as the existence and degrees of thought.

BIBLIOGRAPHY

ARMSTRONG, A. H. (ed.) (1967), *Cambridge History of Later Greek and Early Medieval Philosophy*, Part III, 'Plotinus' (Cambridge).

AX, W. (1986), *Laut, Stimme und Sprache* (Göttingen).

BADAWI, A. (1968), *Transmission de la philosophie grecque au monde arabe* (Paris; 2nd edn. 1978).

BARNES, J. (1983), 'Terms and Sentences: Theophrastus on Hypothetical Syllogisms', *Proceedings of the British Academy*, 69, 279–326.

BEIERWALTES, W. (1975), 'Das Problem der Erkenntnis bei Proklos', in *De Jamblique à Proclus* (Entretiens Hardt, 21; Vandoeuvres–Geneva).

—— (1979), *Proklos²* (Mainz).

—— (1985), *Denken des Einen* (Frankfurt am Main).

BENAKIS, L. (1982), 'Problem of General Concepts in Neoplatonism and Byzantine Thought', in D. J. O'Meara (ed.), *Neoplatonism and Christian Thought* (Norfolk: Vancouver), Greek version plus texts in Φιλοσοφία, 8–9 (1978–9), 311–34.

—— (1987), 'Neues zur Proklos—Tradition in Byzanz', in G. Boss and G. Seel (eds.), *Proclus et son influence* (Actes du colloque de Neuchâtel 1985; Zurich).

BIDEZ, J. (1923), 'Boèce et Porphyre', *Revue belge de Philologie et d'histoire*, 2 (1923), 189–201; repr. in M. Fuhrmann and J. Gruber (1984).

—— (ed.) (1928), *Catalogue des MSS. alchimiques grecs*, vi (Brussels).

BLANK, D. L. (1982), *Ancient Philosophy and Grammar: The Syntax of Apollonius Dyscolus* (Chico: California).

BLUMENTHAL, H. J. (1975), 'Plutarch's Exposition of the *de Anima* and the Psychology of Proclus', in *De Jamblique à Proclus* (Entretiens Hardt, 21; Vandoeuvres–Geneva).

—— (1982), 'Proclus on Perception', *Bulletin of the Institute of Classical Studies*, 29, 1–11.

—— and MARKUS, R. A. (eds.) (1981), *Neoplatonism and Early Christian Thought* (London).

CHADWICK, H. (1981), *Boethius: The Consolations of Music, Logic, Theology, and Philosophy* (Oxford–New York).

COURCELLE, P. (1944), *Lettres grecques en occident de Macrobe à Cassiodore* (Paris).

COULOUBARITSIS, L. (1980), *L'Avènement de la science physique: Essai sur la Physique d'Aristote* (Brussels).

DEVREESSE, R. (1954), *Introduction à l'étude des manuscrits grecs* (Paris).

DONINI, P. (1982), *Le scuole, l'anima, l'impero: La filosofia antica da Antioco a Plotino* (Torino).

EBBESEN, S. (1981), *Commentators and Commentaries on Aristotle's Sophistici elenchi* (Corpus lat. comm. in Aristot. graec., VII, 1; 3 vols., Leiden).

EGLI, U. (1970), *Arbeitspapiere (Universität Bern, Institut für Sprachwissenschaft*, 2).

—— (1978), Stoic Syntax and Semantics, in *Les stoïciens et leur logique* (Actes du colloque de Chantilly 18–22 September 1976; Paris).

EMILSSON, E. K. (1988), *Plotinus on Sense-Perception* (Cambridge).

FINAMORE, J. F. (1985), *Iamblichus and the theory of the vehicle of the soul* (Chico: California).

FOTINIS, A. P. (1979), *The De anima of Alexander of Aphrodisias; A Translation and Commentary* (Washington D.C.).

FUHRMANN, M. (1960), *Das systematische Handbuch* (Göttingen).

—— and GRUBER, J. (eds.) (1984), *Boethius* (Darmstadt).

GERSH, S. E. (1973), ΚΙΝΗΣΙΣ ΑΚΙΝΗΤΟΣ: *A Study of Spiritual Motion in the Philosophy of Proclus* (Leiden).

HADOT, ILSETRAUT (1984), 'Les Introductions néoplatoniciennes à la philosophie d'Aristote', *Annuaire* (Paris, Ecole pratique des hautes études, Vᵉ section, sci, religieuses), t. 92 (1983–4), 337–42.

HADOT, P. (1968), *Porphyre et Victorinus* (2 vols., Paris).

—— (1988), *Plotin, Traité 38 (VI 7): Introduction, traduction, commentaire et notes* (Paris).

HUNGER, H. (1978), 'Hochsprachliche profane Literatur der Byzantiner', *Handbuch der Altertumswissenschaft*, XII/5 (Munich).

JOACHIM, H. H. (1951), *Aristotle: Nicomachean Ethics, A Commentary* (Oxford).

JOANNOU, P. (1954), 'Der Nominalismus und die menschliche Psychologie Christi', *BZ* 47, 369–78.

JOSEPH, H. W. B. (1916), *Introduction to logic²* (Oxford).

KNEALE, W. (1961), 'Time and Eternity in Theology', *Proceedings of the Aristotelian Society* (1960–1), 87–107.

LAMBERTON, R. (1986), *Homer the Theologian: Neoplatonist Allegorical Reading and the Growth of the Epic Tradition* (Berkeley).

LEAR, J. (1980), *Aristotle and Logical Theory* (Cambridge).

LEE, TAE-SOO (1984), *Griechische Tradition der aristotelischen Syllogistik in der Spätantike. Eine Untersuchung über die Kommentare zu den analytica priora von Alexander Aphrodisiensis, Ammonius und Philoponus* (Göttingen).

LEMERLE, P. (1971), *L'Humanisme byzantin* (Paris) Engl. trans. H. Lindsay and A. Moffatt, *Byzantine humanism* (Canberra, 1986).

LEROUX, G. (1974), 'Logique et dialectique chez Plotin', *Phoenix*, 28, 180–92.

LLOYD, A. C. (1956), 'Neoplatonic Logic and Aristotelian Logic', *Phronesis*, 1 (1955–6), 58–72; 146–60.

—— (1962), 'Genus, Species and Ordered Series in Aristotle', *Phronesis*, 7, 67–90.

—— (1971a), 'Neoplatonists' Account of Predication and Mediaeval Logic', in *Le Néoplatonisme* (Colloques internationaux du C.N.R.S. 1969) (Paris, 1971).

—— (1971b), 'Grammar and Metaphysics in the Stoa', in A. A. Long (ed.), *Problems in Stoicism* (London).

—— (1981), *Form and Universal in Aristotle* (ARCA classical and medieval texts, papers and monographs, 4; Liverpool).

—— (1982), 'Procession and Division in Proclus', in H. J. Blumenthal and A. C. Lloyd (eds.) *Soul and the Structure of Being in Late Neoplatonism: Syrianus, Proclus and Simplicius* (Liverpool).

—— (1986), 'Non-Propositional Thought in Plotinus', *Phronesis*, 31, 258–65.

—— (1987a), 'The Aristotelianism of Eustratios of Nicaea', in J. Wiesner (ed.), *Aristoteles Werk und Wirkung*, II (Berlin–New York).

—— (1987b), 'Plotinus on the Genesis of Thought and Existence', *Oxford Studies in Ancient Philosophy*, 5, 155–86.

LLOYD, G. E. R. (1973), *Greek Science after Aristotle* (London).

—— (1978), 'Saving the Appearances', *Classical Quarterly* 28, 202–22.

LONG, A. A. (1988), 'Ptolemy on the Criterion', in J. M. Dillon and A. A. Long (eds.) *The Question of Eclecticism* (Berkeley).

LONG, A. A. and SEDLEY, D. N. (1988), *The Hellenistic Philosophers* (2 vols.; Cambridge, 1987–8).

LUGARINI, L. (1961), *Aristotele e l'idea della filosofia* (Florence).

ŁUKASIEWICZ, J. (1951), *Aristotle's Syllogistic from the Standpoint of Modern Formal Logic* (Oxford).

MANGO, C. (1975), *Byzantine Literature as a Distorting Mirror* (Inaugural lecture; Oxford).

MANSION, SUZANNE (1946), 'La Première Doctrine de la substance: La Substance selon Aristote', *Revue philosophique de Louvain*, 44, 349–69; repr. in id., *Études aristotéliciennes* (Louvain-la-Neuve, 1984).

MINIO-PALUELLO, L. (1970), 'Boezio', in *Diz. biograf. degli italiani* (Rome).

MORAUX, P. (1968), 'La Joute dialectique d'après le huitième livre des *Topiques*', in G. E. L. Owen (ed.), *Aristotle on Dialectic* (Oxford).

—— (1973), *Aristotelismus bei den Griechen*, i (Berlin–New York).

MOREAU, J. (1970), *Plotin, ou la gloire de la philosophie antique* (Paris).

MOUTSOPOULOS, E. A. (1985), *Les Structures de l'imagination dans la philosophie de Proclus* (Paris).

NORMAN, R. (1969), 'Aristotle's Philosopher-God', *Phronesis*, 14, 63–74;

repr. in J. Barnes, M. Schofield, R. Sorabji (eds.), *Articles on Aristotle,* iv. *Metaphysics* (London, 1979).

OBERTELLO, L. (1974), *Severino Boezio* (2 vols.; Genoa).

OGDEN, C. K. and RICHARDS, I. A. (1930), *Meaning of Meaning* (London).

OWENS, J. (1957), '"Common nature"; A Point of Comparison between Thomistic and Scotistic Metaphysics', *Medieval studies,* 19, 1–14; repr. in J. F. Ross (ed.), *Inquiries into Medieval Philosophy: A Collection in Honour of Francis P. Clarke* (Westport, Conn., 1971).

PATZIG, G. (1968), *Aristotle's Theory of the Syllogism,* trans. J. Barnes (Dordrecht).

PÉPIN, J. (1976), *Saint Augustin et la dialectique* (Villanova).

PFLIGERSDORFFER, G. (1953), 'Andronikos von Rhodos und die Postprädikamente bei Boethius', *Vigiliae Christianae,* 7, 98–115.

PODSKALSKY, G. (1976), 'Nicolaus von Methone und die Proklosrenaissance in Byzanz (11./12. Jahrhundert)', *Orientalia christiana periodica,* 42, 509–23.

PRAECHTER, K. [1910a], 'Beziehungen zur Antike in Theodoros Prodromos' Rede auf Isaak Komnenos', *BZ* 19, 314–29.

—— [1910b], 'Richtungen und Schulen im Neuplatonismus', in *Genethliakon C. Robert* (Berlin).

PRIOR, A. N. (1962), 'The Formalities of Omniscience', *Philosophy,* repr. in *Papers on Time and Tense* (Oxford, 1968) and in J. F. Ross (ed.), *Imquiries into Medieval Philosophy* (Westport, Conn., 1971).

—— (1967), *Past, Present and Future* (Oxford, 1967).

RIST, J. M. (1967), *Plotinus: The Road to Reality* (Cambridge).

ROMANO, F. (1985), *Porfirio e la fisica aristotelica* (Symbolon, 3; Catania).

ROSÁN, L. J. (1949), *Philosophy of Proclus* (New York).

RUTTEN, C. (1956), 'La Doctrine des deux actes dans la philosophie de Plotin', *Revue philosophique,* 46, 100–6.

SAMBURSKY, S. (1959), *Physics of the Stoics* (London).

—— (1962), *The Physical World of Late Antiquity* (London).

—— (1965), 'Plato, Proclus and the Limitations of Science', *Journal of the History of Philosophy,* 3, 1–11.

SHIEL, J. (1958), 'Boethius' Commentaries on Aristotle', *Mediaeval and Renaissance studies,* 4, 217–44; repr. in M. Fuhrmann and J. Gruber (eds.), *Boethius* (Darmstadt, 1984).

—— (1982), 'A Recent Discovery: Boethius' Notes on the Prior Analytics', *Vivarium,* 20, 128–41.

—— (1984), 'A Set of Greek Reference Signs in the Florentine MS. of Boethius' Translation of the *Prior Analytics* (B.N. Conv. soppr. J. VI. 34)', *Scriptorium,* 38, 327–42.

SORABJI, R. (1982), 'Myths about Non-Propositional Thought', in M. Nussbaum and M. Schofield (eds.), *Language and Logos: Studies Presented to G. E. L. Owen* (Cambridge).

—— (1983), *Time, Creation and the Continuum* (London).

—— (ed.) (1987), *Philoponus and the Rejection of Aristotelian Science* (London).

STRAWSON, P. F. (1952), *Introduction to Logical Theory* (London–New York).

TATAKIS, B. (1949), 'Philosophie byzantine', in E. Bréhier (ed.), *Histoire de la philosophie*, fasc. suppl. 11 (Paris).

TAYLOR, A. E. (1926), *Plato: The Man and His Work* (London).

TREU, M. (1898), 'Ein byzantinisches Schulgespräch', *BZ* 2, 96–109.

TROUILLARD, J. (1965), *Proclos: Eléments de théologie, traduction, introduction et notes* (Paris).

—— (1982), *Mystagogie de Proclos* (Paris).

WALLIS, R. T. (1972), *Neoplatonism* (London).

WESTERINK, L. G. (1961), 'Elias on the Prior Analytics', *Mnemosyne*[4], 14, 126–39.

—— (1971), 'Ein astrologisches Kolleg aus dem Jahre 564', *BZ* 64, 6–21.

—— (1976), *Greek Commentaries on Plato's Phaedo*, I. *Olympiodorus* (Amsterdam).

WURM, K. (1973). *Substanz und Qualität: Ein Beitrag zur Interpretation der plotinischen Traktate VII, 2 und 3* (Berlin–New York).

ZIMMERMANN, F. W. (1981), *Al-Farabi's Commentary and Short Treatise on Aristotle's De interpretatione, Translated with an Introduction and Notes* (Oxford).

INDEX LOCORUM

GENERAL INDEX